How to do Discourse Analysis

This bestselling textbook is the ideal companion to *An Introduction to Discourse Analysis: Theory and Method*, by leading author, James Paul Gee.

Using a practical how-to approach, Gee provides the tools necessary to work with discourse analysis, with engaging step-by-step tasks featured throughout the book. Each tool is clearly explained, along with guidance on how to use it, and authentic data is provided for readers to practice using the tools. Readers from all fields will gain both a practical and theoretical background in how to do discourse analysis and knowledge of discourse analysis as a distinctive research methodology.

Updated throughout, this second edition also includes a new tool – 'The Big C Conversation Tool'. A new companion website **www.routledge.com/ cw/gee** features a frequently asked questions section, additional tasks to support understanding, a glossary and free access to journal articles by James Paul Gee.

How to do Discourse Analysis: A Toolkit is an essential book for advanced undergraduate and postgraduate students working in the areas of applied linguistics, education, psychology, anthropology and communication.

James Paul Gee is the Mary Lou Fulton Presidential Professor of Literacy Studies at Arizona State University. He is author of many titles including *An Introduction to Discourse Analysis, fourth edition* (2014), *Language and Learning in the Digital Age* (2011) and co-editor of *The Routledge Handbook of Discourse Analysis* (2012).

How to do Discourse Analysis
A Toolkit

Second Edition

James Paul Gee

Routledge
Taylor & Francis Group

LONDON AND NEW YORK

First published 2011
by Routledge

This edition published 2014
By Routledge
2 Park Square, Milton Park, Abingdon, Oxon OX14 4RN

Simultaneously published in the USA and Canada
by Routledge
711 Third Avenue, New York, NY 10017

*Routledge is an imprint of the Taylor & Francis Group, an informa
business*

British Library Cataloguing in Publication Data
A catalogue record for this book is available from the British
Library

Library of Congress Cataloging in Publication Data
Gee, James Paul.
How to do discourse analysis : a toolkit / James Paul Gee. --
Second Edition.
pages cm
1. Discourse analysis. I. Title.
P302.G398 2014
401'.41--dc23
2013029291

ISBN: 978-0-415-72557-6 (hbk)
ISBN: 978-0-415-72558-3 (pbk)
ISBN: 978-1-315-81966-2 (ebk)

Typeset in Berkeley Oldstyle
by Saxon Graphics Ltd, Derby

MIX
Paper from
responsible sources
FSC
www.fsc.org   FSC® C013056

Printed and bound in Great Britain by
TJ International Ltd, Padstow, Cornwall

Contents

Introduction

Discourse analysis is the study of language at use in the world, not just to say things, but also to do things. People use language for lots of different things. They use it to communicate, co-operate, and to help others. They use it to build things like marriages, reputations, and institutions. They also use it to lie, advantage themselves, harm people, and destroy things like marriages, reputations, and institutions.

There are many different approaches to discourse analysis. Some of these are part of the discipline of linguistics and these approaches to discourse analysis are tied closely to the study of grammar. Some approaches to discourse analysis are not as closely tied to the grammatical details of language, but concentrate on ideas, issues, and themes as they are expressed in talk and writing.

In my book *An Introduction to Discourse Analysis: Theory and Method* (Fourth Edition, 2014), I argue that any theory of discourse analysis is made up of a set of *tools* with which to analyze language in use. In my view, no one theory is universally right or universally applicable. Each theory offers tools which work better for some kinds of data than they do for others. Furthermore, anyone engaged in their own discourse analysis must adapt the tools they have taken from a given theory to the needs and demands of their own study.

A book about discourse analysis can take two different approaches. It can offer wide coverage of different theories or it can offer one theory in some detail, a theory that is meant to offer good tools for some purposes and to be a good preparation for learning other approaches for other purposes later on. My book, *An Introduction to Discourse Analysis: Theory and Method* and this one are based on this second approach. The theory in both these books is one that sees discourse analysis as tied closely to the details of language structure (grammar), but that deals with meaning in social, cultural, and political terms, a broader approach to meaning than is common in mainstream linguistics. At the same time, both books are meant to lay a foundation for later learning of other approaches to discourse analysis.

So, then, why two books, both devoted to introducing discourse analysis? People learn and teach differently. An *Introduction to Discourse Analysis: Theory and Method* offers explanations and examples, but it does not give readers lots of work of their own to do. It also does not offer a detailed "how to" approach. This book, while it has explanation and examples, does leave a lot for readers to do and does give detailed instructions of a "how to" sort.

However, readers need to be warned that there is no grand agreed-upon body of content for discourse analysis. There are too many approaches and controversies for that. So I offer my own ideas—what I believe in—but not in the hope that you will believe everything I say, but in the hope that you will make up your own mind and develop your own style and contributions. That is really what "how to" means in this book: learn how eventually to go on your own and choose your own companions on your path to understanding and intervention in the world.

This book is based around 28 tools for doing discourse analysis. In each case, I explain the tool and give an example of how to use it. Then I give readers data and questions that allow them to practice using the tool. The tools are all collected together in an appendix. Readers should also practice using each of the tools on their own data.

What do I mean by a "tool" for discourse analysis? A tool for discourse analysis is a specific question to ask of data. Each question makes the reader look quite closely at the details of language in an oral or written communication. Each question also makes the reader connect these details to what speakers or writers mean, intend, and seek to do and accomplish in the world by the way in which they have used language.

The tools are not ordered. They are all meant to apply at once to any data that is being analyzed. For some data, some tools will yield more illuminating information than for other data. But they can all be asked for each piece of data. In some ways, though, I introduce the tools backwards. A discourse analysis, in my view, would start with the tools in Unit 4 (they are about "the big picture," including things that go beyond language). But this does not mean that starting there is a good way to learn. Once readers have finished this book and want to engage in their own discourse analyses on their own data, they may well want to start with the tools in Unit 4 and work backwards through the 28 tools. On the other hand, each reader may well find their own favored order in which to use the tools.

The approach to discourse analysis in this book applies to both speech and writing. The examples and data in the book come from both. However, because I do not want to have to keep repeating "speech and writing" and "speakers and writers" and "listeners and readers," I will throughout the book just talk about speech, speakers, and listeners. Readers should keep in mind, though, that usually I am talking about both speech and writing (except in obvious cases where only one applies, as when we talk about pausing or pitch changes in the voice).

Because some of the data we deal with comes from speech, the issue of how to transcribe speech arises. With ever more sophisticated recording and computer equipment, it is possible to get incredibly detailed records of speech that include small pauses, slight hesitations, and subtle changes in sound, pitch, rate, and loudness. It is tempting to believe that such detailed records represent some pure, objective, and unanalyzed "reality." In fact, they do no such thing. Speech always has far more detail in it than any recording or transcription system could ever capture.

A discourse analysis is based on the details of speech (and gaze and gesture and action) that are arguably deemed *relevant* in the context where the speech was used *and* that are relevant to the arguments the analyst is attempting to make. A discourse analysis is not based on *all* the physical features present, not even all those that might, in some conceivable context, be meaningful, or might be meaningful in analyses with different purposes.

Any speech data can be transcribed in more or less detailed ways such that we get a continuum of possible transcripts ranging from very detailed (what linguists call "narrow") transcripts to much less detailed (what linguists call "broad") ones. While it is certainly wise to begin one's analysis by transcribing for more detail than may in the end be relevant, ultimately it is the purposes of the analyst that determine how narrow or broad the transcript must be.

In this book we will use broad transcripts. Much more detail could be offered for each transcript, but these details would end up being trees that obscure the forest, and it is the forest we are after in this book. For more on transcription in discourse analysis, see Duranti's book in the Reading list on page 5.

I use a good deal of data in this book and offer readers data to work on. Data has to come from some place. The data here comes from my own work which deals with social, institutional, and educational issues. I believe discourse analysts ought to pick their questions and data because something important bears on the answers they reach. In any case, readers will have their own interests and the data here is for initial practice. Readers should also apply all the tools we introduce to data and issues they have selected and which interest them.

Not all readers will be equally familiar with the data I use. Though much of the data is from the United States it is not even typical of everywhere in the United States and may be more or less "foreign" even to people from there at times. As you will learn later in this book—when we talk about making what we take for granted "strange" and "new"—this is, in many ways, a good thing. At the same time, readers should always think about how the data used in this book could be supplemented by related data from their own area, culture, or country where things may work differently. Readers then could compare and contrast how things work in different cases. Indeed, this would make a good assignment throughout the book.

My approach to discourse analysis is a type of "applied discourse analysis" or "applied linguistics." What does this mean? For me it means this: In areas of empirical inquiry, there are a great many questions to ask, topics to study, and many different types of data to collect. Since there are so many choices here, why not choose questions, topics, and data that bear on issues and problems important to people, society, and the world, rather than ones of less importance? When we make choices based in part on how our inquiry will help speak to wider issues and problems, we are doing applied work. We do not lower our empirical standards, nor do we politicize our work by drawing conclusions more on the basis of desire than data. But we do seek to intervene. You will see in this book that I chose language topics and data that bear on pressing social, cultural, and institutional problems.

This book does not assume that readers know a lot about linguistics or grammar. But I do assume that you will pay attention to the details of language. The book is organized into four units each with a number of sections. Each unit contains explanation and practice for the reader. Throughout the book I also offer what I call "Grammar Interludes." These interludes introduce basic information about grammar as it plays a role in discourse analysis. Each interlude also offers a tool and practice with the tool.

This book was inspired by a professor who told my publisher that she used my book, *An Introduction to Discourse Analysis: Theory and Method* in her class, but that she regretted that it did not tell readers how actually to do a discourse analysis. And I cannot actually tell you "how to" in any full detail. Like good science and good art, some of what it takes to do a good discourse analysis involves things like taste, innovation, risk taking, and good choices (and luck) about what to study. But this book is as close as I can get. I give you specific things to do. I seek to immerse you in asking and answering 28 questions. The questions are not easy and the answers are not obvious. I hope you discuss them and argue over them with others (because science is a social and collaborative enterprise). I hope, after your immersion, you come out having discovered your own perspectives and skills, ready both to learn more and to do your own work of understanding language in the world.

While this book is about language, the tools it develops for analyzing language work for analyzing static images (like a painting), moving or changing images (like a film or video game), and so-called "multimodal" texts that combine words and images and sometimes other modes like music (for example, many ads and video games). This is so because discourse analysis is about communication and, in most cases, images and multimodal texts are seeking to communicate. They use a different "grammar" than does language alone, but they communicate nonetheless. Applying discourse analysis to images and multimodal texts is a very new enterprise and would require a book of its own. Nonetheless, I encourage readers to think about how the different tools in this book might apply outside language proper.

Note on Second Edition: This edition has added one more tool; deleted, added, and corrected data; updated references (which has meant in some cases adding more classics, not just recent work); and revised for clarity in many places. An appendix on multimodal analysis has been deleted, since this is a topic that deserves a fuller treatment than can be done in this book.

Note on Problems: This book has 51 "Problems" or assignments. It is a good idea to ask students to find and bring in data that exemplifies the working of the various discourse tools discussed in this book. Teachers should also supply data and problems that interest their class or that fit well with the backgrounds of the students in their class. It is also a good idea to encourage students to use some or all of the tools on data that they care about and can constitute the basis for their own research. Discourse analysis, like all science, is a collaborative, social endeavor and so students should practice collaborating on analyses, correcting, supplementing, and adding to each other's contributions.

Reading

Throughout this book I will offer reading suggestions. I have tried to keep these to a minimum and to fundamental sources. For a more complete list of references, see Gee, J. P. (2014), *An Introduction to Discourse Analysis: Theory and Method*, Fourth Edition, London: Routledge. The references in this book do not by any means constitute a bibliography of the field. Some are technical and some are not, but all are listed because they are good sources to read along with this book or after it. As I said above, there are many different approaches to discourse analysis. Below I list a few books that will allow you to explore a number of these.

Chafe, W. (1994). *Discourse, consciousness, and time: The flow and displacement of conscious experience in speech and writing*. Chicago: University of Chicago Press. [An important and influential approach to discourse analysis rooted in the flow of ideas in the mind and in speech.]

Duranti, A. (1997). *Linguistic anthropology*. Cambridge: Cambridge University Press. [Excellent overview of discourse analysis within a cultural framework.]

Gee, J. P. and Handford, M., Eds. (2012). *The Routledge handbook of discourse analysis*. London: Routledge. [A good handbook with a very diverse array of articles representing different approaches to and areas in discourse analysis.]

Fairclough, N. (2003). *Analyzing discourse: Textual analysis for social research*. London: Routledge. [Fairclough offers his well-known and widely used approach to "critical discourse analysis."]

Gumperz, J. J. (1982). *Discourse strategies*. Cambridge: Cambridge University Press. [A classic approach to discourse from an anthropological linguist.]

Hutchby, I. and Wooffitt, R. (2008). *Conversational analysis*. Malden, MA: Polity Press. ["CA"—which stand for "conversational analysis"—is a widely used approach to analyzing face-to-face conversations based in sociology.]

Schiffrin, D., Tannen, D., and Hamilton, H. E., Eds. (2001). *The handbook of discourse analysis*. Malden, MA: Blackwell [A good handbook with many articles representing different approaches to and areas in discourse analysis.]

Van Dijk, T. A., Ed. (1997). *Discourse as social interaction*. London: Sage. [This and the book below are both good collections of articles detailing different approaches to and areas in discourse analysis.]

Van Dijk, T. A. (1997). *Discourse as structure and process*. London: Sage.

Van Dijk, T. A. (2008). *Discourse and power*. New York: Palgrave/Macmillan [Van Dijk has done a great deal of work on using his own style of discourse analysis to deal with important social and political issues.]

UNIT 1

Language and Context

1.1 Language and Language Acquisition

Dialects

We will start in this section with some very basic background about language. People often think of grammar as rules that tell them how to speak "correctly." Speaking correctly is often taken to mean speaking in the way educated people do. But this is not really how grammar works.

All human beings, barring serious problems, learn a native language as part of their early socialization in life. Each person learns a certain variety—called a "dialect"—of their native language, the variety their ancestors have passed down to them. In the United States, they might learn Southern English, African-American Vernacular English, New England English, or some other dialect. Dialects can vary in terms of vocabulary, syntax, or pronunciation.

Of course, any region of the United States has people from other parts of the country in it and so there are different varieties of English in any part of the country. Dialects can vary by region (e.g., Southern English), social class (e.g., various working class dialects), and by cultural group (e.g., Appalachian English). In many other countries, the differences between dialects are much more dramatic than in the United States.

What people call "Standard English" is a rather "special" dialect. "Standard English" is the variety of English that is held by many to be "correct" both in the sense that it shows no strong regional variation and that it is used widely in mainstream media and by public figures.

Standard English has its origins in the economic power of a fourteenth-century merchant class in London, people who spoke an East Midland dialect. Because of their growing economic clout, their dialect spread for public business across the country. It became the basis of so-called "Received Pronunciation" ("RP") in England, and eventually gave rise to Standard English in the United States.

Because of its prestige, many people in the United States speak Standard English and pass on that variety to their children, even if earlier in their family histories their ancestors spoke other dialects. For example, many Southerners have given up their Southern dialect in favor of Standard English and speakers of Appalachian Vernacular English or African-American Vernacular English often adopt Standard English for job interviews and interactions within public institutions.

Standard English is something of a fiction. We all speak it, if we do, in somewhat different ways, as is true of all dialects. We all bring to it different linguistic influences from other dialects and languages we know or which are connected to our ancestors. Further, when we are speaking informally (in our vernacular), we all use language forms that are not used in more formal varieties of Standard English as it is used in mainstream media and in writing.

Language Acquisition

For the most part, oral language acquisition for young children is an entirely unconscious process. It does not require overt teaching or correction of any sort. The process of early language acquisition is, at least in large part, under biological control. Humans are creatures of language. They are born ready and able to acquire some variety of a human language.

Young children do not need correction. When they say things like "go-ed" instead of "went," they often do not pay attention to correction even if they get it from adults. They all end up eventually saying "went" as the past tense of "go." In fact, when children say "go-ed" instead of "went," they show they are catching on to the general pattern that English forms the past tense of verbs by adding "ed" to a verb, but with some exceptions to the rule (as with "went"). They are over-extending or over-generalizing the pattern, a common occurrence in language acquisition. This shows that children are actively looking for—making hypotheses about—rules or patterns. They are not just memorizing what they hear.

The grammars of all dialects of all languages follow certain patterns that are, partly at least, controlled by a human biological capacity for language. The human brain sets certain constraints on what a human language can look like and all dialects of all languages follow those basic constraints. Thus, no dialect is "incorrect." Dialects are just different from each other. They do vary, of course, in prestige, thanks to how people think about their speakers and their speakers' social positions.

People often think a structure in a dialect is a mistake or "wrong" because it is different from Standard English. For example, in African-American Vernacular English, some speakers use a "naked *be*" form as in "My puppy, he always be following me" or "We be having leftovers these days." Since Standard English does not use this form, many speakers of Standard English think it is incorrect. They may even say that "People who speak that way don't know English."

However, the naked *be* form has a meaning. It is not a mistake. It is what linguists call a "durative aspect marker," that is, a form that means that an action or event is a regular event, happens over and over, and is characteristic or typical. Lot of languages have a durative aspect marker, even though Standard English does not. This form was added to English by young African-American children acquiring English and looking for a way to express durative aspect. Throughout history, children have changed language as they acquire it (that's why, for example, Spanish and its mother language Latin are so different from each other).

The linguist Noam Chomsky has famously argued that there is a biological capacity for language that sets a basic design for all human languages and sets, as well, parameters of how different languages can vary from this basic design. Language is, thus, for humans, innate or an "instinct" (as is nest building or song for some species of birds, who innately know what their nest or song is like without having to learn it), at least in regard to the core or basic properties of any language. In this sense, at a deep-seated level, all human languages resemble each other in important ways.

According to this view, all varieties of language acquired by humans as native (first) languages are equal, since they all fit the basic pattern or design dictated by our human biological capacity for language. Chomsky's views are controversial. However, it is clear that all humans are born ready to learn language and that human languages do not differ from each other in completely arbitrary ways (i.e., there are language universals, such as the fact that all language have nouns and verbs and subjects and objects).

Language changes all the time. Children change it when they are acquiring it. For example, at one time in the history of English "apron" was said as "nappron." But children heard "a nappron" as "an apron." Once a whole generation said "apron" instead of "nappron," the "correct" form was "apron." The "nappron" form can still be seen in the English word "napkin." Adults change language, as well, as they are influenced by other languages (e.g., bilinguals) or the need to communicate new things.

Speed and Clarity

Human languages must be both fast and clear. We humans want to be able to communicate without undue slowdowns and yet we also want our communications to be clear. These two demands can come into conflict with each other. If we speak quickly and run our words together, communication can get unclear. If we seek total clarity by spelling everything out explicitly, communication can get too slow.

We can see in the history of languages the constant pressure to balance speed and clarity. For example, Latin had "case endings" on its nouns. Different endings on nouns indicated whether a noun was the subject of a sentence or the direct object. So "puella" was the subject form of the word "girl" and "puellam" was the direct object form. Latin had other case endings for other grammatical relations. Because endings on the nouns indicated what was subject and object, Latin did not have to use word order to indicate this (as English does) and could vary word order pretty freely. Sentences like "Puella amat puerum," "Amat puella puerum," and "Puella puerum amat" (the girl loves the boy) were all grammatical.

Old English also had cases on its nouns, much like Latin. But, of course, cases endings make words longer, more complex, and slower. So there is a tendency for these case endings over long periods of time to "erode" (get shorter) and finally disappear. This makes language quicker. But once case endings are gone, there is no way to tell whether a noun like "girl" is being used as a subject or object. So we have lost some clarity. English has lost case endings on its nouns (though they are still on pronouns, as in "he" and "him," "she" and "her"). To indicate what is subject and what is object, English uses the word order "Subject Verb Object," as in "The girl loves the boy," and, thus, has lost the word order freedom Latin had.

So far we are only talking about oral language, not written language. For linguists, oral language is the fundamental form of language. Oral language has been in human history since we became human (and maybe even before). Oral language is part of human biology in the sense that we are certainly creatures prepared and helped to learn oral language by our biology, that is, by structures in our brains.

Written language is much newer in human history, at best it is about 10,000 years old. Not all cultures invented written language (in fact, most did not), while all cultures have oral language today and have had it in the past. Written language is not old enough in human evolutionary history to be part of human biology.

Nonetheless, written language is, of course, an important form of language and important in communication. We will deal with both oral and written language in this book. By the way, American Sign Language counts as "oral language," even though it is signed, since it is acquired as a native language by some children and used for face-to-face communication.

Reading

Chomsky, N. (2006). *Language and mind*. Third Edition. Cambridge: Cambridge University Press.

Clark, E. (2009). *First language acquisition*. Second Edition. Cambridge: Cambridge University Press.

Gee, J. P. (2011). *Social linguistics and literacies: Ideologies in Discourses*. Fourth Edition. London: Taylor & Francis.

Milroy, J. and Milroy, L. (1991). *Authority in language: Investigating Standard English*. Second Edition. New York: Routledge.

Pinker, S. (1994). *The language instinct: How the mind creates language*. New York: William Morrow. [A good introduction to Chomsky's and Pinker's own arguments for the innateness of the language capacity.]

Slobin, D. I. (1977). Language change in childhood and history. In J. Macnamara, Ed., *Language learning and thought*. New York: Academic Press, pp. 185-214. [Slobin's work is the source of the argument about speed and clarity being competing demands in language.]

Wolfram, W. and Schilling-Estes, N. (2006). *American English: Dialects and variation*. Second Edition. Malden, MA: Blackwell.

1.2 Context

Context and Cultural Knowledge

In the last section we argued that human languages must be both fast and clear. We speakers face the trade-off between speed and clarity every day.

When we communicate we do not want to be too slow (or, worse, have our listeners tell us to get on with it). Nor do we want to be unclear (or, worse, have our listeners tell us they don't know what we are talking about). We always have to make a judgment about how much clarity we can sacrifice for speed and how much speed we must give up to achieve an appropriate amount of clarity for the context we are in.

In order to speed things along, any speaker leaves some things unsaid and assumes they will be understood based on listeners' knowledge of the context in which the communication occurs. "Context" is a crucial term in discourse analysis. What do we mean by it? For now, we will define "context" this way: Context includes the physical setting in which the communication takes place and everything in it; the bodies, eye gaze, gestures, and movements of those present; what has previously been said and done by those involved in the communication; and any shared knowledge those involved have, including shared cultural knowledge.

Let's for a moment think about just one aspect of context, namely shared cultural knowledge. For example, in my cultural group, I assume people eat dinner roughly between 6 and 8 o'clock at night. If I invite you out to dinner and ask when you want to meet, I assume, without saying so explicitly, that you will give me a time between 6 and 8. People in other cultures will vary about what their taken for granted "normal" dinner times are. It is hard for us to see how much shared cultural knowledge speakers assume and listeners bring to a communication, since such shared knowledge is usually just taken-for-granted.

A Yucatan Example

Since shared cultural knowledge (one aspect of context) is so often taken for granted, let's look at a communication in what is a foreign culture to most of us. Here we will not know what cultural information speakers assume can go unsaid. My example is from William Hanks' excellent book *Language and Communicative Practices* (1996).

In a small town in Yucatan Mexico, a Mayan shaman named "Don Chabo" is sharing a meal with his daughter-in-law, Margot, and a visiting anthropologist. They are all in Margot's house. A young man, named "Yuum," approaches from the outside. Standing at the window, he asks: "Is Don Chabo seated?" Margot replies: "Go over there. He's drinking. Go over there inside."

The meaning of these utterances is not clear to cultural outsiders. A tremendous amount of cultural knowledge has been taken for granted as already known. For example, the people seated around the table are having a meal, so why does Margo say that Don Chabo is "drinking"? Furthermore, Margot's response implies that Don Chabo is "drinking," despite the fact that he was, at the moment, gazing off into space with a roll in his hand. Indeed, in Mayan, it would have been equally true here to say Don Chabo was "drinking" had he been altogether done with (eating) his meal.

Margot's response implies, as well, that Don Chabo was "seated." Yet, it turns out, it would have been equally true to say he was "seated" had he been standing or even off somewhere else, even taking a bath in his own home.

Or, to take one final example, Margot uses the Mayan word for "there" that means "maximally distant from the speaker," the same word people in Yucatan use for relatives who live outside Yucatan in other states in the Mexican republic. She does this despite the fact that she is telling Yuum to go into her father-in-law's house, not 10 meters away from hers and within the same compound as her house.

How can it be that people can be "drinking" when they are eating or doing nothing at all? That they are "seated" when they are standing or taking a bath? That they are far distant from something 10 meters away?

Things work this way because Mayans (these Mayans, in any case), though they almost always take food with drink and vice versa, use the words "drink" and "eat" in such a way that their morning and evening meals are "drinking" and their larger main meal in the midafternoon is "eating." Furthermore, to these Mayans, as long as the social engagement of mealtime is still going on, regardless of whether the "meal" itself is finished or not, a person is still "drinking" or "eating."

Many Mayans live in walled compounds that contain several houses. They use the word "seated" to mean that one is "at home" and available, regardless of where one is in the compound. Being "available" has, in addition, a special meaning for Shamans. To ask whether a Shaman is "at home" is to ask whether he is available to engage in counseling.

Mayans have their own cultural views of how physical and social space work and are related, as we all do. Margo is excluded from her father-in-law's house, unless she has a specific reason to be there, for social reasons having to do with Mayan cultural views of social relationships and spaces within homes. Thus, she uses the word for "far distant" due to social, rather than physical distance.

In this brief example, I have given you very little of what you really need to know to fully understand these simple utterances (for example, why does Margot, rather than Don Chabo respond?). To really understand them one needs to understand how social hierarchies, gender, meals, social engagements, Shamanism, and a great deal more, work day-to-day in local settings among (certain of the) Mayans. We all take for granted a good deal of cultural knowledge. And, indeed, it is one goal of discourse analysis to uncover and bring to conscious awareness such usually taken-for-granted knowledge.

Making the Taken-for-Granted New and Strange

To do discourse analysis on our own languages in our own culture requires a special skill. We have to make things new and strange that we usually see as completely "normal" and "natural." We can see the Mayan communication above as "strange" because it is brand new to us.

To do discourse analysis, we have to see what is old and taken for granted as if it were brand new. We need to come to see all the assumptions and information speakers leave unsaid and assume listeners know and will add in to make the communications clear. Communication and culture are like icebergs. Only a small "tip" is stated overtly. A vast amount lies under the surface, not said, but assumed to be known or inferable from the context in which the communication is occurring.

By making what is natural to us—what we usually take for granted—new and strange, we can begin consciously to think about all the knowledge, assumptions, and inferences we bring to any communication. And sometimes we will even see aspects of our taken-for-granted cultural knowledge and assumptions—or those of others—that we want to question because we conclude they are doing harm to ourselves or others in terms of things like equity, fairness, and humane treatment of people. What we do in communication with each other is not always benign.

Reading

Duranti, A. (1997). *Linguistic anthropology*. Cambridge: Cambridge University Press.

Duranti, A., Ed., (2009). *Linguistic anthropology: A reader*. Malden, MA: Blackwell.

Duranti, A. and Goodwin, C., Eds. (1992). *Rethinking context: Language as an interactive phenomenon*. Cambridge: Cambridge University Press. [An important book on context, one of the best.]

Hanks, W. F. (1995). *Language and communicative practices*. New York: Westview. [A truly classic book that never gained the wide readership it richly deserves.]

Van Dijk, T. A. (2009). *Society and discourse: How social contexts influence text and talk*. Cambridge: Cambridge University Press.

Grammar Interlude #1: Deixis

When Margo, in the example in Section 1.2, says "Go over there. He's drinking. Go over there inside," she makes crucial use of words linguists refer to as "deictics" (pointing words). Deictics are words whose reference must be determined from context. Common deictics words fall into the categories of (1) person ("I/me," "you," "he/him," "she/her," "we/us," "they/them"); (2) place ("here/there," "this/that"); and (3) time ("now/then," "yesterday/ today"). These words are also called "shifters" because their reference shifts with each different context of use.

If I say "Brad Pitt likes chocolate cake," you know from the words "Brad Pitt," "chocolate," and "cake" what they refer to. But if I say, "He likes it," you have no idea who "he" refers to or what "it" refers to except by considering the context either in terms of what was said previously or what and who are present in the environment. When Margo says "Go over there. He's drinking.

Go over there inside," the listener can only figure out what "over there" refers to by a gesture and what "he" refers to by the previous mention of Don Chabo's name (as we pointed out in Section 1.2, Mayan has a word "there" that means "close" and one that means "far").

Deictics tie speech and writing to context. If listeners do not correctly figure out what deictics refer to (using contextual information), then they do not understand what is meant or they can misunderstand it. At the same time, when speakers use deictics, they assume that their listeners can figure out what the deictics refer to. For example, if I come up to you and say "She's at it again!," I assume our previous talk about some woman and her antics (or some obvious happening in the situation) are salient enough to you that I do not need to name her.

However, the distinction between deictics like "this" and non-deictic words like "cake" is, while clear in linguistics, not always all that clear when we get to actual uses of language. For example, compare the following two utterances: "John had been drinking, so I drove him home" and "John was drinking too fast and dribbled it all down the front of his shirt." In many contexts, "drinking" in the first utterance will mean "drinking alcohol" and in the second it could be any beverage. So even with non-deictic terms, there is often an element of having to use context to figure out what words mean specifically.

To take another example, consider that in "The coffee spilled, go get a mop," we are talking about a liquid and in "The coffee spilled, go get a broom," we are talking about grains. It is the words "mop" and "broom" that serve as the context that tells us what "coffee" means in these sentences specifically. In an utterance like "The coffee spilled, clean it up" only the physical context or something said previously would tell you what was meant specifically by "coffee."

This does not mean that words like "drink" and "coffee"—or that all words (since for any word its specific meaning is determined from context)—are deictics. Such content words do give us more contentful meaning to determine what they refer to in context than do real deictics. But it does mean that in actual use all language has deictic like properties.

The definite article in English ("the") functions like a deictic. If I say to you out of the blue "The woman is at it again!" instead of "She is at it again!," in both cases you have to figure out from interactions we have had previously who "the woman" or "she" is referring to. The definite article ("the") functions like a deictic since it means that that the speaker assumes the listener already knows (from context or previous knowledge) what the noun phrase it is in refers to. The indefinite article ("a," "an") does not have such a deictic function. If I say "A woman came in," I am not assuming the listener already knows who I am referring to. If I say "The woman came in," I am assuming the listener does already know who I am referring to or can figure it out.

We will now introduce the Deixis Tool. This tool serves as one important aid in using the Filling Out Tool we will introduce in Section 1.3.

Tool #1: The Deixis Tool

For any communication, ask how deictics are being used to tie what is said to context and to make assumptions about what listeners already know or can figure out. Consider uses of the definite article in the same way. Also ask what deictic like properties any regular words are taking on in context, that is, what aspects of their specific meanings need to be filled in from context (we will see this latter task again later in the Situated Meaning Tool in Section 4.2).

Problem 1

Below is some data that you will see again in Section 1.4. A teacher is telling a group of people about an episode where an administrator (Mary Washington) at her school told her to call an historian (Sara) from a local university (Woodson). The historian wanted to work with teachers and schools in her town to have children do oral history about their town (i.e., interview people about the past) and other sorts of history. The teacher (Karen) uses the deictic "here" because the meeting is being held at her school. All names of people and places have been changed. Read the data and answer the questions that follow it.

In the transcript below, when words are capitalized it means they were said with emphatic stress, that is, they were emphasized. The symbol "//" means what precedes it was said with what we will call a "final intonation contour" (which is sort of like a period in speech). The symbol "/" means what precedes it was said with what we will call a "non-final intonation contour" (which is sort of like a comma in speech). We will discuss intonation in Grammar Interlude #3 (after Section 1.5). Right now the details are not important.

By the way, when using transcriptions of oral data, be sure to say it out loud as you seek to reflect on what it means. So, now read out loud the data below:

> LAST YEAR /
> Mary Washington /
> who is our curriculum coordinator here /
> had a call from Sara //
> at Woodson //
> And called me /
> and said (pause) /
> "We have a person from Woodson /
> who's in the History Department /
> she's interested in doing some RESEARCH /
> into BLACK history //
> And she would like to get involved with the school /
> And here's her number /
> Give her a call" //

Questions:

1. List all the deictics in this data and say what you think they mean and how the listeners might have figured out what they mean.
2. In the direct quote Karen ascribes to Mary Washington, what is the meaning of the deictic "we" in "we have a person …"? Is the "we" here the royal "we" (so Mary Washington really means only herself)? Does it refer to Mary and Karen? Does it refer to the school as an institution and the people in it? Is it ambiguous? Does this "we" include Sara? What do you think Karen is trying to accomplish with this use of "we"?
3. Why didn't Karen say "There is a person from Woodson …" instead of "We have a person from Woodson"? By the way, a year later it is unlikely Karen remembers the exact words Mary used and, in any case, when speakers quote others they often ascribe words to them that were not actually said but which capture what the speaker herself means and wants to accomplish.
4. When you get to this data again (with the rest of what Karen said) in Section 1.4, return to these questions about "we" and consider how your answers would then fit with your larger analysis of the data at that point.
5. Proper names (like Sara, Mary Washington, and Woodson) are not deictics, since they do not switch their meanings in different contexts. However, proper names do not carry much contentful meaning the way "content words" like "school" and "number" do. How could the people hearing this data have known who Mary Washington is, who Sara is, and what Woodson is?
6. The word "number" in the data above is neither a deictic nor a proper name, but a content word (a noun) with fuller, more contentful meaning (something like a definition) than either a deictic or a proper name. However, this word can have somewhat different specific meanings in different contexts. What is its specific meaning here and how do listeners know what this specific meaning is?

Reading

Brown, G. (1995). *Speakers, listeners, and communication: Explorations in discourse analysis*. Cambridge: Cambridge University Press (see Chapter 4).

Fillmore, C. (1997). *Lectures on deixis*. Berkeley, CA: Center for the Study of Language and Information. [Lecture notes—an old classic.]

1.3 Two Tools: The Fill In Tool and the Making Strange Tool

Communication and Context

Below I sketch out the picture of communication and context we have developed thus far. We will revise it somewhat later, but it is suitable for our purposes now:

WHAT THE SPEAKER SAYS + CONTEXT = WHAT THE SPEAKER MEANS
↓

The physical setting in which the communication takes place and everything in it; the bodies, eye gaze, gestures, and movements of those present; what has previously been said and done by those involved in the communication; any shared knowledge those involved have, including shared cultural knowledge

LISTENER'S WORK = Consider what the speaker has said and the context in which it has been said. On that basis make the assumptions and draw the inferences that will make what the speaker has said clear and complete. I will call this work, the "Filling In Task," because the listener is using what is said and the context in which it is said to fill in or complete what the speaker has said, since speakers always leave a good deal unsaid (but assume it to be known or inferable by listeners).

Tools

So far in our discussion of language and context we have developed the basis for two new tools for discourse analysis. The first tool we will call the "Fill In Tool" and the second we will call the "Making Strange Tool." These tools are related. The Making Strange Tool helps us use the Fill In Tool.

> **Tool #2: The Fill In Tool**
>
> For any communication, ask: Based on what was said and the context in which it was said, what needs to be filled in here to achieve clarity? What is not being said overtly, but is still assumed to be known or inferable? What knowledge, assumptions, and inferences do listeners have to bring to bear in order for this communication to be clear and understandable and received in the way the speaker intended it?

There are ways of being a "resistant listener" (or "resistant reader"). Resistant listeners purposely refuse to make and "buy into" the taken-for-granted knowledge, assumptions, and inferences a speaker intends listeners to make. For example, the speaker might be a racist, asking us to assume that whites are superior to others. However, it is hard to truly understand people—even if we want to oppose them—if we do not first try to get at their underlying assumptions and the reasons they believe and act as they do. This can be very hard to do if we profoundly object to their viewpoints, yet, nonetheless, it makes eventual resistant listening deeper and fairer.

Tool #3: The Making Strange Tool

For any communication, try to act as if you are an "outsider." Ask yourself: What would someone (perhaps, even a Martian) find strange here (unclear, confusing, worth questioning) if that person did not share the knowledge and assumptions and make the inferences that render the communication so natural and taken-for-granted by insiders?

Reading

Shklovsky, V. (1965). Art as technique. In L. T. Lemon and M. J. Reis, Eds., *Russian Formalist criticism: Four essays*, pp. 3–24. Omaha, NE: University of Nebraska Press [An important essay in which the notion of "making strange" and its role in art are introduced.]

1.4 Working with the Fill In Tool

Here we consider some data and put the Fill In Tool to use. I will give you only a little information about the context in which the data occurred. Then I will ask you to think about some questions. These questions are meant to help you think about what you need to know in order to make sense of the data. They are meant to help you think about what you need to "fill in" that is not explicitly said, based on what was said and what you know or can surmise about the context.

I want you to think about the information you need to have (and some of which you may not have in this case), the assumptions you need to make, and the inferences you need to draw to make sense of the communication. Where you do not fully know the context, you have to make guesses about what the context was, based on what was said and your own personal knowledge. This is not an uncommon occurrence even in everyday life, let alone for us discourse analysts.

Your task as a discourse analyst and the listeners' task are similar. The listeners involved in the communication transcribed below needed to draw on certain parts of their knowledge, make certain assumptions, and draw certain inferences to make sense in real time of what they were hearing (based on what was said and the context in which it was said). However, these processes, for them, were, for the most part, unconscious, accomplished rapidly (speech is fast and vanishes quickly), and without much time for reflection. Your analysis of the data will, of course, be conscious and you will have time for reflection. Nonetheless, in your analysis, you will be seeking, in part, to uncover what any listener would have to know, assume, and infer to understand this communication.

It is important to understand that when I say we are trying to understand what someone meant, I mean we are trying to figure out what they were trying to say, what their intentions were, and what goals or purposes they were trying to achieve. We are using the term "meaning" in a quite broad sense.

Of course, we can never be completely sure of people's intentions and purposes, not even our own at times. There is much that goes on in people's minds that is unconscious. Furthermore, even we ourselves are not completely consciously aware of our own reasons, purposes, and intentions. We can discover things about these by talking to others or reflecting on what we have said and done. Nonetheless, both everyday people and discourse analysts do the best they can, make the best and most informed "guesses" they can about meaning.

There is an interesting wrinkle in the data below. There was a group of people listening to this communication. They had different backgrounds and they did not all know the same things. Of course, this is common in life today, where we often communicate with diverse sorts of people. Thus, these people did not all look at the context in the same way. For example, they did not all completely share the same cultural knowledge that the speaker possessed (for example, differences between "teacher culture" and the culture of university academics caused certain conflicts in the project from which the data below came).

Some of the people in the group were in much better shape than others in the group to "fill in" fully the information, assumptions, and inferences the speaker intended them to. The speaker, of course, was aware of this. Like all speakers would, she took it into consideration and, in fact, at points took advantage of the situation. She was communicating—and probably knew she was communicating—somewhat different things to different people in the room based on how much knowledge and culture they shared with her. The speaker is an elementary school teacher and she knows very well the other teachers in the room will be able to do more "filling in" (e.g., recruit more culturally shared background knowledge) than the people in the room who are not teachers.

So this makes the situation complex. As a discourse analyst you want to uncover this complexity. This speaker, like all speakers, is by no means just communicating information. She is also doing other sorts of work, as well, work that involves attempting to create, transform, and negotiate social relationships among the people in the group. We will discuss this sort of work later in this book. For now, "fill in" the best you can and think about what different people in the group brought to the communication (in terms of what they did or did not share with the speaker). Think about what different people in the group might have made of the communication and the speaker's purposes.

So here is a little context for the data to follow: A Research Institute connected to Woodson University (all names have been changed to fictitious names) is working with Sara, a history professor at the university. She wants to work with some local schools to help teachers get their middle school students engaged in doing history by studying their own neighborhoods and town (Middleview). The students will engage in things like interviewing older people and looking at census track data.

A meeting has been called. In attendance are: a few teachers from two schools; Sara and two of her students; a representative from the Institute (herself a university academic); an administrator from one of the schools; and two curriculum consultants from a local history museum. The representative from the Research Institute is chairing the meeting. Since she knows there has been some contact prior to the meeting between Sara and one of the schools, as well as activity around the project, she asks one of the teachers from that school, Karen, to update the group on what has already happened prior to the meeting. Below is reprinted just a part of what Karen said, the beginning part.

The transcript below uses certain conventions, not all of which are relevant right now. A "/" indicates an intonation contour that is heard as "non-final" (more is to come). A "//" indicates an intonation contour that is heard as "final" (closed off, what comes next is separate information, often information that might be in a different sentence in a written text). In real speech, final intonation contours sometimes occur at points that would not be the ends of sentences in a written text. We will look at these matters later and their details need not now be relevant.

When a word is capitalized in the transcript below that means it has been said with what is called "emphatic stress." It is said with emphasis (indicated either by extra loudness or a pitch change). Right now, just take it that such words are emphasized. Listeners have to "guess" why they are emphasized, since Karen does not explicitly say why. This is part of what listeners have to add to Karen's communication in order to make its meaning clear.

> LAST YEAR /
> Mary Washington /
> who is our curriculum coordinator here /
> had a call from Sara //
> at Woodson //
> And called me /
> and said (pause) /
> "We have a person from Woodson /
> Who's in the History Department /
> she's interested in doing some RESEARCH /
> into BLACK history //
> And she would like to get involved with the school /
> And her number /
> Give her a call" //
> And we- I DID call her /
> And we um BOTH expected /
> to be around /
> for the summer institute //
> at Woodson //

I DID /
ah participate in it /
But SARA /
Wasn't able to do THAT //
(Sara tries unsuccessfully to interrupt)

Problem 2

You know only a very little about the context of this language. Based on just what you know (not just what I have told you, but also your own knowledge) and the language in the transcript, answer the questions below. The point here is to see and reflect on what sorts of things you need to add to the language to gain clarity (what sorts of inferences or guesses you need to make; what knowledge you need to bring to bear; what assumptions you must make—all of which are not overtly said in the communication). The point here, also, is to consider, as I later tell you more about the context of this communication, how what you make of the communication (what you take it to mean) changes as you learn more about the context.

Don't bother being timid, feel free to make guesses and go out on a limb. We will see later that it is all right to be bold when making guesses about meaning when you are doing discourse analysis. The point here is not to "be right," but to begin to reflect on the processes by which we humans give meaning to language in use.

Questions:

1. Everyone in the meeting knew Sara was from Woodson University (they had done introductions before Karen spoke). So why does Karen say this explicitly?
2. Why does Karen use Mary Washington's full name, but only Sara's first name (Sara is a tenured professor at the University)?
3. Why is the content of the call from Sara given as a direct quotation and not just summarized (as in "Mary Washington said Sara wanted to get involved with the school and that I should call her")?
4. Why is there emphasis on "last year"?
5. Why is there emphasis on "research" and "Black"?
6. Why is there emphasis on "did" (call her), "both," "did" (participate), "Sara," and "that"?
7. Why did Sara try to interrupt at just the point she did?
8. What in the language tells you that Karen is probably angry or perturbed by something Sara has done?
9. What do you think Sara did that angered or perturbed Karen?
10. What other aspects of context, if any, do you need to know in order to clarify what Karen means and intends?

11. Do you need know who in the room is African-American, who is White, and who is something else in order to fully understand what Karen means and what she trying to accomplish? Do you need to know whether Mary Washington is African-American, White, or something else? Karen? Sara? Anyone else?

12. Karen later says that after talking to Sara, she went to a friend and colleague, Jane, and asked her to get involved with the history project. So at that point there were three people involved with the project: Karen, Sara, and Jane. Karen then says:

Well at that point there were three of us (laughs) //
back in the SUMMER //
And all three of us had not yet /
met together //

Does what Karen says here bear on the answer to any of the questions above (could be more than one)?

These questions are meant to give you a feel for how the Fill In Tool works. Using that tool, you ask what information, assumptions, and inferences are needed for understanding not just what people mean in any narrow sense, but what they are trying to accomplish with their language, what their purposes are, what they are trying to do (all of which are really part of meaning in one sense of the term, as we will see later in this book).

The data and questions above, hopefully, show you that the "Fill In" task isn't easy, either for listeners or us discourse analysts. Lots of questions and issues come up. Everyday people, as they are communicating with each other, usually do not have time to pursue these questions and issues and consciously reflect on them. Sometimes, though, they interrupt (as Sara tried to do) and try to raise some of them overtly (as Sara would certainly have tried to do had she gotten to speak). And sometimes not raising them gets people into trouble later (as happened in this project, when questions and issues that may well have arisen for you as you thought about this data were later overtly raised by participants in the project as, over time, they ceased to understand each other).

Grammar Interlude #2: Subjects and Predicates

All languages in the world are organized grammatically around the basic structure of subjects and predicates. Languages have different ways of indicating what the subject of a sentence is. Some use special marks ("cases") on the ends of nouns to indicate when the noun is a subject (e.g., "puer," "boy," as subject in Latin) and when it is a direct object (e.g., "puerum," "boy," as direct object in Latin) (note in English "he" for subjects and "him" for objects). Other endings are used for other grammatical roles beyond subject and object.

In English we use word order to indicate what the subject is and what the object is by placing the subject before the verb and the object after the verb. Furthermore, the subject agrees with main verbs in the present tense, as in "The girl leaves today" (singular subject, present tense verb) and "The girls leave today" (plural subject, present tense verb). The verb "to be" agrees with its subject in both present and past: "The girl is good," "The girls are good," "The girl was good," "The girls were good."

In a sentence, a verb links the subject (which is always a noun or a noun phrase) to other elements, such as objects (e.g., "Mary loves the man"), complements (e.g., Mary thinks that the boy left home"), prepositional phrases (e.g., "Mary went to the park," "Mary saw the man in the park") or other things (e.g., "The students elected John President," where "President" is called a "predicate nominal"). The verb "to be" is called the copula and links subject to nouns or noun phrases ("Mary is a woman," "Mary is the oldest woman") and adjectives or adjective phrases ("Mary is tall," "Mary is very tall for a woman").

The predicate is the verb and anything following it that the verb links to the subject. Below I have underlined the predicates:

1. Mary loves the man
2. Mary saw the man in the park
3. Mary is the oldest woman in the university
4. The young woman gave the boy a gift yesterday
5. Mary has a hat on her head

The subject of a sentence is "what we are talking about" and we will call it the "topic" of the sentence. The subject is the center of attention, the point around which information is organized. The predicate is "what we are saying about it." The predicate gives information about the subject.

Thus, if I say "Stanford admitted my daughter," I have chosen "Stanford" as the topic, center of attention, and the point around which I am organizing the information in the sentence. If, on the other hand, I say "My daughter was admitted to Stanford" I have chosen "my daughter" as topic, center of attention, and the point around which I am organizing the information in the sentence. The two sentences say much the same thing, but organize the information differently.

Once a speaker has introduced a topic, if he or she wants to keep talking about it, the topic is referred back to via a pronoun as in: "Stanford admitted my daughter. They are lucky to have her" or "My daughter was admitted by Stanford. She is really thrilled." A good deal of everyday speech is made up of an utterance with a full noun phrase subject followed by a number of utterances whose subjects are pronouns referring back to that full noun phrase. In this way, speakers can "chain" on a topic and keep talking about it.

Speakers choose subjects strategically to set up how listeners should organize information in their heads and how listeners should view whatever the speaker is talking about. For example, in the data we saw in Section 1.4, we saw the following sentence:

1. Mary Washington who is our curriculum coordinator here had a call from Sara at Woodson.

The speaker could have said instead:

2. Sara who is at Woodson had called Mary Washington.

In (1) "Mary Washington who is our curriculum coordinator here" is the subject and topic; in (2) "Sara who is at Woodson" is. Going back to the data in Section 1.4, reflect on why the speaker may have made the choice she did (i.e., using "Mary Washington who is our curriculum coordinator" and not "Sara who is at Woodson" as the subject/topic).

Looking at how subjects are chosen and what speakers choose to say about them is one key grammatical tool in discourse analysis:

Tool #4: The Subject Tool

For any communication, ask why speakers have chosen the subject/topics they have and what they are saying about the subject. Ask if and how they could have made another choice of subject and why they did not. Why are they organizing information the way they are in terms of subjects and predicates?

Reading

Finegan, E. (2007). *Language: Its structure and use*. Fifth Edition. Boston, MA: Thomson Wadsworth. [A good introduction with a good take on style differences in language.]
Strawson, P. F. (1974). *Subject and predicate in logic and grammar*. Aldershot, Hants, England: Ashgate. [An old philosophical classic.]

1.5 Working with the Making Strange Tool

When we do discourse analysis we are often dealing with data "after the fact," when a communication is over and done with. Thus, we have to reconstruct the context as far as we can. We have a recording of the data, of course. But that recording gives very little of the full context, even if it is a video. We have to reconstruct as much of the context as we can from notes, interviews, other data, and research.

We argued in Section 1.2 above that when we are dealing with a familiar culture, we have a problem of taking too much for granted. We often miss how much work we and other people like us are doing filling in from context things that the speaker has left unsaid. Thus, we discourse analysts have to learn to make what we take for granted new and strange. This is why it is sometimes good, when doing discourse analysis, for an insider and outsider to study the same data together.

Below is data from a setting with which some readers will be familiar and some unfamiliar. A teacher and a first-grade child are engaged in "sharing time" (sometimes also called "show-and-tell time" or "rug time"). In this classroom—and many others—at the beginning of the school day, the children take turns sharing something with the class. In this case, Mindy is sharing about making candles.

The teacher is sitting close to Mindy, who is standing. The teacher has her arm around Mindy. The teacher interrupts Mindy at several points, as she does all the children when they are sharing. Mindy is not bothered at all by the teacher's interruptions. In fact, the two are quite in synch or in rhythm with each other, like a good dance team.

If you are unfamiliar with elementary classrooms and sharing time, then you are an outsider to this data. You may see things as strange that insiders do not. That is good.

If you are very familiar with elementary school and sharing time, then you are an insider to this data. You may miss things, seeing them as "natural" and normal and not worth commenting on. At the same time, you have a much deeper knowledge of the context and so can sometimes make better judgments about what things mean and why they are being done as they are (if you can bring your unconscious and taken-for-granted knowledge to consciousness).

The outsider can help the insider see old things as new and strange again. The insider can help the outsider use context more deeply to correct judgments about meaning and purposes being pursued.

If you are an insider to the data below and do not have an outsider to work with, you have to learn to look at the data the way an outsider would. You need to see it in a way that lets you see how it could be seen as strange by people to whom it is new. That way you can explicate how meaning is being made and what actions and purposes are being accomplished through the language being used.

If you are an outsider to the data below and you do not have an insider to work with, you have to make guesses and pursue some research. You might have to ask people about what goes on in schools and elementary classrooms. Right now it is also fine, if you can't do this research, for you to make guesses and to reflect on what might be strange in the data. What you find strange as an outsider may well be things that would seem natural to insiders as they apply their insider knowledge.

Whether you are an insider or an outsider in regard to this data, your assignment here is to make it strange. Let me point out that a good deal of research has been done on sharing time. That research has discovered that teachers are not always fully aware of all they are doing and why they are doing it when they are engaged in sharing time. As teachers have helped with such research, read it later, or done their own research, they have sometimes discovered for themselves aspects of what they mean and why they are doing what they are doing. This is true of all of us. We are not consciously aware of all we mean and of all our motives. We can discover new things about ourselves when others study us or we consciously reflect, after action, on what we have said and done.

When I first saw the data below, I knew absolutely nothing about schools. I found this data and other sharing time data quite strange. Just one example: Why does the teacher offer Mindy the false answer "flour"? Indeed, why does she interrupt Mindy and the other children at all?

As I said above, when the teacher interrupts students like Mindy, the child is not bothered or disrupted. This is not so for some (but not all) of the African-American children in this teacher's class and in other classrooms where teachers have behaved in similar ways. Here teacher and student are not in synch. In these cases, the teacher seems to interrupt at the wrong places and the child is disrupted in his or her talk. That seems strange, doesn't it?

Problem 3

So go through the data and point to aspects of the data that an outsider might find strange, worth commenting on, or worth asking about. You are primarily going to be looking at how the teacher interacts with the child. Then hypothesize what the teacher means and what she is trying to accomplish moment by moment. When you are done, consider the following question: What do you think the overall purpose of sharing time is for this teacher and others like her?

MINDY'S SHARING-TIME TURN
Mindy: When I was in day camp /
            we made these /
            um candles //
Teacher: You made them?
Mindy: And uh /
            I-I tried it with different colors /
            with both of them but /
            one just came out/ this one just came out blue /
            and I don't know what this color is //
Teacher: That's neat-o //

Tell the kids how you do it from the very start //
Pretend we don't know a thing about candles//
. . . OK//
What did you do first?
What did you use?
Flour?

Mindy: Um . . . here's some /
hot wax / some real hot wax /
that you /
just take a string /
and tie a knot in it //
and dip the string in the um wax //

Teacher: What makes it uh have a shape?

Mindy: Um / you just shape it //

Teacher: Oh you shaped it with your hand //
mmm //

Mindy: But you have/
first you have to stick it into the wax/
and then water /
and then keep doing that until it gets to the size you want it //

Teacher: OK //
Who knows what the string is for? [asked to the class]

Problem 4

In the advertisement below for Camel cigarettes, it is easy for most of us to see things that are strange. Here the cigarette company is trying to get us to see cigarettes in a new way, trying to get us to begin to take for granted a new way of thinking about cigarettes, a rather hard task for a product that kills people. How would they like us to see their new cigarette in particular and cigarettes in general?

CAMEL SIGNATURE MELLOW
is deliciously smooth with sun-cured
tobacco taste.

Signature Blends are the result of
thousands of passionately creative
adult smokers working together to
help create our most severely
interesting smokes yet.

The art of collaboration never tasted so good.

Get in the Blend@
camelsmokes.com

Reading

Michaels, S. (1981). Sharing time: Children's narrative styles and differential access to literacy. *Language in Society* 10: 423–42 [Mindy's data is from Sarah Michaels' research on sharing time.]

Grammar Interlude #3: Intonation

This section deals with a few aspects of how speech is produced and what this has to do with the sorts of meanings we speakers hope to convey and that we hearers (always actively and creatively) try to "recover" or fill in. Thanks to the way the human brain and vocal system is built, speech is produced in small spurts. These spurts each have their own intonation contour (see below) and often are preceded and/or followed by slight pauses. Unless we pay close attention, we don't usually hear these little spurts, because our ear puts them together and gives us the illusion of speech being an unbroken and continuous stream. In English, these spurts are often, though not always, one "clause" long. The spurts have been called "tone units," "idea units," or "lines." Here I will use the term "idea units."

In a rough and ready way we can define a "clause" as any verb and the elements that "cluster" with it. So in a sentence like "Mary left the party because she was tired," we have two clauses, "Mary left the party" ("Mary" and "the party" cluster with the verb "left") and "because she was tired" ("she" clusters with the very "was tired"). The sentence "Mary left the party" contains only one clause. In a sentence like "Mary intended to leave the party," we have two clauses, "Mary intended" and "to leave the party" (where "Mary" is understood as the subject of "to leave"). Here the second clause ("to leave the party") is embedded in the first clause ("Mary intended") as the direct object of the verb "intend." These two clauses are so tightly bound together that they would most often be said as a single spurt of speech.

In the example below, taken from a story told by a seven-year-old African-American child at sharing time, each speech spurt is one clause long, except 2 and 5 where the child has detached parts of clauses to be spurts on their own (of course, children's speech units tend to be shorter than adults). Each spurt is one idea and each spurt contains one piece of new information:

1. there was a hook
2. on the top of the stairway
3. an' my father was pickin me up
4. an' I got stuck on the hook
5. up there
6. an' I hadn't had breakfast
7. he wouldn't take me down
8. until I finished all my breakfast
9. cause I didn't like oatmeal either

To understand how these spurts work in English (they work differently in different languages), we need to discuss a set of closely interrelated linguistic concepts: function words, content words, information, stress, and intonation. We will start with the distinction between function words and content words.

Content words (sometimes also called "lexical words") belong to the major parts of speech: nouns, verbs, and adjectives. These categories are said to be "open categories" in the sense that they each have a large number of members and languages readily add new members to these categories through borrowing from other languages or the invention of new words.

Function words (also sometimes called "grammatical words") belong to smaller categories, categories which are said to be "closed categories" in the sense that each category has relatively few members and languages are resistant to borrowing or inventing anew such words (though they sometimes do). Such categories as determiners (e.g., "the," "a/n," "this/that," "these/those"— these are also sometimes called "articles"), pronouns (e.g. "he/him," "she/her," "it," "himself," "herself"), prepositions (e.g., "in," "on," "to," "of"), and quantifiers (e.g., "some," "many," "all," "none") are function word categories.

Function words show how the content words in a phrase, clause, or sentence relate to each other, or how pieces of information fit into the overall ongoing communication. For example, the definite determiner "the" signals that the information following it is already "known" to the speaker and hearer. Pronouns signal that their referents have been previously mentioned, or are readily identifiable in the context of communication or on the basis of the speaker and hearer's mutual knowledge. Prepositions link nouns and noun phrases to other words (e.g., in "lots of luck" *of* links *luck* to *lots*; in "ideas in my mind," *in* links *my mind* to *ideas*; and in "look at the girl," *at* links *the girl* to the verb *look*). I have not yet mentioned adverbs. Adverbs are messy and complicated. Very often they function in a way that is midway between a function word and a content word.

Since function words carry less of the real content of the communication (their job being to signal the grammar of the sentence), we can say that they tend to be *informationally less salient* than content words. While they are certainly helpful, they are often dispensable, as anyone who has written a telegram knows (if there is anyone left who has!).

Thus, let us make a distinction between two types of information in a sentence. First, information that is relatively new and relatively unpredictable I will call "informationally salient." The actual specific meaning of any content word in a sentence is unpredictable without knowing exactly what the content word means. If a content word is left out of a sentence it is often hard to predict what it would have been. Thus, content words are usually informationally more salient than function words.

Second, information that is given, assumed already known, or predictable, I will call "informationally less salient." Very often even if you have not heard a function word you could pretty well predict where it should have been and what word exactly it would have been. For example, if you heard "Boy has lots ideas," you could predict that "the" is missing in front of "boy," and "of" between "lots" and "ideas." If, however, you heard "That man has lots of," you could not predict what content word should come after "of." Thus, function words are usually informationally less salient than content words.

In general, then, the content word-function word distinction is a distinction between two types of information. However, beyond this gross dichotomy, the distinction between information that is more or less salient is one that can only be drawn in the actual context of communication. We turn to this matter now.

Information saliency in English is marked by *stress*. In turn, the different stress patterns in a spurt of speech set up its *intonational contour*. To see what these terms mean, consider the little dialogue below:

> Speaker A: Have you read any good books lately?
> Speaker B: Well, I read a shocking book recently. [Goes on to describe the book.]

How speaker B crafts her response is partially set up by the remark made by speaker A, which here represents part of the context in which B's response occurs. Let's think a moment about how the utterance uttered by B might have been said. English speakers mark the information saliency of a word by how much *stress* they give the word.

Stress is a *psychological concept, not a physical one.* English speakers can (unconsciously) use and hear several different degrees of stress in a speech spurt, but this is not physically marked in any uniform and consistent way. Stress is physically marked by a combination of increased loudness, increased length, and by changing the pitch of one's voice (raising or lowering the pitch, or gliding up or down in pitch) on a word's primary ("accented") syllable. Any one or two of these can be used to trade off for the others in a quite complicated way.

In any case, English speakers unconsciously use and recognize stress, and it can be brought to conscious awareness with a little practice (some people are better than others at bringing stress differences to consciousness awareness, though we can all unconsciously use and recognize it). A word with more stress than another word sounds more salient (it often sounds louder, though it may not really be louder, but just be longer or have a pitch change on it, both of which will make English speakers think it sounds louder).

So let's return to speaker B's response and assume it was said as one spurt of speech. It's first word, "well," can be said with little stress, on a relatively low pitch and/or with little loudness, since it carries no content, but simply links speaker's B turn to speaker A's. This is not to say that words like "well" are not important in other ways; such words, in fact, have interesting discourse functions in helping to link and package information across sentences. Since "well" is the first word of speaker B's spurt of speech, and starts her turn, it will be said on a pitch that is taken to be close to the "basic pitch" at which speaker B will be speaking (perhaps, kicked up a bit from B's basic pitch and, too, from where speaker A left off, to mark B's turn as beginning).

"I" is completely predictable in the context of the question speaker A has asked, and it is a function word. Thus, it is not very salient informationally and will receive little stress, just enough loudness to get it said and with a pitch close to the basic pitch speaker B has chosen (for this spurt or related run of spurts as she keeps speaking). The content word "read" is predicable because it has already occurred in speaker A's preceding question. So, too, for the word "book" later in B's remark. Both of these words will have a fairly low degree of stress. They will have more than the function words "well," "I," and "a," since as content words they do carry content, but certainly much less than the word "shocking" which carries new and non-redundant information. The indefinite article "a," of course, is informationally very unsalient and will get little stress. The speaker will mark what stress words like "read" and "book" have by bumping the pitch of her voice a bit up or down from the "basic pitch" she has established or is establishing and/or by increasing loudness a bit relative to words like "I" and "a."

On the other hand, the word "shocking" is the most unpredictable, informationally salient, new information in the sentence. The speaker will mark this saliency by giving this word the most stress in the sentence. Such a word or phrase, which carries the greatest degree of stress in a sentence (or a given spurt of speech) is marked not just by bumping the pitch of the voice up or down a bit and/or by increasing loudness, but by a real *pitch movement* (called a "glide").

The speaker begins to glide the pitch of her voice up or down (or even up-then-down or down-then-up) on the word "shocking," allowing the pitch movement to continue to glide up or down (whichever she has chosen) on the words that follow it, here "book" and "recently." Of course, what sort of pitch movement the speaker chooses, that is, whether up, down, up-then-down, or down-then-up, has a meaning (for example, the speaker's pitch glide rises in certain sorts of questions and falls in certain sorts of statements). We are not now concerned, however, with these meaning differences.

The pitch glide which begins on the word "shocking" marks "shocking" as the *focus* of the *intonation unit*. An "intonation unit" is all the words that precede a pitch glide and the words following it over which the glide continues to move (fall or rise). The next intonation unit begins when the glide is finished. The speaker often hesitates a bit between intonation units (usually we pay no attention to these hesitations) and then steps the pitch up or down a bit from the basic pitch of the last intonation unit on the first word of the next unit (regardless of whether it is a content word or not) to "key" the hearer that a new intonation unit is beginning.

In B's response to A, the content word "recently" is fairly redundant (not too salient) because, while it has not been mentioned in A's question, it is certainly implied by A's use of the word "lately." Thus, it receives about as much stress, or, perhaps a little more, than the content words "read" and "book." The speaker may increase her loudness a bit on "recently" and/or bump the pitch of her voice up or down a bit on its main syllable (i.e., "cent") as her pitch continues basically to glide up or down over "recently" as part of (and the ending of) the pitch glide started on the word "shocking."

Below, I give a visual representation of how speaker B might have said his utterance:

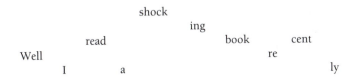

There are, of course, other ways to have said this utterance, ways which carry different nuances of meaning.

There is one last important feature of English intonation to cover here. In English, if the intonation focus (the pitch glide) is placed on the last content word of a phrase (say on "flower" in the phrase "the pretty red flower"), then the salient, new information is taken to be either just this word *or* the material in the phrase as a whole (thus, either just "flower" or the whole phrase "the pretty red flower"). Of course, the context will usually determine which is the case. If the intonation focus (pitch glide) is placed on a word other than the last word in the phrase, then that word is unequivocally taken to be the salient, new information (e.g., if the intonation focus is on "red" in "the pretty red flower," then the salient, new information is taken to be just "red"). In our example above, "shocking" is not the last word in its phrase (it is an adjective in a noun phrase "a shocking book") and, thus, is unequivocally the new, salient information.

An interesting situation arises when the intonation focus (pitch glide) is placed in the last (content) word in a sentence. Then, we cannot tell whether the salient, new information the speaker is trying to indicate is *just* that word or also other words that precede it and go with it in the phrase or phrases to which it belongs. So in an utterance like "This summer, Mary finished fifteen books," if the speaker starts her glide on "books," the new salient information she intends to mark may be just "books" (answering a question like "Mary finished fifteen whats?"), or "fifteen books" ("What has Mary finished?"), since "books" is part of the noun phrase "fifteen books." The new salient information could even be "finished fifteen books," since these words constitute together a verb phrase ending with, and containing, the word "book" (What has Mary done?"). In fact, since "books" is the last word of the sentence, everything in the sentence could be taken to be new and salient ("What happened?"). Of course, in actual contexts it becomes clearer what is and what is not new and salient information.

Ultimately, the context in which an utterance is uttered, together with the assumptions that the speaker makes about the hearer's knowledge, usually determines the degrees of informational saliency for each word and phrase in a sentence. Speakers, however, can also choose to downplay or play up the information saliency or importance of a word or phrase and ignore aspects of the context or what they assume the hearer to know already. This is part of how speakers actively create or manipulate contexts, rather than just simply respond to them. Of course, if speakers take this too far, they can end up saying things that sound odd and "out of context."

In a given context, even a function word's information might become important, and then the function word would have a greater degree of stress. For example, consider the context below:

  A.   Did Mary shoot her husband?
  B.   No, she shot YOUR husband!

In this context, the information carried by "your" is unpredictable, new, and salient. Thus, it gets stressed (in fact, it gets extra stress because it is contrastive—*yours* not *hers*—and surprising). In fact, in (B) given its context (A), it will be the focus of the intonation unit. When speakers want to contrast or emphasize something, they can use extra stress (marked by more dramatic pitch changes and/or loudness)—this is called "emphatic stress."

The intonation contour of an utterance is an important part of its meaning. The intonation contour gives listeners clues about how to interpret what the speaker has said, as well as clues about the speaker's attitude and emotions. There is much more detailed information about intonation available in linguistics than we can cover in this book. However, we can state an Intonation Tool:

Tool #5: The Intonation Tool

For any communication, ask how a speaker's intonation contour contributes to the meaning of an utterance. What idea units did the speaker use? What information did the speaker make salient (in terms of where the intonational focus is placed)? What information did the speaker background as given or old by making it less salient? What sorts of attitudinal and/or affective (emotional) meaning does the intonation contour convey? In dealing with written texts, always read them out loud and ask what sort of intonation contour readers must add to the sentences to make them make full sense.

In this book, we will not transcribe most properties of the intonational contours of utterances. We do often transcribe whether an idea unit (tone unit) ends on a final or non-final pitch glide (remember idea units end on the pitch glide that constitutes the focus of the idea unit). When an idea unit ends on a falling pitch glide (or a rise–fall with a good deal of fall), it sounds "final." Information is closed off and what comes next is treated as a separate piece of information. This is also true when an idea unit ends in a rise, which often signals a question ("Did she leave?"). Final contours, contours that end on final pitch glides, are like a speech equivalent of a period or question mark (or, in some cases, an exclamation mark).

When an idea unit ends in a rise, fall, rise–fall, or fall–rise of pitch, but the rise or fall is small, it sounds non-final, as if the next idea unit following is part of the information being conveyed. Non-final contours, contours that end on a non-final pitch glide, are like the speech equivalent of commas.

Problem 5

Consider the data from the child at the start of this section, reprinted below. If you had said this where would you have placed a final contour (symbolized by "//") and where a non-final one ("/")? Why?

1. there was a hook
2. on the top of the stairway
3. an' my father was pickin me up
4. an' I got stuck on the hook
5. up there
6. an' I hadn't had breakfast
7. he wouldn't take me down
8. until I finished all my breakfast
9. cause I didn't like oatmeal either

The girl placed a non-final contour on each idea unit except the last one ("cause I didn't like oatmeal either"). This girl and some (but not all) other African-American children in the classroom, when they were telling stories, placed a final contour at the ends of "episodes." Other children in the classroom placed them at the ends of what would have been, loosely speaking, sentences in writing (so they might well have placed a final contour at the end of lines 2, 5, 6, and 9 (and perhaps, too, at line 3).

Consider again the data on sharing time in Section 1.5, do you think this fact about the placement of final intonation contours had anything to do with why the teacher's interruptions disrupted some of the African-American children?

The teacher thought some of the African-American children "rambled on." Do the different uses of final intonation contours illuminate why the teacher might have made this judgment, keeping in mind that no speakers are consciously aware of the intonation contours people are using? Listeners from different cultures just expect to hear things like final contours at certain places and get disturbed if they do not, though they do not know why they are disturbed. They have to seek some reason, however spurious it might be. This sort of thing happens often when something in someone's language bothers us, but we do not know what its linguistic basis is or that it even has one.

Written language leaves out intonation—that is, the stress, pitch or tone, loudness, and pacing of the voice. When we read, we can add back these speech elements by "speaking" silently in our own minds (in the Middle Ages people actually mumbled out loud as they read). This way we make guess about and add information about information saliency, emphasis, attitude, and emotion to the text, and, in that sense, "rewrite" it.

Problem 6

Consider the two written passage below. (The first is from Paul Gagnon, *Democracy's Untold Story: What World History Textbooks Neglect*, Washington, D.C.: American Federation of Teachers, 1987, p. 65. The second is from George Saunders' book *The Braindead Megaphone: Essays*, New York: Riverhead Books, p. 251.) Say these passages out loud and pay attention to how you emphasize words, what words you make most important and what words you do not, and what sorts of attitude or emotion, if any, you add to the text as you speak. Can you say each passage in different ways? Can you say them "wrong," in a way that sounds wrong—why does it sound wrong? Compare how you say each passage as speech to how others do.

1. Also secure, by 1689, was the principle of representative government, as tested against the two criteria for valid constitutions proposed in the previous chapter. As to the first criterion, there was a genuine balance of power in English society, expressing itself in the Whig and Tory parties. As narrowly confined to the privileged classes as these were, they nonetheless represented different factions and tendencies. Elections meant real choice among separate, contending parties and personalities.

2. Now it can be told.
    Last Thursday, my organization, People Reluctant To Kill For An Abstraction (PRKA), orchestrated an overwhelming show of force around the globe.
    At precisely nine in the morning, working with focus and stealth, our entire membership succeeded in simultaneously beheading no one. At nine-thirty, we embarked on Phase II, during which our entire membership simultaneously did not force a single man to simulate sex with another man. At ten, Phase III began, during which not a single one of us blew himself/herself up in a crowded public place. ... In addition, at eleven, in Phase IV, zero (0) planes were flown into buildings.

Reading

Bolinger, D. (1989). *Intonation and its uses: Melody in grammar and discourse*. Stanford, CA: Stanford University Press. [A classic.]

Crystal, D. (1969). *Prosodic systems and intonation in English*. Cambridge: Cambridge University Press.

Halliday, M. A. K. and Greaves, W. (2008). *Intonation in the grammar of English*. London: Equinox Publishing.

Ladd, R. D. (1996). *Intonational phonology*. Cambridge: Cambridge University Press.

1.6 The Frame Problem

Falsification

The questions in Sections 1.4 and 1.5 do not have definitive answers. Discourse analysis is an empirical enterprise. Any initial answer to a question is really just a hypothesis. A hypothesis is an educated guess based on some evidence. After we form a hypothesis, then we seek yet more evidence. At some point, we feel the amount of evidence we have makes us confident enough to claim that our hypothesis is true. Yet even then additional evidence—found by ourselves or other investigators—could eventually show that we are wrong or, at least, that additions or changes must be made to our claim.

Empirical inquiry—that is, any investigations whose claims are based on evidence—is about falsification. We seek to make a claim and then see if we or others can falsify it. If it is falsified, we learn something. The field, as a whole, moves forward. In that sense, empirical inquiry is a social endeavor. We look to our colleagues to help us by trying to falsify our claims.

Because fields move forward through falsifying claims, there is no need to be timid about hypotheses. If one seeks to make the safest and most narrow hypothesis, then that hypothesis is harder to falsify. Even if it turns out to be true, we have not learned as much as we could. If we make a bolder and broader hypothesis, it is easier to falsify and we can learn more.

To see how this works, consider an example: Let's say you, in the United States, had seen lots of White swans and no black ones. You could make the narrow hypothesis: "All swans in the U.S. are White" (or even worse, "All the swans I have seen are White"). Or you could make the broader hypothesis: "All swans are White."

This latter hypothesis will turn out to be false and will be shown to be so when someone shows us that there are black swans in Australia (as there are). Now we can retrench to a narrower hypothesis like "All swans outside Australia are White" and see if this can be falsified. Having made the bolder hypothesis we have forced ourselves to learn more about swans by pushing ourselves and others to search more widely for evidence (in this case, to go out and look for black swans well beyond the United States).

Not all people agree with this view of science. Some people think you should only make the safest and most narrow hypotheses. But if you look at the more mature sciences and the best scientists this is not how, in my opinion, they behave. Being wrong in science is not a bad thing; it is a good thing, so long as the claims you make are clear and interesting enough to be tested and lead to further inquiry and further evidence gathering.

The Frame Problem

Discourse analysis has a special and interesting problem when it comes to gathering evidence and falsifying claims. What something means in language—and, thus, the answers to the questions in Sections 1.4 and 1.5—is partly a matter of context, as we have already seen. The same words can have different meanings in different contexts. For example, consider that the word "coffee" means something different in "The coffee spilled, clean it up" when I hand you a mop than when I hand you a broom. "You are one of a kind" can be, in one context, a sarcastic insult (when it means something like you are a one of a kind idiot) and, in another context, a compliment (when it means something like you are a one of a kind friend).

One way we give evidence for claims in discourse analysis is by showing that, given the context in which something was uttered, it must or probably means what we say it does. For example, given that the coffee that spilled was liquid and a mop was involved, "coffee" in "The coffee spilled, clean it up" almost certainly means "coffee as liquid" and not "coffee as beans or grains" ("The coffee spilled, go get a broom") or "coffee as coffee tins" ("The coffee spilled, restack it").

However, context is, in a sense, infinite. We can always learn more about the context in which an utterance was made (the physical, social, cultural, and institutional environment, the previous utterances and interaction of the people involved, their shared knowledge, including shared cultural knowledge). How much of the context should we take into account? Isn't it always possible that if we consider more of the context, we will find out that claims about meaning we thought were true are, in reality, false?

An example: We are sure Joe and Jack are friends—because look at how they smile at each other—and so when Joe says "Jack, you are one of a kind," we are sure he means it as a compliment. But then we research their histories and find out that they have been pretending to be friends all along for business reasons when years ago they had a serious falling out and they actually hate each other. Perhaps, now we think, Joe meant "You are one of a kind" as an insult and Jack knew it, but they both pretended otherwise. More research has shown us the context was not what we thought it was when we just looked at the smiles on their faces.

We can always learn more—or at least this is so in a great many cases—that makes us questions judgments we have made about what people mean. Even if we know a lot about the context, we can still find out more that may make us question judgments we have made about meaning.

This problem has been called "the Frame Problem." The Frame Problem, more formally put, is this: Any aspect of context can affect the meaning of an utterance. Context, however, is indefinitely large, ranging from local matters like the positioning of bodies and eye gaze, through people's beliefs and previous interactions, to historical, institutional, and cultural settings. No matter how much of the context we have considered in offering an interpretation of an utterance, there is always the possibility of considering other and additional aspects of the context, and these new considerations may change how we interpret the utterance.

Where do we cut off consideration of context? How can we be sure any interpretation is "right," if considering further aspects of the context might well change that interpretation?

The Frame Problem is not just the problem that what we think we know about the context may turn out to be false (as it was in the Joe and Jack case). What we know about the context can be true, but too limited. For example, in the data in Section 1.4, it is easy to conclude that Karen is just perturbed by the fact that Sara did not attend the summer institute when she said she was going to. And this is true, as far as it goes. But when we learn more about the context, as we will in a moment, it is easy to conclude that Karen is perturbed about bigger issues, as well, and is using the Sara's failure to come to the institute as but one example of a larger problem.

Let me make it clear that the Frame Problem is a problem both for everyday people and for us discourse analysts. We both face the same problems: How do we know we won't learn more that makes us doubt what we thought people meant? How do know where to stop considering more aspects of context so we can get on with communicating or analyzing?

Everyday people solve the Frame Problem by making judgments about how much and what aspects of the context are "relevant" to what a person has just said; that is, they bring to communication standards of relevance. At the same time, when things seem to be going awry, when communication is becoming confusing or unclear, they consider more of the context and change their judgment about what was and was not relevant.

We will do the same, except we will be yet more vigilant about context than are everyday people (who, after all, must get on with the business of living and acting). We will always be willing to push context a bit further than we would in everyday life to see if we can falsify our claims about meaning.

The Frame Problem in Action

To see the Frame Problem in action consider the data we saw in Section 1.4, which I reprint below:

LAST YEAR /
Mary Washington /
who is our curriculum coordinator here /
had a call from Sara //

at Woodson //
And called me /
and said (pause) /
"We have a person from Woodson /
who's in the History Department /
she's interested in doing some RESEARCH /
into BLACK / history //
And she would like to get involved with the school /
And here's her number /
Give her a call" //
And we- I DID call her /
And we um both expected /
to be around /
for the summer institute //
at Woodson //
I did /
ah participate in it /
But SARA /
wasn't able to do that //
(Sara tries unsuccessfully to interrupt)

In Section 1.4, I asked the following question: What did Sara do that angered or perturbed Karen? Just looking at the transcript and the little bit of context I gave you, one might very well conclude that what perturbed Karen was that Sara had failed to show up for the summer institute. But, as the transcript shows, Sara wanted to interrupt Karen at this point, though she could not do so, as Karen plowed on past her attempt. We know from other data that Sara wanted to explain that she had a good reason to miss the institute and that Karen knew the reason. Under such circumstances we could have imagined Karen not being bothered by Sara's failure to attend, but, nonetheless, she makes a big deal of it.

We know more about the context from another piece of the data I also gave you earlier, reprinted below:

Well at that point there were three of us (laughs) //
Back in the summer //
And all three of us had not yet /
Met together //

From this we know that Karen has done things to get ready for the project, including getting her colleague Jane to be part of it. We can hypothesize here that Karen is bothered by the fact that an official meeting of the project was called so late, so long after Sara's call to the school and Karen's own initial efforts. Since it was Sara's project—she had asked for it—it was her responsibility to move things along, and yet for a long time it was Karen who was moving things along.

So both Sara's failure to call a meeting and her failure to show up at the institute look to Karen like a lack of taking responsibility where one has contracted an obligation to do so. So we can hypothesize now that what bothers Karen is Sara's lack of taking responsibility and, in a sense, putting the burden on Karen.

But now there is another part of the context that many readers of this book will not be familiar with. In the school in which Karen works—and this is true in many other schools—there are "official rules" and an "official chain of command" and there are "unofficial rules" and "unofficial chain of command." In the official rules, an administrator like Mary Washington is the one from whom one would seek permission to involve the school's children in a research project.

In the unofficial rules the teacher "owns" the children in her class (as a teacher says in the data—see below) and one must seek her permission first and informally for the involvement of herself and her children before going to an administrator. Sara, by calling Mary Washington first, and having Mary "order" Karen to call Sara, had unknowingly violated the unofficial rules and unofficial chain of command.

We know from other parts of our data that this issue greatly concerned Karen and her friend Jane (who she had involved in the project). For example, in a much later meeting of the same group, Jane had the following to say:

Well I think /
One thing you need to recognize /
About the STRUCTURE of the Middleview schools
Is that if Su, Lucy, Karen, and I /
Or any combination thereof /
Are involving our classrooms /
We are the people who need to be asked /
And to be plugged into it //
Joe does /
Um as curriculum coordinator for Field Street /
Does not have the right to commit Su Wilson //
Nor Linda Defoe //
Nor does Mary /
Have the right to commit /
Or structure the grant for us //
Uh it becomes a question /
Like Karen said /
This isn't her priority area / [Because Karen teaches English, not History like Jane]
That she wants to be in //
If it is mine /
Or someone else /
We are the direct people //
In a sense we OWN the kids //
If you want the children to be doing the work /
You've got to get the classroom teacher /
Not the curriculum coordinator or [the next speaker interrupts Jane]

Jane is here talking in a context where Sara has written a grant proposal to continue the project in the next year and has, once again, gone to Mary Washington first and not the teachers. Joe is an administrator (and Su and Lucy are teachers at his school) who was also at the first meeting. Mary is, of course, Mary Washington, the same administrator who Sara called and who told Karen to call her. Jane here explicitly says that when someone wants to involve a teacher's classroom that teacher must be asked (and she means asked first, since she is well aware that administrators must give permission eventually).

When Jane says "structure" with emphatic stress she could mean a formal and official structure or an informal and unofficial one. Since Sara and Mary have, by the time Jane is talking, twice gone ahead and agreed to involve the teachers' classrooms without having asked them first, it is clear that the structure to which Jane is referring is an informal, unofficial, but nonetheless binding one for Jane and her friend Karen (who in this meeting strongly agrees with Jane).

So now, with more context—by framing our data in a wider set of contextual data—we can hypothesize that another thing that perturbed Karen was that Sara "broke the rules." She failed to know the rules of the school as a culture even as she wanted the school's involvement and support. At a deeper level, this seems to Karen an example of Sara's lack of taking responsibility. Thus, she uses her utterances to cast Sara as untrustworthy person who does not take proper responsibility.

Karen was not trying to end her involvement with the project. She was not going to walk out. She was still more than willing to go on with the project and she did. She had every intention of dealing with Sara. She wanted to be part of the project and she very much wanted the resources the project would bring her students, since her school was not a wealthy one by any means. What Karen was using language to do here was to "correct the hierarchy" between her and Sara.

By going to the administrator Mary Washington, Sara had set up an "official" hierarchy in which Karen was just a follower to be ordered around. Karen is making it clear that she is not there to be ordered around by Sara, but to be a full and equal participant. She is showing herself to be a do-er and leader and organizer in her own right, while Sara has slacked off in these respects.

Karen is trying to assert the rights of the "unofficial" hierarchy in which the teacher is the boss when it comes to her children and classroom. In fact, she and the other teachers involved in the project will eventually make it clear to all that they are the "protectors" and "nurturers" of their children and not just their "teachers" and these are roles no administrator or university professor can take over from them.

So why doesn't Karen just directly say Sara broke the rules by going first to Mary Washington? Well, these are "unofficial rules" and there is an administrator present in the meeting. The people in the meeting do not all know each other as well as they will after many more meetings. Further, it would take a great deal of time to explicate the whole system for people who don't know it. So Karen uses other examples of Sara's lack of understanding and responsibility, since her main goal appears not to be to explicate how the "rules" work in schools (not yet), but to correct the hierarchy.

Since we have argued that hierarchy and status are at stake here, we can add another piece of the context that would seem to support this. As in many other towns in the United States, in Middleview there is a good deal of tension both between the town and the university (a town–gown problem). The university has been in the town for over a hundred years, but it is a private and elite university and the town is a working class, post-industrial town.

Furthermore, there is a tension between teachers and the university, which trained some of them (though most were trained either by the Catholic college in town or the local state university). The teachers see the university professors, including those in Education (as were the Research Institute people), as disconnected from the realities of teaching and schools. The professors see the teachers as "a-theoretical" and anti-research. This division is made worse by the fact that the vast majority of the teachers in the town were born there and intend to stay there, while the vast majority of the professors at the university were not born there and many do not intend to spend their entire careers there.

All these aspects of context certainly make it likely that issues of hierarchy, status, and leadership will be foregrounded in the interactions between these teachers and university academics. Such issues would have to be dealt with if one wanted to facilitate the workings of this group of teachers and academics. Indeed, this is one role that discourse analysis can help with. We can study how things go wrong and try to help people themselves understand and deal with enough of the context in which they are communicating to make things go right or, at least, "righter."

Remember, however, that even though we have now explicated more of the context, our claims are and will always remain open to falsification. They are, perhaps, at this point a bit beyond mere hypotheses (guesses). We are getting a fair amount of evidence. Nonetheless, we ourselves or others must continue to try to falsify them by learning more about the context. As we learn more and more and then come to a point where we are no longer led to change or deepen our claims, we gain more confidence in our claims and they grow in validity. At that point, we stop and believe our claims, though even then somebody someday may choose later to re-study our data or similar data and question our claims or, at least, modify them. That is all to the good. This is an empirical and social enterprise.

Now, go back to the questions in Section 1.4 and answer them again. Compare your first answers and the ones you give now. Consider areas where you would disagree with claims I have made (if you do) and why. Where do you want more evidence? How would you get it? What other questions would you now ask about the data? If you agree with some of my claims, how would you state them in your own words?

As Karen's data shows, it is hard at times to know just how much information and how many assumptions and inferences that we can make or discover are actually relevant to a communication we are in or are analyzing. How far should we go? That is the Frame Problem and the Frame Problem makes the Filling In task hard at times (whether for everyday people or us discourse analysts).

Reading

Clark, A. (1997), *Being there: Putting brain, body, and world together again*, Cambridge, MA: MIT Press.

Ford, K. M. and Pylyshyn, Z. W., Eds., (1996), *The Robot's dilemma revisited: The frame problem in artificial intelligence*, Norwood, NJ: Ablex.

Popper, K. (2002). *The logic of scientific discovery*. London: Routledge (org. 1935). [This is the classic source for the falsification view of scientific practice.]

1.7 The Frame Problem Tool

The Frame Problem tells us that we should, when we think we are done with an analysis, see if we can look at the context again and widen what we take to be relevant. If looking at more context does not change what we think the language means, then we can be satisfied, at least for the time being, that our analysis is on the right track (though it might always be falsified later). If considering more context or rethinking what is relevant in the context does change what we think, then we have to push the analysis further.

The Frame Problem is a way to keep us honest. We cannot always find out more about the context of data we are analyzing, but we can try. So here is the Frame Tool:

Tool #6: The Frame Tool

After you have completed your discourse analysis—after you have taken into consideration all the aspects of the context that you see as relevant to the meaning of the data—see if you can find out anything additional about the context in which the data occurred and see if this changes your analysis. If it doesn't, your analysis is safe for now. If it does, you have more work to do. Always push your knowledge of the context as far as you can just to see if aspects of the context are relevant that you might at first have not thought were relevant or if you can discover entirely new aspects of the context.

1.8 Working with the Frame Problem Tool

Consider the following discussion drawn from Roger Lewontin's book *Biology as Ideology*. Lewontin (born 1929) is a well-known biologist at Harvard. In his book he tells us that from the point of view of medical science, it is a truism that the cause of tuberculosis is the tubercle bacillus. But then he tells us that tuberculosis was a very common disease in the sweatshops and factories of the nineteenth century, whereas it was much less common among rural people and in the upper classes. So, Lewontin asks, why don't we conclude that the cause of tuberculosis is unregulated industrial capitalism?

In fact, in light of the history of health and disease in modern Europe, Lewontin's explanation makes sense. An examination of the causes of death, first systematically recorded in the 1830s in Britain and a bit later in North America, show that most people did, indeed, die of infectious diseases. As the nineteenth century progressed, however, the death rate from all these diseases continuously decreased. To quote Lewontin:

> Smallpox was dealt with by a medical advance, but one that could hardly be claimed by modern medicine, since smallpox vaccine was discovered in the eighteenth century and already was quite widely used by the early part of the nineteenth. The death rates of the major killers like bronchitis, pneumonia, and tuberculosis fell regularly during the nineteenth century, with no obvious cause. There was no observable effect on the death rate after the germ theory of disease was announced in 1876 by Robert Koch. The death rate from these infectious diseases simply continued to decline as if Koch had never lived. By the time chemical therapy was introduced for tuberculosis in the earlier part of this century, more than 90 percent of the decrease in the death rate from that disease had already occurred. (Lewontin 1991: pp. 43–4)

It was not modern sanitation or less crowding in cities that led to the progressive reductions in the death rate, since the major killers in the nineteenth century were respiratory and not waterborne, and parts of our cities are as crowded today as they were in the 1850s. More likely, the reduction in death from infectious diseases is due to general improvement in nutrition related to an increase in the real wage in "developed countries": "In countries like Brazil today, infant mortality rises and falls with decreases and increases in the minimum wage" (Lewontin 1991: p. 44).

What Lewontin is doing here is widening the contextual frame within which we look at a perfectly "natural" and "obvious" claim from biology. He is juxtaposing the way that medicine or biology looks at a claim (the cause of tuberculosis is the tubercle bacillus) with how other areas, such as public health or a sociopolitical discussion of capitalism, would look at the claim.

Another example that Lewontin gives is the way in which biologists talk about genes "self-replicating." Yet, genes cannot make themselves (any more than a blueprint can make a house). Genes are made by a complex machinery of proteins that uses the genes as models for more genes. It is not the genes that are self-replicating, it is the entire organism as complex system. Isolating genes as "master molecules," and effacing the "manufacturing machinery" of proteins that actually carry out the work of making other proteins and genes themselves, is "another unconscious ideological commitment, one that places brains above brawn, mental work as superior to mere physical work, information as higher than action" (Lewontin 1991: p. 48).

Lewontin is using what we have called The Frame Problem Tool in a certain way. He is aware that when biologists say something like "the cause of tuberculosis is the tubercle bacillus," they mean "cause" in the narrow sense of "physical/medical cause," if they actually consciously think about and reflect on the matter at all. Thus, they are considering the social and political parts of the context of their utterance (i.e., the social and political facts Lewontin points to as true about who dies from tuberculosis and who does not) as irrelevant to their meaning and, thus, too, not part of what listeners are meant to fill in.

Lewontin broadens the frame within which we look at the statement—increases the amount of context he takes as relevant—to change how we think about the original statement. We now, perhaps, see the statement as less than the whole story, not completely true, as ignoring or effacing important issues. This sort of broadening of the contextual frame is one way to engage in a politically committed discourse analysis and to engage in what we can call "resistant" listening and reading (i.e., resisting the limits the speaker or writer wants listeners or readers to put on what is relevant information in the context).

Problem 7

Here are some questions for you to think about in terms of using the Frame Problem Tool:

1. Do you "buy" Lewontin's analysis? Do you think it is "fair"?
2. What do you think the purpose is (or purposes are) of Lewontin's analysis? Do you think that his way of broadening the contextual frame is a good way to achieve these purposes?
3. Lewontin clearly has deep political commitments (he has sometimes identified himself as a Marxist or at least as left-leaning). Do you think this invalidates his analysis? Does it make his analyses "unscientific"? "Unempirical"?
4. Malaria, an infectious disease, is one of the most severe public health problems worldwide. It is a leading cause of death and disease in many developing countries, where young children and pregnant women are the groups most affected. Worldwide, one death in three is from an infectious or communicable disease. However, almost all these deaths occur in the

non-industrialized world. Health inequality effects not just how people live, but often dictates how and at what age they die (see: www.cdc.gov/malaria/impact/index.htm and http://ucatlas.ucsc.edu/cause.php). Given this information, do you find the following dialogue odd? If you do, why? If you don't, why not?

Question: Why do so many children in Africa die before they are five years old?
Answer: Because they get infectious diseases like malaria and others.

Reading

Lewontin, R. C. (1991). *Biology as ideology: The doctrine of DNA*. New York: Harper.

UNIT 2

Saying, Doing, and Designing

2.1 The Doing and Not Just Saying Tool

People Do Things with Language, Not Just Say Things

What is the purpose of human language? Many people, especially in modern societies, think the major purpose of language is to convey information. However, we do a lot more with language than give each other information.

In fact, language may not be an ideal form for giving information. Many academic disciplines, which are in the business of discovering and communicating new information, have found the need to develop more explicit and clearer forms of communication through mathematics and other sorts of symbol systems (as, for example, in physics).

Even when they use language, academic disciplines tend to use varieties of language that are more arcane and complex than everyday language. For example, a biologist might say something like "Hornworm growth displays a significant amount of variation" for what we might say in everyday life as "Hornworms sure vary a lot in how well they grow."

In our everyday lives, even when we are conveying information to someone, we are also trying to do other things, as well. In fact, for all their emphasis on information, we will eventually see that this is true of academic disciplines and their forms of language as well. Not only do we use language to do many different things, but any one utterance is often meant simultaneously to carry out more than one action.

Because language is used for different functions and not just to convey information (which is but one of its functions), it is always useful to ask of any communication: What is the speaker trying to DO and not just what is the speaker trying to SAY? We humans use language to carry out various sorts of actions and informing someone else is only one sort of action that we accomplish through language.

For example, consider the little the utterances below:

1. It's a cold one today. [From one neighbor to another as they pass by each other.]
2. Teacher: What is 5 + 2? Student: 7.
3. I pronounce you man and wife. [Said by minister.]
4. I promise to be there by five.
5. Can you lift a hundred pounds?
6. Can you pass me the salt?
7. Pass me the salt?

What are the purposes (functions) of these utterances? The neighbor who says "It's a cold one today" surely knows the neighbor to whom he said it already knows it is cold. So why say it? What is the speaker trying to do?

Normally when we ask questions, we do not know the answer. But the teacher in (2) does know the answer to the question she is asking and school is one place (one context) where we accept and expect questions that are not really asking for information the asker does not already know. Why? The purpose of the teacher's question is not to find out the answer to the question. What is its purpose?

Saying "I pronounce you man and wife" only works to carry out the action of marrying two people if the person saying it is a minister or other sort of appropriate official. If I say it to two friends, it doesn't work. Institutional arrangements (ministers and marriage ceremonies) are required here for the language to work. But if I say "I promise to be there at five" I have engaged in the action of promising and no institutional arrangements are required. Why can I promise with no need of institutional support, but not pronounce two people man and wife without such support?

When I ask if you can lift a hundred pounds, I am asking if you have the ability to do it. The action in which I am engaged is asking a question. But when I ask if you can pass me the salt at dinner, I am not asking if you have the ability, but asking you to pass me the salt. The action in which I am engaged is a request. In the first case you can say "yes," but in the second you cannot just say "yes" and leave it at that. You actually have to pass me the salt. How can "can" mean such different things in these two utterances? How do we know it means these different things? Can we imagine settings in which "Can you lift a hundred pounds?" (or, say, "Can you lift a hundred pounds for me?") means "Will you lift a hundred pounds for me?" and "Can you pass me the salt?" means "Do you have the ability to pass me the salt"?

"Pass me the salt" is not a request, but an order. Why is it usually ruder to say this than "Can you pass me the salt?"? Even if I say, "Pass me the salt, please?" this sounds ruder or blunter than "Can you pass me the salt?," at least to me. Why? "Please, pass me the salt" sounds less rude or blunt than "Pass me the salt, please." Why?

There are some verbs in English—like "pronounce" (in "pronounce you man and wife"), "promise," "ask," "tell," "request," and "forgive"—that name actions directly. These are called "direct speech acts." There are also indirect ways to perform speech acts. If I say "I promise you I will come at five," the word "promise" directly names the action of promising. But I can also promise less directly by saying something like "I will be there at five" or even "I WILL be there at five," though, of course, a statement like "I will be there at five" has other uses, as well. It could be a simple statement of fact (an act of informing) or a prediction (as in "I will win the match next Friday").

Asking "Will you pass me the salt?" is a direct question; it is one of the structures we use in English to signal that we are asking a question. "Can you pass me the salt?" sounds like a question (about your ability)—and this structure can be used as a direct question (as in "Can you lift a hundred pounds)—but it can, as we have seen, be an indirect and polite way to perform a request. A direct way to make a request would be: "I request you to pass me the salt," a form we would rarely actually use (sounds too formal, though we would say something like: "I request your presence at the inquest").

We are concerned here with actions in a much broader sense than just direct speech acts (like "I promise to come") and indirect speech acts (like "I will come" when it is used not just to inform, but to make a promise). These are all verbal actions ("speech acts"), acts tied closely to speaking and language. But here we are concerned also with actions that given uses of language carry out, but which themselves have nothing particularly to do with speaking (in the way in which promising and requesting do, since these are actions that can only be carried out in language), actions like insulting you (something I can also do without language, e.g., by a gesture) or making you feel important (also something I can do without language, e.g., by saluting you).

Anything we say performs some sort of action. Even if you ask me the time and I say "It's five o'clock," I am engaged in the actions both of answering you and informing you. If you and I are fellow lawyers and you say to me, after a tennis match, "You are not so great at tennis" and I say "But I am a better lawyer than you are," my remark can be, depending on how we read the context (see the Fill In Tool and The Frame Problem Tool), performing different actions (some of them even all together): informing you I think I am a better lawyer than you; bragging; getting back at you for insulting my tennis; correcting my feelings of being inferior to you at sports; needling you; joking with you; acting out further our competitive relationship; threatening your face (that is, your identity as a good lawyer), and others. Here we are concerned with actions as broad as these. They are not inherently verbal. While it is often easier to carry them out in language, they can be carried out in other ways, as well, unlike promising and requesting.

The relationship between language and action is a very complex one and we will have a good deal more to say about later in this book. For now, what is important is that you learn to ask of any communication not just "What is the speaker trying to say?" but also "What is the speaker trying to do?."

In this section we have developed the basis for a new tool, although we develop this basis further later in the book. Our new tool is "The Doing and Not Just Saying Tool?":

Tool #7: The Doing and Not Just Saying Tool

For any communication, ask not just what the speaker is saying, but what he or she is trying to do, keeping in mind that he or she may be trying to do more than one thing.

Reading

Austin, J. L. (1975). *How to do things with words.* Second Edition. Cambridge, MA: Harvard University Press.

Searle, J. (1979). *Expression and meaning: Studies in the theory of speech acts.* Cambridge: Cambridge University Press.

2.2 Working with the Doing and Not Just Saying Tool

Below I reprint some data that will allow us to work with the Doing and Not Just Saying Tool. However, this data is also a good opportunity to work more with the Making Strange Tool. The data is the beginning of a conversation at home between a mother and her three-year-old. In some families parents do not talk and interact with their three-year-olds this way. In some other families such talk and interaction is common. The Frame Problem Tool can be used here, too, as you think about how much of the context is relevant to what this mother is doing and push the relevant context beyond the home.

In this interaction, the mother and child have in front of them a plastic dinosaur, a plastic replica of a dinosaur's egg, and a little card on which is written the name of the dinosaur and information about it and its egg. As you think about this data, ask what the mother is trying to do and not just say. Ask, too, where the mother is trying to give the child information and why. Even when she is giving the child information, is this the only thing she is trying to do, her only purpose?

Problem 8

This data is from Crowley and Jacobs' paper "Islands of expertise and the development of family scientific literacy." I have reprinted the transcript as they have printed it. The bold print on "egg" means emphatic stress and "..." means a noticeable pause. "C" is the child and "M" is the mother:

C: This looks like this is an **egg**.
M: Ok well this...
       That's exactly what it is!
       How did you know?
C: Because it looks like it.
M: That's what it says,
       see look **egg**, **egg**...
       ...Replica of a dinosaur **egg**.
       From the oviraptor.

Here are questions to think about in trying to apply the Doing and Not Just Saying Tool to this data:

1. When the child says "This looks like this is an egg" the mother says "That's exactly what it is!" in an energized way. The exclamation point means her intonation contour was one of excitement or surprise (as does her use of "exactly" here). Why does the mother say this in such an energized, excited way? Is she actually excited or surprised? Is her excitement or surprise real or "faked"? If you think it is faked," why is it? What is the mother trying to do?

2. Why does the mother ask the child "How did you know?" after he has says: "This looks like this is an egg." The child in saying "this looks like" seems actually to making a guess, rather than claiming to know. Why does the mother take him to making a claim to know, rather than just a guess?

3. The child answers the mother's question about how he knew it was an egg by saying "Because it looks like it." Then the mother says "That's what it says [here on the card]." Why does she say this? The child has answered "how do you know" by making an observation based on how things look to him. The mother is pointing to print as an answer to the question. Why?

4. After the mother says "That's what it says" [here on this card], she says "see look *egg, egg*... Replica of a dinosaur *egg*." From the oviraptor." The mother is telling the child to look at the printed card. He is three years old and cannot read, so why is she telling him to look at the card? Why is she emphasizing the word "egg" (which is printed on the card)?

5. The mother reads off the card "Replica of a dinosaur egg. From the oviraptor." This is hardly three-year-old language ("replica," "oviraptor"). Why does she read it to the child? The mother doesn't just read this sort of language to her child, she speaks it as well. Later she says:

    Do you have a . . . You have an oviraptor on your game! You know the egg game on your computer? That's what it is, an oviraptor. And that's from the Cretaceous period. And that was a really, really long time ago.

    Why does she speak this way ("oviraptor," "Cretaceous period") to the child? Why is she bringing up the child's game?

6. Do you think this three-year-old knows a lot about dinosaurs? Do you think he is a "little expert" on dinosaurs? Can three-years-olds know a lot about something like dinosaurs by adult standards? Does what the child know about dinosaurs have anything to do with what the mother is trying to do in the way she talks to and interacts with the child here?

7. When people communicate, they are trying to do things with each utterance and with a whole set of utterances taken together. They have

local goals or purposes for each utterance and larger, more global goals for a whole set of connected utterances. What is the mother trying to do or accomplish with the whole set of utterances we have transcribed above? Does school (though the child is not in school yet) have anything to do with what she is trying to do?

It may be useful for readers at this point to reconsider earlier data in this book in terms of the Doing and Not Just Saying tool.

Reading

Crowley, K. and Jacobs, M. (2002). Islands of expertise and the development of family scientific literacy. In Leinhardt, G., Crowley, K., and Knutson, K., Eds., *Learning conversations in museums*. Mahwah, NJ: Lawrence Erlbaum, pp. 333–56.

2.3 Using Grammar to Build Structures and Meanings

The Container/Conduit View of Language

We said in the last section that language is about doing and not just saying. The traditional view of language pays attention only to saying and not doing. It sees meaning as something that resides in the head of the speaker as "concepts" or "ideas." When speaking, the speaker encodes these concepts into words and phrases as if they were containers and then conveys them to the listener. The listener decodes the language received and removes the concepts from their containers. Then the listener stores these concepts in his or her head. This is a "conveyor belt" and "container" view of language in which speaking is like putting things (concepts) into containers (made of language) and conveying them to listeners who take them out of the containers and put them in their heads.

We already know this view is seriously wrong. For one thing it has nothing to say about the role of context and the listener's need to use context to engage in "filling in" what the speaker has left unsaid. For another thing, it leaves out all we do with language beyond conveying information and ideas to each other. We have seen that in speaking, people are actively doing things, not just conveying messages.

The "conveyor belt" and "container" view of language is, of course, based on a metaphor, a metaphor that treats speaking and writing as like putting things in a container and conveying them to others. Metaphors are important for understanding complex things. They can illuminate things, allowing us to see them in new and useful ways. Or they can blind us to things they leave out of the picture (things like context and doing and not just saying). The conveyor belt and container metaphor is a poor one, however common a way it is to think about language and communication.

Grammar as Tools for Building Structures and Meanings

A better view of language than the "conveyor belt" and "container" view of language is what I will call a "building and designing view." I have already said that when we speak, we are always doing things and not just saying things or communicating information. In order to do things with language (including informing), we use grammar to build and design structures and meanings.

Imagine you were making a car. You have to build (put parts together) and design (choose what parts to put together). There are lots of choices to make. Making a car means choosing what sort of car (e.g., compact, SUV, convertible, station wagon) to build in the first place. It means, as well, choosing for each part what type of part to use and what specific part to use. For example, while building any car requires that you have an engine, you must choose what type of engine (e.g., gas, diesel, rotary, four cylinder, V6, V8) to have and what specific engine (of that type) actually to put in.

Some parts are optional, so you must choose whether to include these or not. For example, do you want a hood ornament or not? Hood ornaments are optional on cars. Finally, you must choose what different parts should go together. For example, you may not want monster tires on a car that looks like a Honda Civic. Monster tires and the other parts in a Honda Civic just don't go well together. Monster tires are better on trucks.

Cooking from recipes works the same way. We make food by combining ingredients; we choose which ingredients to buy (e.g., organic tomatoes or genetically modified), and there are ingredients that are optional.

Of course, most of us don't build our own cars (and, indeed, many Americans do not cook their own food). We buy a car from a car lot or buy precooked and processed food at a market or fast food restaurant. But when we use language we are all expert builders and designers. Of course, there are situations where we also take language "off the lot," so to speak, when we just repeat what someone else has said or written. But, in most situations, we do not just repeat what others have said, but build and design our own structures and meanings.

We can think of language in a similar way to how we thought of building and designing a car or cooking a meal. In language, too, we have parts of different types. We must choose what types of phrases we want in our utterances and how we want to put them together. We must choose what words we want to use in these phrases. And, here, too, some choices of phrases and words are optional and some are required (e.g., an English sentence must have a subject and a transitive verb must have a direct object).

Just as there are rules or procedures to follow in building a car that will work, the rules of English grammar tell us how we can build things out of words and phrases. For example, English grammar tells us that connecting an Article (e.g., "the" or "a(n)") with an adjective (e.g., "happy" or "tall") and then with a noun (e.g., "girl" or "boy") gets us an acceptable bigger structure, called a "noun phrase": "Art. + Adj. + Noun" (e.g., "the happy girl"). Thus, we can view grammar, in part, as rules telling us how to use smaller parts to build bigger things, in this case one type of a noun phrase.

Grammar also tells us how to build prepositional phrases. One way is to connect a preposition (e.g., "from") and a noun (e.g., "home"). This will get us the structure "Prep. + Noun" (e.g., "from home," "to home," and "from Newark"), which is one type of prepositional phrase. Grammar also tells us that anywhere a noun can occur a noun phrase can occur. So this rule tells us that if we can have "Prep. + N" ("from home") as a prepositional phrase, then we can also have "Prep. + noun phrase" (e.g., "to the happy girl") as a prepositional phrase.

Another rule of grammar tells us that a prepositional phrase can be added to the end of a noun phrase. So to the end of a noun phrase like "Art + Adj. + Noun" (e.g., "the happy girl"), we can add a prepositional phrase and get: "Art + Adj. + Noun + Prep. Ph." (e.g., "the happy girl from home" or "the happy girl from the sad town"), a yet bigger noun phrase.

Just as there are rules in grammar for how to build noun phrases and prepositional phrases, there are rules for how to build verb phrases. So one sort of verb phrase is composed of a verb followed by a noun or noun phrase, thus: "Verb + Noun" (e.g., "go home") or "Verb + Noun Phrase" (e.g., "love the puppy"). Another type of verb phrase is composed of a verb followed by a noun or a noun phrase that is in turn followed by a prepositional phrase, thus: "Verb + Noun + Prep. Ph." (e.g., "go home to the country") or "Verb + Noun Phrase + Prep. Ph." (e.g., "love the girl with brown hair").

There are other grammatical categories, other sorts of blocks or bricks with which we can build beyond the parts of speech. For example, there are the categories "subject," "predicate," and "direct object." English grammar says that you can build a sentence if you connect a subject and predicate. A subject must be a noun or noun phrase and a predicate can be a verb or verb phrase (there are other types of predicates). In turn, a verb phrase, as we saw above, is made up of a verb followed by a noun or noun phrase and possibly, too, a prepositional phrase.

So we can build sentences like: "Noun + Verb" (e.g., "Girls laugh"); "Noun Phrase + Verb" (e.g., "The happy girl laughed"); "Noun + Verb + Noun" (e.g., "Boys like girls"); "Noun Phrase + Verb + Noun" (e.g., "The happy girl likes boys"); "Noun + Verb + Noun Phrase" (e.g., "Girls like the tall boy"); and "Noun Phrase + Verb + Noun Phrase" (e.g., "The happy girl likes the tall boy").

There are yet other grammatical categories; for example, clauses, that serve as other sorts of bricks (themselves made up of smaller bricks). A clause is any string of words that has a subject and a predicate, but does not stand as a complete sentence by itself. Clauses too can be connected to build larger things. For example, two clauses can be combined with a conjunction (e.g., "and," "but") to get us a structure or pattern like: "Clause + Conjunction + Clause" (e.g., "The happy girl laughed and the tall boy left"). Or we can combine a clause with a subordinating conjunction (e.g., "while," "because") and then combine this with another clause in any order to get a structure or pattern like: "(Subordinating Conjunction + Clause) + Clause" (e.g., "While the happy girl laughed, the tall boy left") or "Clause + (Subordinating Conjunction + Clause)" (e.g., "The tall boy left, while the happy girl laughed").

So we can see grammatical categories (like nouns, adjectives, verbs, adverbs, articles, and prepositions), or subjects, predicates, and direct objects, or conjunctions and clauses as blocks or bricks or parts with which we can build larger structures or patterns. But just as with building cars, we also have to make lots of design decisions as we build.

The design choices we make are these: We choose what to build in the first place (i.e., what sorts of phrases and sentences we want to build). For example, I can combine much the same concepts or ideas in a noun phrase (e.g., "children's growth") or a sentence ("Children grow"). I choose to build a noun phrase or a sentence based on what I want to mean and do.

We choose what types of words and specific words we want to put in the phrases and sentences we build. For example, we choose what type of noun we want to put in a noun phrase we build (e.g., a proper noun like "California" or a common noun like "state") and what specific noun we want to use (e.g., "state" rather than "province").

We choose what optional elements to put in or leave out. For example, not all noun phrases must have an adjective, so both "the happy girl" and "the girl" are acceptable noun phrases.

We choose what sorts of words should or should not be put together in order to achieve our own style and purposes. For example, the sentence "Please find enclosed our contractual agreement" (from a business letter) puts together a number of formal words ("please," "enclosed," "contractual," and "agreement") and thereby creates a formal tone. A sentence like "Give our contract a look over when you get a chance" combines words in a way that sounds much less formal and, perhaps, seems a bit odd when talking about something as official as a contract.

Each way of combining words has a meaning. For example, "John married Sue" makes John the topic, center of attention, and sees the marriage from his perspective. "Sue married John" does the same for Sue. "John broke the clock" focuses on John and his agency more than "The clock was broken by John." "Load the wagon with hay" means the wagon is full, while "load hay on the wagon" does not require the wagon to be full with hay.

Each design choice you make about building language structures determines certain aspects of what you mean (we have already seen that some meaning is determined not by what you say, but by the context in which you say it). Each different choice has a different meaning. You might choose to call someone "a brave freedom fighter" and I might call the same person a "a cowardly terrorist." These are both noun phrases, but what words we choose to put in the noun phrases clearly make a difference, even if we are talking about one and the same person.

Compare saying "I don't eat beef" (where "beef" is a mass noun) with saying "I don't eat cows" (where "cow" is a count noun). Here it is not only the choice of nouns, but also the type of noun (mass versus count) that makes a difference. "Beef" treats cows as "stuff," in particular as food. Saying "I don't eat cows" makes them living animals again and makes us aware we are eating what was once alive.

As an example of different types of verbs (in this case involving the same word) making a difference, compare "Your clock broke" (where "break" is being used an intransitive stative verb, that is, a verb with no direct object and that names a state) with "I broke your clock" (where "break" is now being used as an transitive, active verb, a verb with a direct object and that names an action). To use these different type of verbs I also have to choose different structures ("Your clock broke" versus "I broke your clock"). Even if I broke the clock, if I tell you "Your clock broke," I imply it may just have happened. This is why government bureaucrats so often say things like "Mistakes were made" rather than "I made some mistakes."

If you say "The queen died and then the king disappeared" you imply that the king disappeared because the queen died. If you say "The king disappeared and then the queen died" you imply that the queen died because the king disappeared. English grammar allows you to build "Clause + Conjunction + Clause" structures or patterns, but it matters what order you put the clauses in.

I can choose to say "The child grew" using a sentence with a verb ("grow") or I can choose to say "the child's growth" using a noun phrase with a noun ("growth"). The first choice, the sentence version, treats growing as a process and the second choice, the noun phrase, treats it as an abstract thing. The second choice also allows me to use the noun phrase to build a bigger, more complex sentence, for example: "The child's growth is within normal variation."

When we build with language, we follow the rules of grammar, putting the bricks together in a grammatically acceptable way (according to the rules of your dialect). We also make design choices about what to build (what types of phrases and sentences to use); what words and types of words to use; what options to take when grammar allows options; and what words should or should not go together in order to achieve our own style and desired meanings, nuances, and purposes. Every different design choice has a different meaning, though sometimes meaning differences can be nuanced and subtle.

We want to view words and grammatical rules as tools for active building and designing. Using language is all about making choices about what and how to build (design choices) so that we can mean what we want to mean. But, as we know, this active process also always involves choices about what not to say and to leave to the listener to fill in based on context.

We want to view speakers and writers as designers. They design meanings by designing and building language structures. It is much like cooking where we create nutrition by combining food ingredients. When we just parrot what others have said we get the language equivalent of processed food, food made by someone else (often an institution), someone else who may or may not have our interest at heart.

Reading

Ortony, A., Ed., (1992). Metaphor *and* thought. Cambridge: Cambridge University Press.
Reddy, M. J. (1979). The conduit metaphor: A case of frame conflict in our language about language. In A. Ortony (Ed.), Metaphor and thought. Cambridge: Cambridge University Press, pp. 284–310.
Thomas, L. (1993). *Beginning syntax*. Malden, MA: Blackwell.

Grammar Interlude #4: Vocabulary

English is a Germanic language, that is, it is in the same family as German. Germanic languages are a family of languages that includes, besides English and German, Dutch, Yiddish, Swedish, Danish, Icelandic, and Norwegian. Thus, a good number of English words are, of course, "Germanic." But English also contains a large number of words that were borrowed from Latin or from French (a Romance language derived from Latin). So English has two large stocks of vocabulary, one Germanic and one Latinate. Of course, English has also historically borrowed from other languages (e.g., Greek) as well. But Germanic and Latinate words make up the great majority of the English vocabulary. [Linguists tend to use the word "lexicon" instead of "vocabulary" and often call words "lexical items".]

English contains a great number of Latinate words (words borrowed from Latin and French) because of two historical events: the conversation of England in 597 AD to Roman Christianity and the Norman Invasion of England in 1066 AD. Latin was the language of the Roman Church and the Normans spoke an early version of French, a daughter language of Latin.

Today, for the most part, Germanic words and Latinate words compose two different types of vocabulary in English. Germanic words are used more often in more informal and everyday contexts and Latinate words are used more often in more formal and specialist contexts (though some of both can be found in each sort of context). The Latinate vocabulary is the vocabulary of books and people whose talk is influenced by books. Thus, "see" and "think" are Germanic, while "perceive" and "conceive" are Latinate. Other examples are, with Germanic first and Latinate second: "alive"/"animate"; "dog"/"canine"; "cat"/"feline"/ "god"/"deity"; "tell"/"narrate"; "land"/"terrain"; "manly"/"virile."

Some educators make a distinction in English vocabulary among three "tiers" of words. Tier 1 words are basic everyday words that occur often in spoken language, words like "go," "home," "dinner," and "dog." Tier 2 words are more formal words that occur across many academic, specialist, and public-sphere domains and in a wide variety of written texts, words like "process," "state," "account," "probable," "occurrence," "maintain," "benevolent," and so forth. Such words do not occur regularly in everybody's everyday conversation. Tier 3 words are specialist technical terms used in narrow meanings in specialist domains, words like "electron," "spelunker," and "hydrogen." There are also many seemingly everyday words like "work," "heat," and "temperature" that have become technical terms in science and do not mean in science what they mean in everyday life.

This educational distinction among tiers of words is made because, by and large, schooling involves a good deal of learning about tier 2 words, words people use in non-vernacular speech and in school-based academic writing. Many tier 2 words are from the Latinate vocabulary of English (and some are derived from Greek).

So vocabulary in English is one marker of different styles of languages—different registers or social languages. A preponderance of Germanic words marks a style as less formal and more vernacular than a preponderance of Latinate words, which marks a style as more formal. Many specialist and academic domains incorporate a good deal of Latinate vocabulary and this can be a barrier to people with limited education or literacy skills or who consider such language off-putting for any of several reasons even if they have these skills.

We can state another discourse analysis tool, the vocabulary tool:

Tool #8: The Vocabulary Tool

For any English communication, ask what sorts of words are being used in terms of whether the communication uses a preponderance of Germanic words or of Latinate words. How is this distribution of word types functioning to mark this communication in terms of style (register, social language)? How does it contribute to the purposes for communicating?

Problem 9

Consider the two utterances below. They were said by the same person, a young woman (see Section 2.8 below for more on this data). In the first case, she was talking to her boyfriend and in the second to her parents at dinner. Discuss these two utterances in terms of the use they make of Germanic and Latinate vocabulary. Think back also to our view that speakers and writers are often active designers and builders. How is this young women designing and building with language? Why has she done so differently in each case?

1. He was hypocritical, in the sense that he professed to love her, then acted like that.
2. What an ass that guy was, you know, her boyfriend. I should hope, if I ever did that to see you, you would shoot the guy.

Reading

Beck, I. L., McKeown, M. G., and Kucan, L. (2002). *Bringing words to Life: Robust vocabulary instruction*. York: Guildford Press. [A good source for educators.]

Jackson, H. and Amvela, E. Z. (1999). *Words, meaning, and vocabulary: An introduction to modern English lexicology*. New York: Continuum.

2.4 The Why This Way and Not That Way Tool

In the last section, we argued that we can look at words and phrases as bricks and mortar for building (following the rules of grammar) structures and meanings. We also argued that building also always involves making design choices. We make choices about what to build (e.g., a noun phrase like "children's growth" in a sentence like "Children's growth is spectacular" or a verb like "grow" in a sentence like "Children grow spectacularly"), words and types of words, available options, and ways to combine or avoid combining certain words.

If we were to build a car, we would do so because we wanted to drive the car (and maybe for other reasons, as well, for example to impress the neighbors). In turn, we drive for all sorts of different reasons, in order to do all sorts of things, for example to get to work, go shopping, take a vacation, visit friends, and other things. So why do we build things with grammar? We do so in order to make meanings. But, like driving, we make meanings for all sorts of different reasons, in order to do all sorts of things (see the Doing Not Saying Tool).

Having studied the Doing Not Saying Tool, we already know some of the things we do with the meanings we make. Consider, for example, the following utterances:

1. I will be at your party tonight
2. See you at the party tonight
3. We're gonna party hard tonight, bro!

Each of these utterances informs the listener that the speaker will be at the listener's party, so one thing they are doing is informing. Utterance (1) says so directly, and (2) and (3) say so indirectly. Utterances (2) and (3) do something else, as well. They express bonding or solidarity with the listener, while (1) is much more socially and emotionally neutral. In turn, (3) is much more expressive of bonding and solidarity than is even (2).

The speaker has made different choices about how to build with grammar, that is, made different design choices. Each different choice means something different and in each meaning is being used to do something different.

Our discussion of building and designing with grammar allows us to state a new tool, "The Why This Way and Not That Way Tool."

Tool #9: The Why This Way and Not That Way Tool

For any communication, ask why the speaker built and designed with grammar in the way in which he or she did and not in some other way. Always ask how else this could have been said and what the speaker was trying to mean and do by saying it the way in which he or she did and not in other ways.

This is not really a separate tool from the Fill In Tool or the Doing Not Saying Tool. Rather, it is another way to get at what those tools are getting at. In reality, we need to use all three of these tools together and hope they converge on the same answers, since each of these tools gives us a somewhat different angle on the data.

Grammar Interlude #5: Integrating Information

A clause is any string of words composed of a subject and predicate as in "The boys liked the cakes." In traditional grammar, a sentence is any clause that stands complete by itself (e.g., "The boys liked the cakes"). A non-sentential clause is any string of words with a subject and predicate that does not stand complete by itself (e.g., "John thinks that the boys like the cakes," where "the boys like the cakes" is a clause, but "John thinks that the boys like the cakes" is a sentence). Since I do not want to keep having to say "clause or sentence," I will call anything with a subject and predicate a clause, whether it is a clause or a sentence in traditional terms.

The subject of a clause is always a noun or noun phrase (e.g., "Boys like cake" or "The tall boys liked cake"). The direct object of a verb is also always a noun or noun phrase (e.g., "like cake" or "like very small cakes"). The predicate of a clause is always a verb or a verb phrase (e.g., "eat" or "eat small cakes").

Since a noun phrase can occur wherever a noun can occur and a verb phrase can occur wherever a verb can, many linguists just count single nouns and verbs as if they were phrases and call them (single word) noun phrases and verb phrases. A small part of the syntactic rules for English are given below. When an element is in parentheses it means it is optional. It can be there or not:

Clause → Noun Phrase + Verb Phrase
(e.g., The boys liked the cakes)
Noun Phrase → (Art) (Adj.) Noun (Prep. Ph.)
(e.g., boys, the boy, the happy boys at the school, etc.)
Verb Phrase → Verb (Noun Phrase) (Prep. Ph.)
(e.g., eat, eat the cakes, eat at home, eat the cakes from home)
Verb Phrase → Verb (that) Clause
(e.g., think that the boys liked the cakes)
Prep. Ph. → Prep. + Noun Phrase
(e.g., into the house)
Clause → Clause and Clause
(e.g., John likes cake and Mary likes pie)

The subject, the object of the verb, and any prepositional phrases that go with the verb are called the "arguments" of the verb. They are the phrases that spell out what the verb means in the sense of being the actors and locations in the drama the verb names. Thus, in a sentence like "The girl hit the boy on the head," the subject "the girl" (the "hitter"), the object "the boy" (the one being hit), and "on the head" (where the hitting occurred) are the arguments of the verb "hit."

English has verbs like "be" and "have" whose arguments are a subject and either an adjective phrase (e.g., "Mary is very happy") or a noun phrase ("Mary is the queen" or "Mary has the book"). These are called "predicate adjectives" and "predicate nouns" in traditional grammar.

The simplest clauses are made up of a verb and only the elements the verb's meaning requires to be present ("required arguments"):

1a.	Mary touched John	[Subject verb Object]
1b.	Mary is healthy	[Subject be Predicate Adjective]
1c.	Mary has a brother	[Subject have Predicate Noun]

Clauses can be expanded by adding optional arguments to the verb:

2a.	Mary touched John on the head
2b.	Mary touched John with her lips
2c.	Mary touched John on the head with her lips

Clauses can also be expanded by optional elements that are not arguments of the verb but which modify either the verb or the whole clause in some way:

3a. Mary lightly touched John ["lightly" modifies the verb "touched"]
3b. Yesterday, Mary touched John ["yesterday" modifies the clause "Mary touched John"]
3c. Fortunately, Mary is healthy ["fortunately" modifies the clause "Mary is healthy"]
3d. Mary, fortunately, has a brother ["fortunately" modifies the clause "Mary has a brother"]

Clauses can be combined or integrated more or less tightly together in four ways. First is a "loose" way, when two or more clauses are combined by coordination and each is a "main clause." A "main clause" is any clause that stands alone as a sentence or bears no relationship to any larger clause other than coordination. So in "The boys like cake and the girls like pie," the whole sentence ("The boys like cake and the girls like pie") is a main clause and both sub-clauses ("The boys like cake," "The girls like pie)—linked by coordination— are main clauses:

4a. The boys like cake and the girls like pie
4b. The boys like cake but the girls like pie

Second, clauses can be combined in a somewhat less loose way, when one or more clauses is juxtaposed as a subordinate clause to a main clause:

5a. While John was not looking, Mary touched him on the head. ["while" introduces subordinate clause]
5b. Mary touched John on the head because he was causing trouble. ["because" introduces subordinate clause]

Third, two clauses can be tightly integrated by having one clause embedded inside another one:

6a. John felt Mary touch him on the head [= "Mary touched him on the head" is embedded inside "John felt …"].
6b. John believed that Mary had touched him on the head [= "Mary touched John on the head" is embedded inside "John believed …"].
6c. Mary planned to touch John on the head [= "(Mary) touched John on the head" is embedded inside "Mary planned …"].

Note in (6c) that "Mary" is understood as the subject of "to touch John on the head" but not expressed. This is common with infinitives ("to verb" forms like "to eat" or "to plan").

Fourth, in the tightest form of integration, a clause can be turned into a phrase (losing its status as a clause). This can be done by changing a verb into a noun as when we turn the verb "grow" into the noun "growth." This process is called "nominalization." It allows us to change a clause like "Hornworms grow" into the noun phrase "Hornworm growth."

What I mean by "change a clause into a noun phrase" is that a noun phrase like "Hornworm growth" contains a full clause's worth of information ("Hormworns grow"). When we turn a clause into a noun phrase we can then use that noun phrase (which contains a full clause's worth of information) in a new clause and make new and quite complicated and complex clauses, for example: "Hornworm growth exhibits significant variation."

We can also turn an adjective (e.g., "healthy," "happy") into a noun (e.g., "health," "happiness") and thus go from clauses like "John is healthy" and "Mary is happy" to noun phrases like "John's health" and "Mary's happiness."

Verbs (e.g., "abuse," "smile") can also be turned into adjectives (e.g., "abused," "smiling"). This allows us to go from clauses like "He abuses children" and "Children smile" to noun phrases like "abused children" ("Abused children deserve help") and "smiling children" ("Smiling children are cute").

So far, in all of the cases above, we have been moving from clauses to combinations of clauses or to clauses disappearing into phrases. But in discourse analysis we usually must go the other way round. We have to start with sentences that are composed of two or more (sometimes many more) clauses (combined or integrated in the ways we have just discussed above and a few others) and then take these sentences apart. That is, we have to ask what clauses the sentences combine or integrate or transform. So, to give one example, consider the case below:

> 7.   When I was reading my textbook, I discovered that scientists think that hornworm growth exhibits significant variation.

This sentence is quite complex and integrates a good deal of information. To see how it integrates this information we have to take it apart. The main clause is "I discovered that scientists think that hornworm growth exhibits a significant amount of variation." "When I was reading my textbook" is a subordinate clause that has been added to this main clause by the subordinator "when." "Scientists think that hornworm growth exhibits significant variation" is an embedded clause that has been embedded as the object of the verb "discover" using the word "that" (which is optional). "Hornworm growth exhibits significant variation" is another embedded clause that has been embedded as the object of the verb "think" using the word "that." The phrase "hornworm growth" encapsulates the clause "hornworms grow" (it is a clause's worth of information). The phrase "significant variation" encapsulates the clause "something varies significantly."

We can visually represent this complexity—the way several clauses worth of information are integrated in various ways into a single sentence—as per diagram on the next page.

We can also just list the clauses:

1.   Main Clause: I discover that scientists think hornworm growth exhibits significant variation.
2.   Subordinate Clause: While I was reading my textbook
3.   Embedded Clause: That scientists think hornworm growth exhibits significant variation
4.   Embedded Clause: That hornworms exhibit significant variation
5.   Nominalization: Hornworm growth (hornworms grow)
6.   Nominalization: Significant variation (something varies significantly)

Subordinate Clause	Main Clause
↓	↓
(1) When I was reading my textbook, growth exhibits significant variation	(2) I discovered that scientists think that hornworm

↓

Embedded Clause

↓

(3) That scientists think that hornworm growth exhibits significant variation

↓

Embedded Clause

↓

(4) That hornworm growth exhibits significant variation

↓   ↓

(5) Hornworms grow   (6) Something varies significantly

The point is that the single sentence "While reading my textbook, I discovered that scientists think that hornworm growth exhibits significant variation" integrates or packages together six clauses worth of information. Further, each clause worth of information is integrated into the whole more or less tightly (coordination is looser than subordination which is looser than embedding which is looser than turning clauses into phrases).

Integrating or packaging clauses allows speakers to organize how they want to present and represent information. It allows them to take a particular perspective on the information they want to communicate. It is a key part of designing and building with language.

For example, material placed in a subordinate clause is assumed and not asserted; material placed in a main clause is foregrounded and asserted. So if I say, "Even though they are different parties, Republicans and Democrats both serve the rich (people in society)," I am assuming that Democrats and Republicans are different parties and asserting that they both serve the rich. I take their being different parties as less significant than the fact they serve the rich and not significant enough to override the similarity that they both serve the rich.

If, on the other hand, I say "Even though Democrats and Republicans both serve the rich, they are different parties," I am assuming that they serve the rich and am asserting they are different parties. Now I am taking the fact that they serve the rich as less significant than that they are different parties and taking the fact they are different parties to be significant enough to override the fact that they both serve the rich.

Embedded clauses are not asserted either. If I say "John told Jane's husband that she had cheated on him," I am not myself asserting that Jane cheated on her husband, though I might well, in some contexts, be suggesting it. But if I say "Jane cheated on her husband and John told him so," I am asserting that she cheated on her husband.

When we turn a clause into a phrase often information is left out. If I say "physically abused children need support," "physically abused children" is a noun phrase that encapsulates a clause's worth of information: "someone abuses children physically." When we turn the clause into a phrase (use the phrase version rather than a clause version) we can leave out the subject, that is, we do not have to name who did the abusing. Thus, consider the sentence below from a published piece of research (Pollak, S. D., Vardi, S., Putzer Bechner, A. M., and Curtin, J. J. (2005), Physically abused children's regulation of attention in response to hostility," *Child Development* 76.5: 968–77):

> 8.   The present data suggest that once anger was introduced abused children maintained a state of anticipatory monitoring of the environment.

The phrase "abused children" refers to the subjects in the experiment, so it really means "the abused children (in this experiment)." The phrase is related to the clause "someone abused the children." If this was said as a clause, the abuser would have to have been named in some fashion, since clauses require subjects. In fact, in this study the children were physically abused by their parents. The article says this at the beginning and thereafter uses the phrase "physically abused children" or "abused children."

The authors might have done this because, as in all technical writing, they wanted to be concise. Or, perhaps, they did it, too, in part, because normally in an experiment on children one gets permission from the children's parents, but in this case these were the same people who abused the children. The authors never really confront this fact in the paper and the constant use of "abused children" effaces both the parents and the dilemma about experimenting on children whose parents are not necessarily in a good position to represent the best interests of their children.

We can state another grammatical tool for discourse analysis, The Integration Tool:

Tool #10: The Integration Tool

For any communication, ask how clauses were integrated or packaged into utterances or sentences. What was left out and what was included in terms of optional arguments? What was left out and what was included when clauses were turned into phrases? What perspectives are being communicated by the way in which information is packaged into main, subordinate, and embedded clauses, as well as into phrases that encapsulate a clause's worth of information?

Problem 10

Apply The Integration Tool to the sentence below (from the same research paper as 8 above). That is, take the sentence apart in terms of what clauses it is composed of and what phrases encapsulate a clause's worth of information:

> 9.   First, we sought to further examine the ways in which physically abused children can regulate attentional processes when confronted with anger or threat.

In this experiment the experimenters exposed five-year-old children who had been physically abused by their parents to voices of adults getting angry at each other. What has been left out in 9? ["processes" is a noun related to the verb "process," so it encapsulates the information "someone processes something"; "attentional" is an adjective related to the verb "attend," so it encapsulates the information "someone attends to something"; "anger" is a noun related to the predicate adjective "be/get angry," so it encapsulates the information "someone is/gets angry with someone" and "threat" is a noun related to the verb "threaten," so it encapsulates the information "someone threatens someone"]. Who confronted the children with anger or threat? Does "confront someone with threat" mean to "threaten them"? Who (if anyone, in your view) threatened whom here?

Problem 11

Package or integrate the clauses below in as many ways as you can. [One way, of course, is just to leave them all separate as in: "The book belonged to John. It had a cover. The cover was green. The cover was torn." You can add or leave out "little words" to make the integrations work (e.g., "John's book had a green cover that was torn"). Reflect on whatever differences of meaning there are among the different ways of combining these clauses:

10a. The book had a cover
10b. The book had a green cover
10c. The cover was torn
10d. The book belonged to John

Do the same for the clauses below (again, you can add or leave out "little words" like "how" and you can change "significantly" to "significant," "develop" to "development," and "vary" to "variation"). Of course, we can leave the two clauses separate as in: "All children develop. But they develop in significantly different ways."

11a. All children develop
11b. Children vary significantly in how they develop

Reading

Halliday, M. A. K. and Matthiessen, C. (2004). *An introduction to functional grammar.* Third Edition. London: Hodder Arnold.

2.5 Working with the Why This Way and Not That Way Tool

The Why This Way and Not That Way Tool tells us to always ask why something was said the way it was and not some other way. One way to operate with this tool is to ask yourself the ways in which any data you are analyzing could have been said differently. Then ask why it was said the way it was and not the other ways. Below, you will get some practice with the Why This Way and Not That Way Tool.

Problem 12

Consider the following sentences from Paul Gagnon's book *Democracy's Untold Story: What World History Textbooks Neglect* (Washington, D.C.: American Federation of Teachers, 1987, pp. 65–71):

> Also secure, by 1689, was the principle of representative government, as tested against the two criteria for valid constitutions proposed in the previous chapter. As to the first criterion, there was a genuine balance of power in English society, expressing itself in the Whig and Tory parties. As narrowly confined to the privileged classes as these were, they nonetheless represented different factions and tendencies. Elections meant real choice among separate, contending parties and personalities.

Consider the sentence: "As narrowly confined to the privileged classes as these were, they nonetheless represented different factions and tendencies." Let's change it slightly to: "As narrowly confined to the privileged classes as these were, the Whig and Tory parties nonetheless represented different factions and tendencies." Below I give two different ways to say this information:

1. As narrowly confined to the privileged classes as these were, the Whig and Tory parties nonetheless represented different factions and tendencies.
2. Though they represented different factions and tendencies, nevertheless, the Whig and Tory parties were narrowly confined to the privileged classes.

What is the difference grammatically and in meaning between these two? Why didn't Gagnon write version (2) instead of (1)?

Problem 13

Consider the next two sentences:

1. Hornworms sure vary a lot in how well they grow.
2. Hornworm growth exhibits a significant amount of variation.

These two sentences are built and designed in very different ways. Why did the speaker of (1) say it that way and not some other way, for example as in (2)? Why did the speaker of (2) say it that way and not some other way, for example as in (1)?

List all the grammatical differences between (1) and (2)—all the different choices the speakers made about how to use grammar, how to build and design with grammar. For each difference, say why the speaker said it that way and not the other way. For example, why is the subject of (1) "hornworms" and the subject of (2) "Hornworm growth"?

Considering all the choices made, what do you think the speaker of each utterance is trying to do, to accomplish?

Though these are both spoken utterances, if you did not know that, which utterance would you have thought more likely to have been written and why?

It sounds odd to say or write "Hornworm growth sure exhibits a significant amount of variation?." Why?

Grammar Interlude #6: Topics and Themes

We saw in Grammar Interlude #2 in Unit 1 that clauses are made up of subjects and predicates. There we said that the subject of a clause is its "topic." The word topic has a lot of different meanings. Here it means the entity in the clause that the predicate is about. If I say "Mary got into Stanford," I am saying about Mary that she got into Stanford. If I say "Stanford admitted Mary," I am saying about Stanford that it admitted Mary. If I ask "Did Mary get into Stanford?," I am asking about Mary whether she got into Stanford.

While the subjects of clauses are always "topics" (this is their general meaning), in different situations of use, subjects take on a range of more specific meanings. In a debate, if I say, "The constitution only protects the rich," the subject of the sentence ("the constitution") is an entity about which an assertion is being made; if a friend of yours has just arrived and I usher her in saying "Mary's here," the subject of the sentence ("Mary") is a center of interest or attention; and in a situation where I am commiserating with a friend and say something like "You really got cheated by that guy," the subject of the sentence ("you") is a center of empathy (signaled also by the fact that the normal subject of the active version of the sentence—"That guy really cheated you"—has been "demoted" from subject position through use of the "get-passive"). There are other possibilities as well.

There is another important discourse notion, closely related to the notion of "topic," and that is "theme." [This word has been used in many different ways in the linguistics literature; I am using here in the way in which the linguist M. A. K. Halliday does.] The "theme" of a clause is the point of departure of the message, a framework for the interpretation of the clause. The theme orients the listener to what is about to be communicated. In English, the theme of a clause is whatever comes before the subject. If nothing comes before the subject, then the subject is both the theme and the topic. So in "Stanford admitted Mary last year," "Stanford" is the subject, topic, and theme. In "Last year, Stanford admitted Mary," "last year" is the theme and "Stanford" is the subject and topic.

Theme is really a position in the clause, not just necessarily one constituent. So in a sentence like "Well, last year, on her birthday, Mary got into Stanford," all the material before the subject—"Well, last year, on her birthday"—is a multi-part theme. Grammatical words like "well" and other interjections, conjunctions (e.g., "and," "but," "so"), and conjunctive adjuncts (e.g., "however, because, though, therefore) are often called "textual themes," since they help tie clauses and sentences together and have less content than things like "last year" and "on her birthday." So we can distinguish between textual themes (like "well") and what we might call non-textual more contentful themes (like "on her birthday"; Halliday calls them "interpersonal themes"). I will use "textual theme" for textual themes and just the word "theme" for the more contentful themes.

Sometimes the subject of a sentence is left out of a clause because it can be recovered from context, as in the sentence: "In this project, we lay the ground work for developing a potentially transformational approach to assessment in the twenty-first century." Here "we" is understood as the subject of "developing" (i.e., "our developing"), but has been left out. So, too, in "John left my house at five and went home," where "John" is understood as the subject of "went home." Subjects that are left out still count as topics and themes (if there is nothing in front of them in their clause).

The "theme" creates the perspective from which everything else in the clause or sentence is viewed. It is the launching off point for the rest of the information in the clause or sentence. It sets the framework or context in which we view the information in the rest of the clause or sentence. The normal or usual case in English—what linguists call the "unmarked" case—is for the subject of the clause to be both theme (thereby first) and topic. When something other than the subject is first and thereby theme (as in "Last year, Stanford admitted Mary"), the choice of theme is what linguists call "marked" (less usual).

If I say, "Regrettably, the big girl hit the small boy" (theme = "regrettably"; topic = "the big girl"), then I am viewing the claim that the big girl hit the small boy through the lens of my regret about the matter. If I say, "The big girl, regrettably, hit the small boy" (theme = topic = "the big girl"), then I am viewing both the action of hitting and my feelings of regret about the matter through the lens of what I think or feel about the big girl.

Each clause has its topic and theme. When a sentence contains more than one clause, the whole sentence can have a theme in addition to each clause in it having its own theme. Anything that occurs before the subject of the main clause is the theme of the multi-clause sentence. If nothing occurs before the main clause subject that subject is the theme of the multi-clause sentence.

So consider the sentence: "Though Mary loves John, she treats him poorly." Here "though" is a textual theme and "Mary" is the topic/theme of the clause "Mary loves John" and "she" is the topic/ theme of the clause "she treats him poorly." However, since "Though Mary loves John" precedes the subject of the main clause ("she" in "she treats him poorly), it is the theme of the whole two-clause sentence. In "Mary treats John poorly, though she loves him," nothing is before the main clause subject ("Mary" in "Mary treats John poorly") and, thus, "Mary" is the theme of its own clause and the whole sentence.

In Section 1.4 we saw the following utterance:

> LAST YEAR / Mary Washington / who is our curriculum coordinator here / had a call from Sara //

The speaker is a teacher in the first official meeting of a project organized by academics (including Sara) at a local university. She has been asked to open the meeting by catching everyone up to date on what has gone on among various people prior to the meeting. The meeting is being held in her school.

The teacher, later in the meeting, makes clear that she and other teachers had put in a good deal of effort in helping to organize the project prior to the first meeting and that it had, from her point of view, taken the academics too long to call the first official meeting. Thus, she makes "last year" the theme of her opening clause and even gives it emphatic stress. This is a marked theme (less usual), since the usual (unmarked) way to say this would have been to say "Mary Washington who is our curriculum coordinator here had a call from Sara last year." By making the less usual (marked) choice the speaker is making "last year" significant.

By making "last year" the theme of her opening clause, the teacher is making that the framework within which what follows is to be interpreted. In this case, this includes not just the clause of which "last year" is the theme, but a good deal of what else follows this clause in her extended turn at talk. She wants to make clear that what has gone on prior to the meeting, in terms of her efforts and those of other teachers, has gone on too long without the academics calling a meeting and getting involved themselves. She wants listeners to use the lapse of year as a framework with which to understand what she is saying.

We can state another grammatical tool for discourse analysis:

Tool #11: The Topic and Theme Tool

For any communication, ask what the topic and theme is for each clause and what the theme is of a set of clauses in a sentence with more than one clause. Why were these choices made? When the theme is not the subject/topic, and, thus, has deviated from the usual (unmarked) choice, what is it and why was it chosen?

In Section 1.4 we saw the following utterance (I print the data here to look more like print with clear sentence boundaries):

> And we um BOTH expected to be around for the summer institute at Woodson. I DID participate in it. But SARA wasn't able to do THAT.

"And" and "but" are textual themes. How is "but" functioning here to create a context or framework for interpretation (the role of themes)? What difference would it made if the speaker had said "I did participate in it. Sara, however, wasn't able to"? How do putting emphatic stress on "did" and "Sara" and "that" and using "but" as textual theme all work together to communicate here?

Problem 14

Consider the written sentences below from a grant proposal:

> In this project, we lay the ground work for developing a potentially transformational approach to assessment in the 21st century. Today, work that requires only basic skills flows overseas where labor is cheaper.

Discuss what themes were chosen in this communication and how they function (i.e., how are they setting up frameworks for interpretation?). This is from a proposal asking for funds (a grant proposal). Does this help explain the choice of themes? How is the version below different from the version above?

> We lay the ground work for developing a potentially transformational approach to assessment in the 21st century in this project. Work today that requires only basic skills flows overseas where labor is cheaper.

Problem 15

Consider the four following sentences, sentences which say pretty much (but, of course, not exactly, the same thing). Say what the topics and themes are in each case, why they might have been chosen as they were, and how the different choices in each case communicate somewhat different things:

1. For no good reason, the stupid company she works for fired my daughter.
2. The stupid company she works for fired my daughter for no good reason.
3. For no good reason, my daughter was fired by the stupid company she works for.
4. My daughter was fired by the stupid company she works for for no good reason.

Reading

Halliday, M. A. K. and Matthiessen, C. (2004). *An introduction to functional grammar.* Third Edition. London: Hodder Arnold.

2.6 Why We Build and Design with Grammar

In Section 2.5, I asked you to think about the two utterances below:

1. Hornworms sure vary a lot in how well they grow.
2. Hornworm growth exhibits a significant amount of variation.

Let's look at some of the different choices in how to build with grammar these two utterances represent. Then we can ask why these choices were made, what they mean, and what they allow the speaker to accomplish (do).

Subjects of sentences name what a sentence is about (its "topic"). They also name the perspective from which we are viewing the claims we want to make (its "theme") if they are initial in the sentence.

Sentence (1) above is about hornworms (cute little green worms) and launches off from the perspective of the hornworm. Sentence (2) is not about hornworms, but about a trait or feature of hornworms, namely "hornworm growth," in particular one that can be quantified, and launches off from this perspective.

In sentence (1) "sure" is an emotive or affective marker indicating that the speaker is impressed or surprised. The affective marker communicates the attitude, interest, and even values of the speaker/writer. Sentence (2) not only does not have "sure" in it, the presence of "sure" would make the sentence sound odd: "Hornworms sure display a significant amount of variation." Attitudes, interest, and/or values seem out of place or "odd" in sentence (2). Why do you think that is?

Sentence (1) involves dynamic processes (changes) named by verbs ("vary," "grow"). Sentence (2) turns these dynamic processes into abstract things ("variation," "growth") through a linguistic device known as "nominalization."

Sentence (1) has a contentful verb ("vary"). Sentence (2) has a verb of appearance ("exhibit"), a class of verbs that is similar to copulas (i.e., verbs like "be"). Such verbs are not as deeply or richly contentful as verbs like "vary." Such copulative and appearance verbs are basically just ways to relate things to each other (in this case, abstract things, namely hornworm growth and significant variation).

Sentence 2 contains the phrase "vary a lot in how well they grow" (a verb phrase). What determines that the hornworms do, indeed, vary a lot? The fact that the speaker has seen them. This utterance is from a child who was raising hornworms in her classroom. The claim that the hornworms vary a lot in how well they grow is her opinion based on raising, studying, and looking at her hornworms. Some seem so small and others so big. The standard by which she judges that this difference is "a lot" is her own viewpoint ("the evidence of her own eyes"), that it just seems like a big difference.

Sentence (2) contains, not the phrase "vary a lot in how well they grown," but "display a significant amount of variation." What determines here that the variation is, indeed, "significant" (the "equivalent" of sentence (1)'s "a lot")? Not the speaker's opinion or what he or she has seen. "Significant" here is about an amount that is evaluated in terms of the goals and procedures of an academic discipline (here a type of biology), not just a single person. It is a particular area of biology, its theories, and its statistical tests that determines what amounts to significant variation and what does not. All our hornworms could be stunted or untypical of well grown hornworms ("well grown" from non-specialist everyday perspective) and still display a significant amount of variation in their sizes in terms of a statistical test of significance. How they look is "trumped" by the statistical tests the discipline of biology gives us.

So there are lots of differences between sentence (1) and (2) in how they were built and designed from the rules of grammar. But what do these differences mean and accomplish? Sentence (1) and (2) are, in fact, different styles or varieties of language. They are what we will later call two different "social languages" (see Section 4.4).

Sentence (1) is in a vernacular style. The vernacular is the style we use when we are speaking as "everyday people," making no claims to expert or specialist status or knowledge. Each of us has a vernacular style, though this style differs for different dialects and cultures.

Sentence (2) is in a specialist style of language. Specialist styles are used by experts or specialists when they are speaking and acting as experts and specialists (when they are not, they use a vernacular style).

The choices of how to use grammar in sentence (1) are partly meant to convey that one is speaking as an "everyday person" making claims based on one's own opinion and inspection of the world. The choices in sentence (2) are partly meant to convey that one is speaking as an expert or specialist making claims based not just on one's own opinion and inspection of the world, but also on the basis of a discipline's formal theories, tools, and practices.

Of course, when we speak as "everyday people" we have our own informal theories and ways of saying and doing things that we share with others in our families and cultures. But experts and specialists make their theories and practices more overt and public and share them well beyond their families and cultures.

Sentence (2) uses grammar to build and design meanings that are part of an enterprise that seeks to develop knowledge explicitly as part of a disciplinary group of people engaged in a communal search for that knowledge (communal in the sense of things like shared training and peer review). This group of people has a number of tools they have developed and which they share for producing knowledge, tools like experimental apparatus, measuring devices, and statistical tests. Their way of speaking and writing—their specialist style of language—is also one of these tools, a tool for attempting to produce knowledge.

Sentence (1) is in its own way communal too. The speaker, though expressing her own opinion, one that is not backed up by a specialist group, is surely assuming that if the hornworms look to her to vary a lot in how well they grow, they will look that way to others. Her claim, especially with the presence of "sure," says that what she sees is or should be obvious and apparent to "anyone." But "anyone" here means "everyday people" not specialists. Specialists have different standards than "everyday people" (remember, it could look to us everyday people as if there were big differences among our hornworms and yet the specialist's statistical tests might claim these differences were not "significant").

What is important and what I want to stress is this: By using grammar to build and design their utterances in different ways the speakers of sentences (1) and (2) are helping to build something else, as well, something out there in the world. The speaker of sentence (2) is helping to build and sustain the domain of biology. By speaking biology's style of language the speaker is reproducing the domain of biology, keeping it going, even if he or she turns out to be wrong about his or her specific claim.

The speaker of sentence (1) is helping to build and reproduce (continue, sustain) what we can call the "life world." The life world is the domain where we speak, value, and act as "everyday people" making claims based on "everyday knowledge," "common sense," or the sorts of evidence gathering any "everyday person" can do.

People's life worlds differ by their cultures. Different cultures, even within a country like the United States, have different standards for what counts as "everyday knowledge," "common sense," and evidence open to anyone. However, in the modern world, there is often a conflict between the life world and specialist claims to knowledge. We often have trouble knowing which we should trust. Furthermore, specialist knowledge over the last two centuries has, for better and worse, greatly eroded the space within which everyday people can comfortably claim to know things.

Reading

Gee, J. P. (2004). *Situated language and learning: A critique of traditional schooling.* London: Routledge.

Halliday, M. A. K. and Martin James R. (1993). *Writing science: Literacy and discursive power*. Pittsburg, PA: University of Pittsburg Press.
Schleppegrell, M. (2004). *Language of schooling: A functional linguistics perspective.* Mahwah, NJ: Lawrence Erlbaum.

2.7 Using Language to Build Things in the World

So far in this unit, we have discussed how grammar allows us to build phrases and sentences so we can convey meanings and carry out actions. When we choose words and build phrases and sentences with grammar, we are giving clues or cues or recipes (whatever we want to call them) to listeners about how to construct a picture in their heads. Our choice of what sorts of phrases to use, what words to put in them, and how to combine words and phrases is determined by the sort of picture we want listeners to form in their heads.

For example, imagine someone says to you: "My daughter got a PROMOTION at the agency" (with emphatic stress on "promotion"). This utterance has been built in a certain way. The word "daughter" tells you, the listener, to form a picture of a female child (in this case an adult female child). "My" tells you to connect the daughter to the speaker as his child. "My daughter got a PROMOTION" tells you to connect a promotion to the daughter in your head.

Every aspect of the choices a speaker has made has implications for the picture the listener is supposed to build in his or her mind. The speaker here has chosen "my daughter" as the subject (and, thus, too the topic). He could have chosen "the agency" as the subject and topic (e.g., "The agency promoted my daughter"). He chose the wording "got a promotion" instead of "was promoted" (e.g., "My daughter was promoted at the agency"). He chose to put emphatic stress on "promotion" when he could have failed to do so ("My daughter got a promotion at work"). He chose to say "the agency" rather than, say, "her company" or "the FBI."

The way this utterance is built tells you to construct a picture in your head in which the agency promoted the speaker's daughter. Since "my daughter" is the subject and topic (and theme), you must make the picture about her and not, say, the agency.

The use of "the agency" implies you will already know what agency the daughter works for (e.g., from previous encounters). So you have to take this information out of memory and put it into your mental picture (let's say you know it's the FBI). Indeed, the picture you form in your mind is determined, as we know, not just by what was said, but by the context in which it was said.

The phrasing "got a promotion," rather than the more neutral "was promoted," expresses the speaker's empathy for the daughter and the feeling that something specially good happened to her. So this is added to your mental picture as well.

The emphatic stress on "promotion" shows that the promotion was a surprising, happy, or otherwise special event. You determine which from your knowledge of the context and put that in your mental picture, too.

Based on context (e.g., what you know about the speaker and your previous interactions with the speaker), you may (using the "Fill In Tool") put a good deal more in your mental picture than this. You may know, for example, that the speaker's daughter is just a beginner at the FBI and, thus, that the speaker intends you to take the promotion as an unexpected big deal. Or you may know the daughter has worked at the FBI for years and been regularly passed over for promotion and, thus, that the speaker really means something like "My daughter FINALLY got a promotion at work."

Listeners may take the pictures they form in their minds (based on the way utterances are built, as well as on context) to be real (true), possible, or unreal (untrue). For example, you may know that the speaker is an inveterate liar, but you still form a picture of his daughter getting a somehow special promotion in your mind. You just count this picture as at best possible, if not unreal.

We do not know from research, as of yet, what these pictures in the mind are made of in terms what is in the brain. They may be based on our capacity to form images or on some sort of language-like symbol system in our heads, or some combination of these. They have been called by a variety of names, such as "mental models," "discourse models," "discourse records," and "possible worlds."

So in building with grammar we make meanings that combined with context allow listeners to build pictures in their minds that are taken as true, possible, or as untrue of the world. This is what building with grammar amounts to.

However, we use language to get people to construct pictures in their minds for many different purposes. We speak and put pictures in people's heads because we want to make things happen in the world. We want to do things and not just say them. And in order to do these things we engage in yet another sort of building, what we might call "world building." We build (or destroy, for that matter) not grammatical things, but things out in the world.

For instance, in the last section, we saw that a biologist who speaks and writes in the language of biology (makes choices about grammar that fit that style of language) is actually helping to build, produce, reproduce, and sustain the enterprise of biology out in the world. And that enterprise involves not just people, but institutions, like university biology departments, biology journals, and biology associations and conferences, as well.

We use language (we build with grammar) so that we can also build things out in the world, make things happen, try to make them true. Let me give one example (we will study this process in the next unit). The example will be oversimplified to make my point.

How do spouses build and sustain relationships? They do things for and with each other and they speak to each other in certain ways. Consider, then, the following. A wife has given her husband two ties as a gift. He comes happily into the room wearing one. She says: "You didn't like the other one?" This is a "double-bind" communication. The husband cannot win, whatever tie he puts on, his wife will say this and imply he did not like the other one. Enough communication like this and the wife has not built something in the world with language, but, rather, destroyed it, namely her relationship.

On the other hand, formulating one's communications with one's spouse in supportive, collaborative, and loving ways can solidify and sustain a relationship. Two things are clear from this simple example. First, how we speak has consequences in the world, it can build things up or tear them down. In this case, we are talking about building up or tearing down relationships, but we will talk about building up and tearing down other sorts of things, as well, later.

Second, language is rarely used all alone in this building up or tearing down process. Actions and bodies count, as well, so do circumstances in the world. A husband who works in the garage all day and spends no time with his wife is tearing down the relationship. A wife who fails to ever look at or touch her husband is tearing down the relationship. Dire poverty can tear apart relationships as well. In the world, language almost always works in tandem with non-language "stuff" (bodies, actions, objects, and circumstances).

What this means is that the meanings we build through grammar—and the mental pictures this lets us help people construct—are really tools. They are tools for doing things and one of the things we do with these tools is build things (such as academic disciplines like biology) and destroy things (such as marriages) in the world.

Reading

Bolinger, D. (1980). *Language, the loaded weapon: The use and abuse of language today.* New York: Longman.

Gee, J. P. (2004). *Situated language and learning: A critique of traditional schooling.* London: Routledge.

Grammar Interlude #7: Stanzas

We saw in Grammar Interlude #3 that speech is produced in tone units or idea units. These units are usually, but not always, one clause long. The information embraced within a single idea unit of speech is, of course, most often too small to handle all that the speaker wants to say. It is usually necessary to integrate several idea units into a larger block of information.

Speech is often organized into groups of idea units that I will call "stanzas." Each stanza is a group of idea units about one important event, happening, or state of affairs at one time and place, or it focuses on a specific character, theme, image, topic, or perspective. When time, place, character, event, or perspective changes, we usually get a new stanza. I use this term ("stanza") because these units are somewhat like stanzas in poetry.

Within a larger genre of language—like a narrative, a description, an explanation, and exposition—the stanzas are themselves often grouped into larger blocks of information that serve a role in the whole narrative, description, explanation, exposition, or whatever genre is being used.

Below, I lay out the idea units and stanzas in the opening of the story a seven-year-old African-American told in school during sharing time. Each numbered line is an idea unit:

SETTING OF STORY:
STANZA 1 (getting stuck):
1.   last yesterday
2.   when my father
3.   in the morning
4.   an' he ...
5.   there was a hook
6.   on the top of the stairway
7.   an' my father was pickin me up
8.   an' I got stuck on the hook
9.   up there

STANZA 2 (having breakfast):
10. an' I hadn't had breakfast
11. he wouldn't take me down
12. until I finished all my breakfast
13. cause I didn't like oatmeal either

Note here how the first stanza is about getting stuck on the hook and the second is about having breakfast. The two together serve as the setting for the girl's story, which we will see in a moment. These are two blocks of information.

Connected speech is like a set of boxes within boxes. Idea units, most of which are single clauses, are grouped together into a stanza as one block of information. Then one or more (usually more) stanzas can constitute a yet larger unit like the setting for a story or an explanation within an argument.

Larger pieces of information, like a story about my summer vacation, an argument for higher taxes, or a description of a plan for redistributing wealth, have their own characteristic, higher-level organizations. That is, such large bodies of information have characteristic parts much like the body has parts (the face, trunk, hands, legs, etc.). These parts are the largest parts out of which the body or the information is composed. The setting of the child's story we have been discussing is a piece of the larger organization of her story. It is a "body part" of her story.

Below, I reprint this child's story as whole. Each larger "body part" of the story is numbered with a Roman numeral and labeled in bold capitals

(SETTING, CATALYST, CRISIS, EVALUATION, RESOLUTION, and CODA). In order to see the patterning in the little girl's story all the more clearly, I do something a bit different below in the way I represent the numbered lines and stanzas. I remove from the girl's story the various sorts of speech hesitations and dysfluencies that are part and parcel of all speech (and that tell us something about how planning is going on in the speaker's head). I also place the little girl's idea units back into clauses when they are not full clauses (save for "last yesterday" which is a temporal adverb with scope over most of the story). What I have produced here, then, is an idealized representation intended to make the structure of the girl's story clearer.

A Seven Year Old Child's Story

PART I: SETTING
STANZA 1
1. Last yesterday in the morning
2. there was a hook on the top of the stairway
3. an' my father was pickin' me up
4. an I got stuck on the hook up there

STANZA 2
5. an' I hadn't had breakfast
6. he wouldn't take me down
7. until I finished all my breakfast
8. cause I didn't like oatmeal either

PART II: CATALYST
STANZA 3
9. an' then my puppy came
10. he was asleep
11. he tried to get up
12. an' he ripped my pants
13. an' he dropped the oatmeal all over him

STANZA 4
14. an' my father came
15. an he said "did you eat all the oatmeal?"
16. he said "where's the bowl?"
17. I said "I think the dog took it"
18. "Well I think I'll have t'make another bowl"

PART III: CRISIS
STANZA 5
19. an' so I didn't leave till seven
20. an' I took the bus
21. an' my puppy he always be following me
22. my father said "he—you can't go"

STANZA 6

23. an' he followed me all the way to the bus stop
24. an' I hadda go all the way back
25. by that time it was seven thirty
26. an' then he kept followin' me back and forth
27. an' I hadda keep comin' back

PART IV: EVALUATION
STANZA 7

28. an' he always be followin' me
29. when I go anywhere
30. he wants to go to the store
31. an' only he could not go to places where we could go
32. like to the stores he could go
33. but he have to be chained up

PART V: RESOLUTION
STANZA 8

34. an' we took him to the emergency
35. an' see what was wrong with him
36. an' he got a shot
37. an' then he was crying

STANZA 9

38. an' last yesterday, an' now they put him asleep
39. an' he's still in the hospital
40. an' the doctor said he got a shot because
41. he was nervous about my home that I had

PART VI: CODA
STANZA 10

42. an' he could still stay but
43. he thought he wasn't gonna be able to let him go

This girl's story has a higher-order structure made up of a SETTING, which sets the scene in terms of time, space, and characters; a CATALYST, which sets a problem; a CRISIS, which builds the problem to the point of requiring a resolution; an EVALUATION, which is material that makes clear why the story is interesting and tellable; a RESOLUTION, which solves the problem set by the story; and a CODA, which closes the story. Each part of the story (except the Evaluation and Coda) is composed of two stanzas.

In some ways this is the structure of all stories, regardless of what culture or age group is telling them. However, there are also aspects of story structure that are specific to one cultural group and not another. For example, devoting a block of information to an Evaluation prior to a story's Resolution is more common among children than it is among adults. Adults tend to spread such Evaluation material throughout the story or to place it at the beginning. Some

African-Americans engage in a good many "performance" features, which are a type of Evaluation, and tend to use Evaluation material to "key" a hearer into the point of the story, rather than to hit them over the head with the point bluntly indicated. Of course, such cultural information is never true in any very exclusive way: there are many varieties of African-American culture, as there are of any culture (and some African-Americans are in no variety of African-culture, but in some other variety of culture or cultures). And other groups do similar or overlapping sorts of things.

Another aspect of this story that is more specific to African-American culture, though also in a non-exclusive way, is the large amount of parallelism found in the way language is patterned within the stanzas. Note, to take one example of many, how Stanza 3 says "an' then my puppy came" and then gives four things about the puppy, and then Stanza 4 says "an then my father came" and then says four things (all of them speech) about the humans involved. This parallel treatment of the father and the puppy forces the hearer to see the story as, in part, about the conflict between the puppy as a young and exuberant creature and the adult world (home and father) as a place of order and discipline. As a seven year child, the teller of the story is herself caught in the conflict between her own urges to go free and her duty to go to school and ultimately enter the adult world.

Notice that the part of the story labeled Evaluation makes clear that the essential problem with the puppy is that he wants to freely *go* places where he cannot go, just as, we may assume, a child often wants to go where she is not allowed to go and must go where she doesn't want to go. In line 21, the child says "My puppy he always be following me," and repeats this in the Evaluation. This "naked *be*" is a form in African-American Vernacular English that means an action is habitual (regularly happens). Here it indicates that the puppy's urge to follow and go with the girl is not just a once or sometime thing, but a regular and recurrent event that follows from the nature of the puppy. It is a problem that must be resolved.

The resolution of the conflict between the puppy and the adult world takes place at a hospital where a doctor (an adult) gives the puppy a shot and puts him to "sleep." Thus, the adult world dictates that in the conflict between home and puppy, the adult norms must win. The child is working through her own very real conflicts as to why she can't have her puppy and, at a deeper level, why she must be socialized into the adult world of order, duty, and discipline (by the way, while it is not clear what the hook in the first stanza is, it does appear be just a dramatic device—the child seems to be trying to say that her parents require discipline in the home; she is not, by any means, accusing anyone of mistreatment). This, in fact, is the basic function of narrative: narrative is the way we make deep sense of problems that bother us.

Children have clearer and simpler stanza structure than adults and it is easier to find their stanzas. Adult language is often more complex—idea units can be longer and stanzas more complicated. Below is a stretch of speech from a curriculum consultant talking to the teachers in the history project we have seen several times before (you will see this data again in Section 3.15).

PART I: CURRICULUM DEVELOPMENT
STANZA 1: Curriculum Development
1.   There's a there's a big complicated process /
2.   Of working through the materials /
3.   Figuring out how to teach it //
4.   Which is called curriculum development //

STANZA 2: Complicated
5.   And that's what we're involved in now /
6.   And it's very murky /
7.   And it's very complicated /
8.   And we we don't know where we're going /
9.   But that's an innate part of curriculum development /
10. Unfortunately /
11. Especially when you work with a group of people /
12. And you're not just doing it yourself //

PART II: HELP
STANZA 3: WHY CURRICULUM CONSULTANTS ARE THERE
13. Um so and that's where Sandy and I were hired /
14. As sort of the hired guns /
15. To come in and help facilitate it /
16. Because we know you don't have the time //

STANZA 4: Sara and Ariel are different
17. Um and and um Sara and Ariel [two university professors] /
18. Didn't don't have the experience /
19. Of working in the classroom /
20. And they teach in a different structure /
21. Which is very different //

STANZA 5: Here to help
22. And so, so we're there as the helping hands to give you /
23. To help you where you need /
24. And to act as sort of the interpreters /
25. And the shapers,
26. But in response to what is necessary //

STANZA 6: Here for you
27. I mean we're not coming in to do something that we want to do //
28. We're trying to facilitate what you want to do //

Note that the stanzas here are close to what in some forms of writing would have been one complex sentence (e.g., "It's an innate part of curriculum development, unfortunately, that it is very complicated and people do not always know where they are going, especially when they work with a group of people and not just by themselves"). Note also that stanzas often (but not always) start with some hesitation or a discourse particle like "so" and end with a final intonation contour ("//").

When looking for stanzas, look for how idea units cluster into one small topic, perspective, or "take" on things. Then look at how stanzas themselves cluster together to form larger units of sense (e.g., a setting in a story) as part of a larger stretch of speech (e.g. a story or an explanation). Note above how two stanzas are devoted to defining curriculum development and then three are devoted to explaining why the curriculum consultants are around. When you are engaging in your own analyses, do not worry about being "exactly right" about where the stanza boundaries are. You are trying, by placing speech in stanzas, to be clear about what clusters of sense or meaning you as a listener or interpreter have seen in a stretch of speech.

We can introduce another grammatical discourse tool:

> ### Tool #12: The Stanza Tool
>
> In any communication (that is long enough), look for stanzas and how stanzas cluster into larger blocks of information. You will not always find them clearly and easily, but when you do, they are an important aid to organizing your interpretation of data and of how you can display that interpretation.

Problem 16

The data below is from the same long turn of speech by the curriculum consultant above. Place this stretch of speech into stanzas and any higher order blocks of information you think are present. You will see that one of the virtues of looking for stanzas is that the process forces you to think hard about how information is organized. You may well find ambiguous situations, cases where it is hard to decide what clusters with what, but that is just the sort of thing you want to discover as you seek to find meaning. Sometimes speakers are clear about their blocks of information and sometimes they are less clear or elide one thing into another.

1. So but we also don't want to put any pressure /
2. I mean there shouldn't be any pressure //
3. There should be something that's fun to do /
4. And what works works /
5. And what doesn't work goes by the wayside //
6. And um that's all it can be /
7. You know something small /
8. That accomplished by the end of the semester //

9. But if it goes into something that is exciting /
10. And has potential /
11. And should be continued next year /
12. And should be given to other teachers /
13. And should maybe affect other schools in Middleview /
14. Then that's where Sara's working towards something more long term //
15. Where this could be maybe funded by NEH /
16. And to pay teachers /
17. And to pay for release time /
18. And pay for materials /
19. And pay for resources to come in /
20. And make it work on a larger scale //
21. So this is like a little pilot project that is /
22. I agree /
23. It's very murky /
24. And it's very frustrating /
25. But I see that as sort of inevitable /
26. And we can make that work for us /
27. Instead of against us //

Reading

Gee, J. P. (2011). *Sociolinguistics and Literacies: Ideology in Discourses*. Fourth Edition. London: Taylor & Francis.

Hymes, D. (1996). *Ethnography, linguistics, narrative inequality: Toward an understanding of voice*. London: Taylor & Francis.

Labov, W. and Waletzky, J. (1967). Narrative analysis: Oral versions of personal experiences. In J. Helm, Ed., *Essays on the verbal and visual arts: Proceedings of the 1966 Annual Spring Meeting of the American Ethnological Society*. Seattle: University of Washington Press, pp. 12–44.

UNIT 3

Building Things in the World

3.1 The Context is Reflexive Tool

In the first unit we saw the importance of context. In the second Unit we saw that we use grammar and words to design and build language structures with meaning. We then argued that we use these meanings as cues or clues to guide people to build (with the help of context, as well) pictures in their heads. We want our listeners to build such pictures in their heads because we want to do things in the world and we need other people to think and act in certain ways in order to get them done. We use language to build and destroy things in the world, things like our academic discipline, our church membership, our ethnic affiliation, or our marriage. In this unit we are going to talk about the sorts of things we use language (along with non-verbal actions, things, and circumstances) to build in the world.

But first, we have to discuss context again. So far I have given you an oversimplified view of context. In Section 1.2, I defined "context" as follows:

> Context includes the physical setting in which the communication takes place and everything in it; the bodies, eye gaze, gestures, and movements of those present; all that has previously been said and done by those involved in the communication; any shared knowledge those involved have, including cultural knowledge, that is, knowledge of their own shared culture and any other cultures that may be relevant in the context.

So far we have treated context as something that is just "there" surrounding speech. Listeners consult both what a speaker has said and the context in which it was said, put these together—kind of add them up—and thereby give meaning to the speaker's words. This view of context is too static. It leaves out the power speakers have to shape how listeners view context. It also leaves out the power of listeners to construe what counts as relevant in the context and how the context should be viewed.

Language has a rather magical property: When we speak we build and design what we have to say to fit the context in which we are communicating. But, at the same time, how we speak—what we say and how we say it—helps to create that very context. It seems, then, that we fit our language to a context that our language, in turn, helps (in part) to create in the first place.

This is rather like the "chicken and egg" question: Which comes first? The context we're in, for example a university committee meeting? Or the language and interactions we use, for example our committee ways of talking and interacting (e.g., calling a question to force a vote)? Are we speaking and acting this way *because* this is a committee meeting or is this a "committee meeting" *because* we are speaking and acting this way? If institutions, committees, and committee meetings didn't already exist, our committee ways of speaking and interacting wouldn't mean anything or be possible. But, then, too, if we did not speak and act in certain ways, committees would cease to exist.

Another way to look at the matter is this: We always actively use spoken and written language to create or build the world of activities (e.g., committee meetings), identities (e.g., committee chairs, members, facilitators and obstructionists) and institutions (committees in universities and universities themselves) around us. However, thanks to the workings of history and culture, we often do this in more or less routine ways. These routines make activities, identities, and institutions seem to exist as contexts apart from language and action in the here and now. Nonetheless, these activities, identities, and institutions have to be continuously and actively rebuilt in the here and now. If we do not rebuild them again and again, they will cease to exist. If we start rebuilding them in different ways, which modify them, then they change. This is what accounts for change and transformation.

This property of context—namely that it is both there (and gives meaning to what we do) and that we help to create it with our ways of speaking and acting—is called the "reflexive" property of context. Speaking reflects context and context reflects (is shaped by) speaking (what was said). If I stand in front of a classroom as a professor and start to lecture, my way of speaking and acting creates the context of a class session. On the other hand, if class sessions and classrooms did not already exist as an institutional context in the world I could not speak and act this way.

We can introduce a new tool for discourse analysis, based on the reflexive property of context: the Context is Reflexive Tool. The tool is given below:

Tool #13: The Context is Reflexive Tool

When you use the Fill in Tool, the Doing and Not Just Saying Tool, the Frame Problem Tool, and the Why This Way and Not That Way Tool, and all other tools that require that you think about context (and not just what was said), always ask yourself the following questions:

1. How is what the speaker is saying and how he or she is saying it helping to create or shape (possibly even manipulate) what listeners will take as the relevant context?
2. How is what the speaker is saying and how he or she is saying it helping to reproduce contexts like this one (e.g., class sessions in a university), that is, helping them to continue to exist through time and space?
3. Is the speaker reproducing contexts like this one unaware of aspects of the context that if he or she thought about the matter consciously, he or she would not want to reproduce?
4. Is what the speaker is saying and how he or she is saying it just, more or less, replicating (repeating) contexts like this one or, in any respect, transforming or changing them? No act of speaking in a context is ever totally identical in every respect to another (e.g., every lecture is different somehow), but sometimes the differences are small and not very significant and other times they are larger and more significant.

Reading

Duranti, A., Ed., (2009). *Linguistic anthropology: A reader*. Malden, MA: Blackwell.

Duranti, A. and Goodwin, C., Eds., (1992). *Rethinking context: Language as an interactive phenomenon*. Cambridge: Cambridge University Press.

Kramsch, C. (1993). *Context and culture in language teaching*. New York: Oxford University Press. [An excellent book for anyone interested in language or language teaching.]

3.2 Working with the Context is Reflexive Tool

In this section we will investigate some data in order to use the Context is Reflexive Tool.

Problem 17

In the data below a college student has done an activity in class where the students had to read a story and rank the characters in order from worst to best in terms of how they had behaved morally. In the story, Gregory is Abigail's boyfriend. Abigail has done something bad in order to be able to see Gregory, but when he finds out what it was, he disowns her. In the first communication below, the young woman is telling her parents at the dinner table about the task and why she ranked Gregory as the worst character in the story. In the second, she is telling the same thing to her boyfriend in her bedroom. Both of these are, of course, just portions of what she said.

> **To Parents at Dinner**:
> Well, when I thought about it, I don't know, it seemed to me that Gregory should be the most offensive. He showed no understanding for Abigail, when she told him what she was forced to do. He was callous. He was hypocritical, in the sense that he professed to love her, then acted like that.

> **To Boy Friend Late at Night**:
> What an ass that guy was, you know, her boyfriend. I should hope, if I ever did that to see you, you would shoot the guy. He uses her and he says he loves her. Roger never lies, you know what I mean?

Questions:

1. How is the way this young women is speaking—what she says and how she says it—helping to create or shape the way the listener views the context?
2. How are the contexts of being at dinner with her parents and being in her bedroom with her boyfriend determining how she speaks?
3. Which is more important here do you think, the way the young women uses her language to shape the context or the way in which aspects of the context that are in place (e.g., dinner, parents, boyfriend, bedroom) shape

how she speaks? Do all young people speak this way to their parents at dinner? Do you think she is actively trying to create or shape the contexts in which she is speaking or more just reflecting what she assumes the context to be?

4.   Which version leaves more interpretive work (more Filling In) to be done by the listener? Why does the young woman demand more such work in one case than in the other? What does this have to do with creating or assuming a context of a certain sort?

5.   In which communication does the language sound more like the style of language we expect at school? Why does the speaker speak "school like" in one case and not the other? What does this have to do with creating or assuming a context of a certain sort?

Problem 18

A foreign doctoral student in graduate school in the United States has, after several years in her program, lost her PhD advisor. She needs to get another one. She is talking to a professor who she wants as an advisor, but who is reluctant to take her on as a student. Facing this reluctance, she says: "It's your job to help me, I need to learn."

Questions:

1.   What sort of context is this student seeking to create—or, at least, assuming—given what she says and how she says it?

2.   Do you think this is a successful thing to say to the professor to convince him? How do you think the professor views the context?

3.   If you say something like "It's your job to help me, I need help," who is this more likely to work on, a nurse or an accountant? What about a priest versus a business executive? What do your answers to these questions tell you about how the student viewed the context or what context she was trying to create?

4.   Do you think this student was actively trying to manipulate the context, that is, actively to shape how the listener saw the context and responded to her language or that she did not understand the context of university PhD students and their professors?

5.   The professor in this case, after hearing this utterance, was even more reluctant to take the student. Why do you think this was so? Would this be true of all or most professors? Would the field they were in make any difference?

6.   The student is trying to get the professor to overcome his reluctance to take her on as a student. She says "It's your job to help me, I need to learn." Formulate in your own words another way to seek to accomplish her goal here. What sort of context does your formulation assume or seek

to create? Does your formulation pretty much assume the context is a certain way and try to fit it or does it actively seek to shape the context? Or is it a mixture of the two? In what ways?

7. This student was in ESL (English as a Second Language) classes for a few years. What she says is grammatical. In fact, her English grammar was good. Is there anything else her ESL class should have taught her. Why?

3.3 Building Tasks and Building Tools

In the last unit we argued that we use grammar and words to design and build structures and their accompanying meanings. We build these structures and meaning so that we can do things with language. One thing we do with language is think: we use it to think with in our minds. In fact, some types of human thought are much like silently talking to oneself. It also appears humans think in terms of images and a mental language shared by all humans regardless of their language.

Another thing we do with language is use it to perform actions in the world. The actions we accomplish using language allow us to build or destroy things in the world, things like institutions and marriages. We do not usually just engage in a single isolated action and leave it at that. Rather, we have plans and goals and engage in series of related actions in related contexts over long periods of time. These longer term chains of action are usually done in order to build something in the world (like an institution or a marriage) or to sustain it across time. In this unit we are going to talk about the things we use language to build in the world.

We continually and actively build and rebuild our worlds not just through language, but through language used in tandem with other actions, interactions, non-linguistic symbol systems, objects, tools, technologies, and distinctive ways of thinking, valuing, feeling, and believing. Sometimes what we build is quite similar to what we have built before (e.g., sustaining a good marriage); sometimes it is not (e.g., starting a new career).

So language-in-use is a tool, not just for saying and doing things, but also, used alongside other non-verbal tools, to build things in the world. Whenever we speak or write, we always and simultaneously build one of seven things or seven areas of "reality." We often build more than one of these simultaneously through the same words and deeds. Let's call these seven things the "seven building tasks" of language in use. In turn, since we use language to build these seven things, a discourse analyst can ask seven different questions about any piece of language-in-use. This gives us, in turn, seven new tools for discourse analysis.

Below, I list the seven building tasks. We will take up each one in turn in the following sections where we will develop a discourse analysis tool connected to each one.

1. Significance:
We use language to make things significant (to give them meaning or value) in certain ways. We build significance. As the saying goes, we make "mountains out of mole hills." Things are often not trivial or important all by themselves. We humans make them trivial or important or something in between. If I say, "Guess what? My daughter got a PROMOTION at the agency" I make the event more significant and attention worthy than if I say "My daughter was finally promoted at the agency."

2. Activities:
I have already said that language is used not just to say things but to do them and that even informing is a type of action. Thus, we use language to carry out actions like promising and encouraging and a great many others. This is what the Doing Not Just Saying Tool was about. However, we humans also enact what I will call "activities," using the word in a special and restricted way. By an "activity" I mean a socially recognized and institutionally or culturally supported endeavor that usually involves sequencing or combining actions in certain specified ways. Encouraging a student is an action, mentoring the student is an activity. Telling someone something about linguistics is an action (informing), lecturing on linguistics is an activity. Often the term "practice" is used for what I am calling an activity.

We use language to get recognized as engaging in a certain sort of activity. A graduate student who has lost her advisor after some time in a graduate program and asks a professor "Will you be my advisor?" is making a request (an action we do with language). But she is also engaged in the activity of seeking a new graduate advisor in graduate school. This requires more than just the request. There is more that needs to be said and done. For instance, the student has to be able to talk about her background in the program, her knowledge and skills, and her accomplishments in ways that impress the advisor without seeming too arrogant or exaggerated.

3. Identities:
We use language to get recognized as taking on a certain identity or role, that is, to build an identity here and now. For example, I talk and act in one way and I am speaking and acting as the chair of the committee; at the next moment I talk and act in a different way and I am speaking and acting as just one peer/colleague speaking to another. Even if I have an official appointment as chair of the committee, I am not always taken as acting as the chair, even during meetings.

Doctors talk and act differently to their patients when they are being doctors than they do when they are talking as acquaintances or friends, even in their offices. In fact, traditional authoritarian doctors and new humanistic doctors talk and act differently to the patients, are different types of doctors. Humanistic doctors try to talk less technically and more inclusively to their patients. One and the same doctor can even switch between the two identities at different points or in different activities in his or her treatment of a patient.

4. Relationships:
We use language to build and sustain relationships of all different kinds. We use language to build relationships with other people and with groups and institutions.

For example, in a committee meeting, as chair of the committee, if I say "Prof. Smith, I'm very sorry to have to move us on to the next agenda item," I am constructing a relatively formal and deferential relationship with Prof. Smith. On the other hand, suppose I say, "Ed, it's time to move on." Now I am constructing a relatively informal and less deferential relationship with the same person.

5. Politics (the distribution of social goods):

I am going to use the term "politics" in this book in a special way. By "politics" I do not mean government and political parties. I mean any situation where the distribution of social goods is at stake. By "social goods" I mean anything a social group or society as a whole takes as a good worth having.

We use language to build and destroy social goods. For example, for most people, treating them with respect is a social good and treating them with disrespect is not. Speaking and acting respectfully and deferentially is to create and distribute a social good.

However, there are also circumstances where people want to be treated not deferentially, but with solidarity and bonding. Speaking and acting with solidarity and bonding towards someone who wants my friendship is in that circumstance to create and distribute a social good.

Why do I refer to this as "politics"? Because the distribution of social goods and claims about them—goods like a person being taken as acceptable, normal, important, respected, an "insider" or an "outsider," or as being connected to acceptable, normal, or important things (in the right circumstances)—are ultimately what give people power and status in a society or not.

People obviously disagree about what are social goods in various circumstances. They also sometimes fight over the distribution of social goods and demand their share of them.

Let me give an example that shows that how we construct our sentences has implications for building or destroying social goods. If I say "Microsoft loaded its new operating system with bugs," I treat Microsoft as purposeful and responsible, perhaps even culpable. I am withholding a social good from them as an institution, namely respect and a good reputation.

If I say, on the other hand, "Microsoft's new operating system is loaded with bugs," I treat Microsoft as less purposeful and responsible, less culpable. I am still withholding social goods, but not as much as before. Now it seems they did not act intentionally, but, nonetheless, still put out a bad product.

If I say, "Like any highly innovative piece of new software, Microsoft's new operating system is loaded with bugs," I have mitigated my withholding of social goods further and even offered Microsoft some social goods, namely treating them as innovative and as not really responsible for the bugs. How I phrase the matter has implications for social goods like guilt and blame, legal responsibility or lack of it, or Microsoft's bad or good motives, and Microsoft's reputation.

6. Connections

Things in the world can be seen as connected and relevant to each other (or not) in a great many different ways. For example, if I say "Malaria kills many people in poor countries" I have connected malaria and poverty. If I say "Malaria kills many people across the globe," I have not connected the two (though, in reality, Malaria kills many more poor people than richer ones). Some connections exist in the world regardless of what we say and do (like malaria and poverty). Nonetheless, we can still render these connections visible or not in our language.

Other connections do not exist so clearly in the world until we have worked— partly through how we use language—to make them real. For example, many politicians and media pundits have connected "socialism" and "government public health care" in the United States so often that a great many Americans think the two are inherently connected. However, these same people often do not see Medicare and socialism as connected, despite the fact that Medicare is a government public health plan for the elderly. Medicare has been around a long time now, many people use it, and past debates about it are forgotten.

7. Sign Systems and Knowledge

We use language to build up or tear down various sign systems (communicational systems) and different ways of knowing the world. There are many different languages (e.g., Spanish, Russian, English). There are many different varieties of any one language (e.g., different dialects, as well language varieties like the language of lawyers, biologists, and hip-hop artists). There are communicative systems that are not language (e.g., equations, graphs, images) or at least not just language (e.g., hip hop, poetry, video games, ads with pictures and words). These are all different sign systems.

All these different sign systems are important to the people who participate in them. People are often deeply connected to and committed to their dialect. Lawyers are committed to talking like lawyers. Hip hop fans are passionate. There are even violent arguments over where and when Spanish should be spoken in the United States. Physicists believe the language of mathematics is superior to languages like English for explicit communication.

Furthermore, different sign systems represent different views of knowledge and belief. As we said, physicists believe the language of mathematics is superior to English for producing and communicating knowledge about the physical world. Poets believe poetry is a higher form of knowing and insight; people who use religious varieties of language believe these are a higher form knowing and insight. Speakers of African-American Vernacular English believe there are some things that can be expressed or felt in that dialect better than they can in Standard English. So, too, for Spanish-English bilinguals who favor one language or the other for different topics or emotions. Statisticians believe statistics is a deep way of understanding reality, while some qualitative researchers do not or, at least, believe the language of statistics has spread too far in our understanding of the social world.

We can use language to make certain sign systems and certain forms of knowledge and belief favored or not, relevant or privileged, "real" or not in given situations, that is, we can build privilege or prestige for one sign system or way of claiming knowledge over another. For example, I can talk and act so as to make the knowledge and language of lawyers relevant (privileged) or not over "everyday language" or over "non-lawyerly academic language" in our committee discussion of facilitating the admission of more minority students.

I can talk and act as if Spanish is an inferior language or not. I can talk and act so as to privilege the language of "controlled studies" (e.g., "controlled studies of classrooms") as "real evidence" or "real science," or not. I can talk and act so as to constitute the language of creationism as "scientific" and as a competitor with the language of evolution, or not.

The Sign System and Knowledge Building task is clearly related to the Politics task, since constructing privilege for a sign system or way of knowing the world is to create and offer a social good. But the domain of sign systems (including the world's languages) and ways of knowing are especially important domains. Consider the effort people have spent trying to build or destroy astrology or creationism ("design science") as "acceptable" and "true" ways of talking and acting.

3.4 The Significance Building Tool

One thing we build with language is significance. We use language to make things significant in certain ways or to downplay their significance in certain ways. Things are not always trivial or important all by themselves. We humans make them trivial or important or something in between. Thus, we can state the first of our seven building tools:

Tool #14: The Significance Building Tool

For any communication, ask how words and grammatical devices are being used to build up or lessen significance (importance, relevance) for certain things and not others.

It is important to realize that any use of language is usually engaged in more than one building task at once. Furthermore, often more than one word or grammatical choice is contributing to any one building task.

There is one key grammatical choice that is central to building significance, though many other grammatical devices are used to build or lessen significance as well. What we choose to put in a main clause is foregrounded information. What we choose to put in a subordinate clause is backgrounded information. Foregrounded information is taken to be what is being focused on here and now and, thus, is treated as the most significant information here and now.

In a sentence like, "While I know I did wrong, I am basically a good person," the clause "I am basically a good person" is the main clause. It is also a declarative clause (and not, for example, a question), thus it is the asserted information, what the speaker is asserting or claiming. "While I know I did wrong" is a subordinate clause and, thus, is not asserted, but just assumed as background information. If listeners want to be cooperative listeners (and they don't always), they are supposed to respond to (agree with or disagree with) the asserted information and not the background information. Background information is information they are supposed to assume or take for granted.

A sentence like "While I am basically a good person, I know I did wrong" reverses the foreground and background. Now "I know I did wrong" is foregrounded and asserted and "I am basically a good person" is background and assumed taken-for-granted information.

In a question like "Since I haven't heard yet, what was the outcome of the meeting?," the clause "what was the outcome of the meeting?" is foregrounded and achieves the main speech action here (asking a question). "Since I haven't heard yet" is background information. Cooperative listeners don't say "What do you mean you haven't heard yet?" or "Why haven't you heard?," but answer the question.

In Section 2.5 you reflected on some data from Paul Gagnon's book *Democracy's Untold Story: What World History Textbooks Neglect* (Washington, D.C.: American Federation of Teachers, 1987, pp. 65–71). Here I want to reflect on that data a bit to make my point about foregrounding information and backgrounding as a way to engage in the Significance Building Task. Below I repeat the quote from Gagnon's book:

> Also secure, by 1689, was the principle of representative government, as tested against the two criteria for valid constitutions proposed in the previous chapter. As to the first criterion, there was a genuine balance of power in English society, expressing itself in the Whig and Tory parties. As narrowly confined to the privileged classes as these were, they nonetheless represented different factions and tendencies. Elections meant real choice among separate, contending parties and personalities.

Let me rewrite a part of Gagnon's text, changing what is a main clause and, thus, foregrounded and what is a subordinate clause, and, thus, backgrounded:

> Though they represented somewhat different factions and tendencies, the Whig and Tory parties were narrowly confined to the privileged classes. Elections meant real choice among separate, contending parties and personalities.

Gagnon foregrounded and asserted "they [the Whig and Tory parties] nonetheless represented different factions and tendencies" by making it the main clause and, thereby, asserting it. He backgrounded the information that they were narrowly confined to the privileged classes. My version did the reverse. I made "the Whig and Tory parties were narrowly confined to the privileged classes" the main clause and, thereby, asserted it. I made "they represented different factions" the subordinate clause and, thereby, backgrounded it and took it as assumed information.

Note that my version makes Gagnon final sentence ("Elections meant real choice ...") sound odd, since asserting the two parties were narrowly confined to the same class of people mitigates any claim that choosing between them in an election was much of a "real choice."

Of course, just because we have asserted something or asked a question via the use of a main clause does not alone make it of great significance. It simply makes it the main speech action we are engaged in and the information on which we are currently focusing, which is, indeed, a type of significance. I can add other things to my assertions and questions to render what I am asserting or questioning yet more significant (or less), as in:

1.   It is important that the Whig and Tory parties represented different factions.
2.   The Whig and Tory parties did indeed represent different factions.
3.   The Whig and Tory parties crucially represented different factions.
4.   The Whig and Tory parties barely represented different factions.

Examples 1–3 increase the significance of the information that the Whig and Tory parties represented different factions. Example 4 downplays or mitigates that significance. Of course, one way to decrease its significance is to remove it from the main clause and make it a subordinate clause.

I can even increase the significance of information in a subordinate clause, as in "While it is, indeed, important that the Whig and Tory parties were narrowly confined to the privileged classes, nonetheless they represented different factions." Though I have here increased the significance of the information in the subordinate clause, that clause is still not asserted, but assumed and taken as background.

There are times when people assert or ask questions about information that seems trivial. For example, a neighbor might say in passing, "It's a nice day" or "Nice day, isn't it?." Commenting on the weather seems trivial, so listeners reason this way: My neighbor has asserted (questioned) something that seems trivial and taken for granted, thus, making it foregrounded and significant. Since this information is not important, the neighbor must mean something else and be taking something else as significant. What he must be trying to do is to be cordial to me as his neighbor, either to be nice, to be polite, or to keep peace in the neighborhood. This is "phatic" communication, in which the purpose is largely just to keep the peace, so to speak, and keep a channel of social interaction open.

It is the fact that the neighbor has asserted (or questioned) something trivial, which we usually do not do, that makes us as listeners reflect on what may be his real purpose. Of course, by now, for most of us this sort of "weather talk" or "small talk" is taken for granted and operates pretty much automatically.

3.5 Working with the Significance Building Tool

We use lots of grammatical devices to build or lessen significance, beyond what we choose to put in a main clause and what we choose to put in a subordinate clause, though it is always important to consider this. Below I give some data that will allow you to reflect on and use the Significance Building Tool.

Problem 19

The exchange below is from a meeting of a team of college students who are learning to be engineers. They are part of a project from five colleges across the country that together are supposed to build and design a model race car that will be raced in a competition with the cars from other multi-school teams. Two of the colleges are in the same state and in the transcript below students from these two schools are meeting. Alex is from a very prestigious engineering program at a very prestigious university. Katherine is from a much less prestigious program from a much less prestigious university.

The data below is from the research of Kevin O'Connor at the University of Rochester (not yet published). The marks in the transcript below mean the following:

":" means a sound was lengthened
"/" is a non-final intonation contour
"?" is a final rising intonation contour
"//" is a final falling intonation contour
"(.)" marks a short pause
"(inaud")" means a portion of the speech was inaudible on the tape
Brackets mean the two speaker said the two things marked in brackets at the same time

Alex:	And just to: sort of update the (inaud) right here uh /
	I had a question on what the objective is /
	Of this uh sort of uh sort of fi- five school team?
	Was it to actually produce a working model /
	Or was it to design somethin?
	Because if it is to design somethin /
	Then uh we have to dedicate more time towards uh (.) designing //
	Rather than uh (.) building //
	[Wuh- wuh- what (inaud-)
Kath:	[It's to produce the car //
Alex:	It's actually to produce a car?
Kath:	Yes.

Questions:

1. What does Alex do that gives significance to designing and indicates that he considers designing more important or significant an engineering activity than building?
2. What does Alex do that downplays the significance of the five school consortium?
3. How does Katherine make producing the car important? Do you think her bluntness and conciseness plays a role in this?

4.   It turns out that the students from Alex's (prestigious) engineering program (where many of the students come from professional families) take design rather than actually building to be the more important aspect of engineering. Alex's program was primarily responsible for designing in this project. On the other hand, the students from Katherine's (less prestigious) engineering program (where many of the students come from working class families) take building to be as important (or more so) than designing. In this project, Katherine's program was primarily responsible for building what was designed. Does this contrast surprise you? If not, why not? How does it bear on what Alex and Katherine see as significant?
5.   Why do you think Alex hesitates ("uh") and pauses ("(.)") before both "designing" and "building" near the end of his turn at talk?

Problem 20

Below I reprint a small portion of a letter from a department chair to a university tenure committee. Several members of the committee had voted against the tenure of a person from this chairman's department because they questioned the ethics of some of his research:

> I wish to convey deep concern over the validity of the committee's actions. I don't believe that it is up to your committee to assess the ethics of someone's research. This university has in place rigorous procedures for assessing this issue.

Questions:

1.   How does the writer build significance in each sentence and what is he making significant? Include word choice and phrasing choices in your answer.
2.   The chairman obviously did not care to mitigate his objections. Perhaps being this blunt might offend some members of the committee. In this case, the candidate won a majority of the committee's votes and only a minority voted no on ethical grounds. But let's say a majority had voted no on ethical grounds and the chairman's letter needed to convince the committee to reconsider their vote. Now such bluntness might not work so well. Can you rewrite this portion of the letter in way that might be more conducive to getting the committee to reconsider its vote? How does significance building work in your version and compare to the chairman's?

3.6 The Activities Building Tool

One thing we build with language, as we saw in earlier sections, are actions. We do things with language like promising and encouraging. But action goes further than this. We also use language to build what I will call "activities," using the word in a special limited sense. Activities are just another way to look at actions. When I call something an action, I am focusing on doing and what is being done. When I call something an activity I am focusing on how an action or sequences of actions carries out a socially recognizable and institutionally or culturally normed endeavor. Often the word "practice" is used for what I am calling an activity.

Let me give some examples of the contrast I am trying to make in distinguishing between actions and activities. If I say someone is "playing a video game," I am naming an action. If I say they are "gaming," I am naming an activity or practice, which names a way of engaging in various actions so as to be socially recognized by others as a "gamer."

If I say a parent is "reading a book to her child," I am naming an action. However, there are established ways that some parents read and interact with their small children to get them ready for school and advantaged (ahead) when they go to school. They read with lots of expression, ask the child questions, encourage the child to comment on the text, respond to the child's remarks, ask the child what a given word "says" or picture means, and other such things. This activity or practice does not have a set name, though some people just call it "book reading" or "reading with your child." In any case, many parents recognize this activity as an established routine that gets kids ready for school.

Not all parents, however, read this way to their small children. Some read and tell the child to sit quietly and not interrupt. This is an activity or practice that is not as good for getting kids ready for and ahead in school.

These two different ways of reading to a child or to engage in book reading with a child are partially class and culturally based. Working class parents and parents from cultures which value authoritarian parenting tend to adopt the latter form where the child listens quietly. The other more interactional form is carried out more often by middle class parents and parents from cultures which value less authoritarian forms of parenting. The interactional form is also adopted at school by many kindergarten teachers and is supported by schools as a way to get children ready for learning to read.

If I say John is "playing baseball at the park" I am naming an action. If I say "John plays baseball for the Yankees" I am naming an activity, professional sports. If I say "Mary is writing on her computer" I am naming an action. If I say "Mary is writing a review of a novel for the school newspaper" I am naming an activity or practice. If I say, "Professor Smith is talking to the students" I am naming an action. If I say "Professor Smith is lecturing to the students," I am naming an activity or practice.

The distinction between actions and activities is not air tight. It is really about whether we are concentrating on doing in the here and now (actions) or the meaning, the social significance, and the social, institutional, or cultural norms being followed (activity). When we look at something as an action we are focused on what is being done; when we look at something as an activity or practice, we are focused on its social, institutional, and cultural significance. Activities usually involve a set of actions and ways of sequencing or combining them that are normed by a given institution, culture, or some socially recognizable group (e.g., video "gamers," i.e., people who "game").

Of course, all actions are also socially and culturally normed in the sense that social groups and cultures have norms and standards about how actions should be done. But activities (practices) are larger sociocultural endeavors and when we focus our attention on them we are also focusing particularly on institutional, social, and cultural support systems and values.

So we can now state our second building tool:

Tool #15: The Activities Building Tool

For any communication, ask what activity (practice) or activities (practices) this communication is building or enacting. What activity or activities is this communication seeking to get others to recognize as being accomplished? Ask also what social groups, institutions, or cultures support and norm (set norms for) whatever activities are being built or enacted. [The Doing and Not Saying Tool in Section 2.1 deals with actions; this tool deals with activities/practices.]

Note that activities like (video) gaming or "book reading" (say of the middle-class interactive sort) have to be built, enacted, or produced anew each time someone wants to accomplish them. At the same time, when they are built, enacted, or produced they are done in more or less similar ways as they have been so before, by ourselves and others, otherwise people would not know (recognize) what was being done. It is, however, always worth asking of any activity (practice) being built, enacted, or produced just how similar a given performance is to the "normal" way this activity is carried out. If there are significant differences, then the current performance is potentially a source of disruption or innovation in social life.

Let me turn now to some data. The data below is from the same meeting that Karen's data in Section 1.3 is from. The meeting, as we said before, was composed of an historian from Woodson University, a representative of an educational research center at the university, several teachers, students, and one school administrator. The goal of the project was to help middle-school teachers engage their students with doing history, especially studying the local history of their own neighborhoods.

As is typical of such meetings, the person chairing the meeting, the representative of the educational research center in this case, asked the people in the meeting to take turns introducing themselves. An introduction to a group in a formal meeting is an activity or practice.

Part of the job of discourse analysis is to analyze the structure or patterning of activities. We also need always to ask how routinized or rigid an activity is. Some activities are carried out in very similar ways each time they are done. Little variation is allowed. These activities are highly routinized. Other activities allow more variation (but are still recognized as the "same" or similar sorts of activities).

Introductions at formal meetings are particularly rigid or routine in how they are carried out. While any activity has to bear some similarity to the same sorts of activities that have been carried out before (or people would not know what is going on), not all activities are as rigid and routine as formal introductions in such meetings as this one. For example, much more variation is allowed in how people carry out an activity like giving a report at such a meeting, though, of course, there are norms to follow for reports, as well.

We also want to ask, no matter how routinized an activity is or is not, what sorts of other communications and actions—what sorts of social work—people can and do carry out while still respecting the structure of the main activity in which they are engaged. For example, when we analyze the data below we will see that even though people follow the pattern for an introduction quite faithfully and closely, they still manage to engage in communicating and acting out their own agenda. Even though they are heavily constrained by the rather rigid pattern of introductions, they still manage to communicate and act creatively in their own right.

The Activities Building Tool tells us to look at how various actions are carried out as people build, often together, various activities. Some of these actions are integral to building the activity. Others are ones people engage in inside the activity to carry out their own goals and agendas. These actions are often, as we will see, carrying out others of our seven building tasks.

Even in the type of introduction we will study below, rigid in its demands though it is, there is still some variation to how it is done, variation across people and settings. Nonetheless, everyone in this meeting (14 people) used the very same pattern with which to introduce themselves. Each person first stated their name. Next they said what role they held that was relevant to why they were invited to the meeting. Next they gave a rationale for why they were at the meeting. And finally there was a coda where they "signed off." It is just such patterning or structure we are seeking when we analyze the activities people are building or constructing. Of course, as we said, this patterning or structure is not always so straightforward and regular.

Below I print the introductions of the two undergraduate students in the meeting. Both Melissa and Sandy were students in the history professor's (Sara Vogel) course at the university. Because they were Sara's students, they were recruited by the representative from the university research center (Ariel Dante) to help on the project. Melissa was a White student. Sandy was an African-American student.

Both Melissa and Sandy were going to work for both Ariel and Sara, the two women who headed the project, though ultimately Sara was the lead person, since the project was her idea and she had asked the research center for their help. There is one crucial piece of context you need to know, however.

Sara, the history professor, was teaching a course on Black History. The course was concentrating on local Black History (in Middleview), in part because the project we are discussing was going to be devoted to local history and students in the course would have the opportunity to work on the project. This was the course both Melissa and Sandy were in. Most of the African-American students on campus had chosen to boycott the course, because Sara was White. Sandy, an African-American, had chosen not to boycott the course. She had not only joined the course, but the project as well.

So here is the data:

Melissa's Introduction:

Name:	1. My name is Melissa Smith //
Role:	2. I'm a student at Woodson University //
Rationale:	3. And I'm working directly with Ariel /
	And the Literacy Center on this project //
	4. And I'm also working with Sara /
	In a seminar around something about history /
	In Black Middleview //
Coda:	5. So that's about it for me

Sandy's Introduction:

Name:	1. My name is Sandy Wilson //
Role:	2. I'm a Woodson student also //
Rationale:	3. I'm working directly with Ariel Dante and Prof. Vogel on the same things that Melissa—[stops, pauses, then continues]
	4. We're in the same class as I am, this project also //
Coda:	5. That's about it for me I think //

It is clear that such introductions, as an activity, are pretty constrained. They follow a pretty rigid pattern and the speaker is not supposed to hold the floor for too long (though we have all known people who did). Despite the form's rigidity, speakers can still get significant social work done.

Melissa splits the rationale in her introduction into two parts. In the first part she says she is "working directly with Ariel" (the representative of the research institute) "on this project." In the second part of her rationale, she says: "and I'm also working with Sara /in a seminar around something about history /in Black Middleview //."

Despite the fact that Sara is the true head of the project, Melissa only states her relationship to Sara through Sara's (contested) course, not the project itself. She could well have said she was working "directly" on the project with both Ariel and Sara (after all, Ariel was there to facilitate Sara's work with the teachers and schools).

When Melissa says "in a seminar around something about history / in Black Middleview" this is both distancing (from Sara) and somewhat impolite. It is somewhat insulting for a student in a professor's course to say the course is about "something about history" and then, almost as an afterthought (in a separate intonational unit), say "in Black Middleview," when the course was entirely about Black history with a focus on Middleview. It sounds as if Melissa does not really know what the class is about or, worse, that Sara has not made it clear. However, the content of the course had been the subject of much controversy on the campus—and people very well knew what its content was—and Melissa was well aware of this.

Melissa, perhaps due to the controversy, is distancing herself from Sara and her course and connecting herself more "directly" to Ariel. This is a good example of how people can engage in more than one building task at once. In constructing her introduction (an activity), Melissa is also building connections and disconnections, in this case her connections and disconnections to people on the project (Ariel and Sara), as well as to the project and the course. She is also, of course, building and mitigating social relationships she has with Ariel and Sara in the project.

Melissa's introduction puts Sandy in a hard place. Sandy is loyal to Sara and has stood up for her in the face of the controversy. She is African-American and Melissa is White, and, since it is the African-Americans who are boycotting the course, she is more directly involved with the controversy. Yet she has remained loyal to Sara. However, formal introductions as a form do not allow speakers to explicitly undo what previous speakers have said in their introductions or to directly confront them. Of course, a speaker could do this, but it would be perceived as confrontational and a violation of the norms of such introductions.

Worse, it is common in introductions that subsequent speakers follow, even imitate, the format of the previous speaker, as Sandy tries to do here. And this is all the more likely here, given that Melissa and Sandy are in almost exactly the same positions in the project and in their relationships to Ariel and Sara.

Sandy says: "I'm working directly with Ariel Dante and Prof. Vogel on the same things that Melissa." She imitates Melissa's "directly," but connects herself "directly" to both Ariel and Sara. Furthermore, she uses their full names, treating them as higher in status than her (they are older and leaders in the project), something Melissa did not do. Thus, both her connections and relationships building are done differently than Melissa's.

However, when Sandy says "on the same things that Melissa ...," she stops, unfinished. She has the same relationship to Ariel and Sara on the project as does Melissa in a formal sense of their duties, but she is loyal to Sara and not just Ariel. She and Melissa are not the same in that respect and Sandy does not want to replicate Melissa's disconnection from Sara.

At the same time, she does not want to confront Melissa directly and correct her. So she says "we're in the same class as I am, this project also ." She is flummoxed by how Melissa has set up her (Sandy's) turn at introducing herself and so this comes out wrong. But she clearly wants to connect the class and project and say that both she and Melissa are, in actuality, in both of them together and that they are, in fact, connected. However, saying this explicitly would have been confrontational with her fellow undergraduate in front of many people she did not know.

Melissa has deftly built her introduction to follow the rather rigid format this activity or practice requires, while still engaging in social work, in this case, the work of building a connection to Ariel and a disconnection to Sandy, as well as building her social relationship with them in very different directions.

In the process, Melissa has made Sandy's introduction much harder, as Sandy tries to follow Melissa's introduction pattern. This requires Sandy to do things in a similar way to how Melissa has done them, while not replicating Melissa's distancing from, and even impoliteness towards, Sara, all the while not explicitly responding to and contradicting Melissa. In a sense, her "speech errors" actually help this to happen.

We have used this data to show how Melissa built (enacted) an activity, namely doing a formal introduction at a meeting. The building requirements here are fairly narrow and strict, things have to pretty much be done in one way: Name, Role, Rationale, Coda, all done in short compass. Nonetheless, Melissa communicates and acts out her desires about connections and disconnections and social relationships. At the same time, she situates Sandy in a difficult position: Sandy has to follow the introduction pattern, even imitate Melissa, yet not confront Melissa directly, and still not disconnect from Sara the way Melissa did. This, too, Sandy manages to pull off, speech errors and all.

Introductions look harmless. But all social activities (practices) are rife with opportunities for people to engage in social work, all the while "hiding" behind the activity and its rules. People rarely disrupt activities in which they are engaged jointly to confront others since that would "break" the activity. One thing this data is meant to make clear is that even activities we take for granted as "trivial" or routine can be important, hiding a good deal of important social work.

3.7 Working with the Activities Building Tool

The Activities Building Tool tells us to ask how people are building a socially recognizable activity, what actions this takes, and what actions they manage to accomplish within the activity that realize their own goals and agendas. People can be building more than one activity at a time. We discourse analysts always want to ask, as well, how rigid (routine) or not the activity we are studying is (How much freedom are people normally allowed in how they carry out the activity?) and how much innovation, if any, is occurring in how the activity is being carried out.

Problem 21

Below is printed a dialogue. What activity are these people engaged in? You may have to do some research (ask around) to find out what sort of activity this is. How does the ways in which these people use language reflect and help build this activity? What actions are Bead and Allele carrying out inside this activity? This data is good data with which to work with the Making Strange Tool. What is strange about this communication? How did it ever come to seem to normal and natural to some people?

> Bead: Are you really dead
> Allele: Yes, did you get the heart?
> Bead: I got the heart—another guy was helping
> Allele: Good
> Bead: I am standing over your body—mourning
> Allele: I died for you
> Bead: So touching
> Allele: It's a long way back
> Bead: I know—I've done it

Does knowing that Allele and Bead are brothers, identical twins in fact, help you in any way better understand the data?

Problem 22

Below is reprinted a warning on a bottle of aspirin I once had. Answer the questions below.

> Warnings: *Children and teenagers should not use this medication for chicken pox or flu symptoms before a doctor is consulted about Reye Syndrome, a rare but serious illness reported to be associated with aspirin.* Keep this and all drugs out of the reach of children. In case of accidental overdose, seek professional assistance or contact a poison control center immediately. As with any drug, if you are pregnant or nursing a baby, seek the advice of a health professional before using this product. IT IS ESPECIALLY IMPORTANT NOT TO USE ASPIRIN DURING THE LAST 3 MONTHS OF PREGNANCY UNLESS SPECIFICALLY DIRECTED TO DO SO BY A DOCTOR BECAUSE IT MAY CAUSE PROBLEMS IN THE UNBORN CHILD OR COMPLICATIONS DURING DELIVERY.

Questions:

1. What activity or activities is this language seeking to build or construct? Is the only activity here an official (legal) warning?
2. Why doesn't the sentence "In case of accidental overdose, seek professional assistance or contact a poison control center immediately?" leave out the word "accidental"? Why is the word there? Is the label telling us to let people die who take an overdose on purpose?
3. Why does the first sentence mention this medication (the medication in the bottle) directly ("this medication"), but the second sentence says "this and all drugs" and the last says "as with any drug"? Why is the label sometimes direct about the actual medication in the bottle and sometimes generic and talking about "all drugs" and "any drug"? Why does the first sentence use the phrase "this medication," rather than "aspirin" (after all it uses "aspirin" at the end of the sentence)?
4. The first sentence (in italics on the label) and the last (in capitals on the label) were added later. Originally the warning had only the sentences in the middle (in regular print). Why do you think these additions were added? The style of language in these additions is different than the style of language in the middle sentences. How so? Why?
5. People often say that warnings on medicine are meant to protect people and, thus, should be written in a simple way so that people with poor reading levels can read them. Is this "warning" written in a way that people with poor reading levels could read it? Do people usually read these warnings? Why are they so often in small print? Who is the primary audience for this "warning"? Who is the "author" of this "warning"?

Problem 23

The data below involves a second grade teacher teaching reading. The teacher is working with a small group of students. She first dictates a sentence that the students have to write down. The sentence was "I love the puppy." Then she dictates a list of words, one at a time, which the children are to write down with correct spelling. After they have gone through the list, the teacher asks the children how the word "love" in the sentence is spelled and how each word on the list (one after the other) is spelled. The children are supposed to correct each spelling, if they have made a mistake, after the teacher has elicited the correct spelling orally from the children.

Below is what one African-American girl's list looked like. Note that "sume" ("some") and "shuve" ("shove") are spelled incorrectly:

dove
sume
glove
one
shuve
come
none

As we said, the teacher has the children correct the original sentence and then each word in the list one-by-one, eliciting the correct spelling of each item from the group of as a whole. When she gets to "some," the second word on the list, the African-American girl corrects it, then notices what the pattern is and goes ahead and corrects "shuve" further down the list. The teacher stops her and sharply reprimands her, saying that they have to go "one at a time" and she shouldn't "go ahead."

The teacher moves on to have the small group of children engage in a "picture walk" of a book. This is an activity where children "read the pictures" in a book, using each picture in turn to predict what the text in the book will say. The African-American girl bounces in her chair repeatedly, enthusiastically volunteering for each picture. The teacher tells her to calm down. The girl says, "I'm sorry, but I'm SO happy?." The teacher responds, "Well, just calm down."

Questions:

1. What activity is the teacher building in the spelling task? What is the nature of this activity? What are her goals in this activity? Is there more than one activity she is building?
2. Is there any way that the teacher's response to the girl's "going ahead" in correcting the spelling on her list could seem to contradict what could be seen as a key goal of this lesson (i.e., recognizing a spelling pattern in English)? Why would she contradict this goal?
3. What does the teacher's response to the girl's, "I'm sorry, but I'm so happy" (namely, "Well, just calm down") and her response to this girl in the spelling task tell you about how she views what she is doing when she engages in the activity of teaching reading?
4. A well-known British sociologist of education, Basil Bernstein, said that in every classroom there is a regulatory discourse and an instructional discourse and often the instructional discourse is in the service of the regulatory discourse. Do you have any idea what he meant by this? Does the data about this teacher and child bear on this remark?

Reading

Bernstein, B. (2000). *Pedagogy, symbolic control, and identity*. Lanham, MD: Rowman and Littlefield.

3.8 The Identities Building Tool

We use language to get recognized as taking on a certain identity or role. We build an identity here and now as we speak. We each act out different identities in our lives in different contexts. For example, a person might, at one and the same time or at different times, be acting as a parent, a male, an African-American, a professor, an avid video gamer, an evangelical Christian, a committee chairman, and other such identities. And, too, each of these identities can influence the others when any one of them is being performed.

We are all members of different cultures, social groups, and institutions and have different sorts of roles and relationships. In each of these, we have to talk and act so as to get recognized as having the "right"—or an "appropriate"—identity. Evangelical Christians or gamers will not recognize just anyone as a fellow Evangelical or gamer. They expect those they see as sharing their identities to talk and act in certain ways. The same goes for bird watchers, gang members, lawyers, and feminists.

Further, there are different types of Evangelical Christians, African-Americans, gamers, feminists, lawyers, or any other identity. When we act and speak as a particular "type of person," that is, in a particular socially recognizable identity, we act and speak specific types of these. There are multiple ways of being an African-American, a gamer, an executive, a working class person, or any other identity. Identities, as I am using the term, are about being and recognizing different socially significant "types of people."

Since we all have a number of different identities in different contexts, the issue comes up as to whether there is some core identity or sense of self that underlies and unifies all these multiple identities. Let's call this our "core identity." Some scholars do not think any such core unified identity really exists, though almost all humans feel they have one. They feel there is someone they are that is behind or stands apart from all their social identities and roles.

Other scholars feel that we humans actively create our core identity by the way we tell the stories of our lives—and what we have to say about who we are—to others and to ourselves. And yet this story, and what we say about who we are, can change in different contexts and across time. At the same time, it is clear that our sense of having a body (and mind) that is ours and that moves across all different sorts of contexts is part of our sense of having a unified, core identity.

In any case, as discourse analysts, we do not care whether there is really a core self or exactly what it is. We care about how people express their sense of who they are and their multiple other identities through language.

There is one identity that we can all perform that is important to single out. We are all capable of being an "everyday person," not a specialist or expert of any sort, in certain contexts. When we talk and act as everyday people, we all talk and act differently depending on our own dialects and cultures, though there are also certain shared norms about this across a wider society like the United States. I will call this identity our "life world identity." The life world is all those contexts in which we speak and act as everyday people.

Even specialists like doctors, lawyers, physicists, and so forth, do not always speak and act as specialists or experts. There are contexts where they are expected to speak and act as everyday people, appealing to commonsense, "what everybody knows," and what everyday humans are expected to share. Using highly specialist language over drinks to talk to friends or intimates who are seeking to fraternize and socialize is usually considered rude. Sometimes a group of people who all share the same specialty or expert knowledge may talk "shop" as they socialize, but even in some of these cases they do not.

Let me repeat, however, that people from different social classes and cultural groups in a society use different sorts of language and act in different ways when they are communicating as everyday people in their life worlds. They even vary on what counts as "commonsense" (the sense of everyday people). Furthermore, there is still variation across different contexts, in how any one person talks and acts as an everyday person. We do not talk the same way at a bar as we do to our spouses when we are being intimate as we do when we are talking to people we do not know particularly well (e.g., at a bus stop). But in each case, we normally talk and act as everyday people and consider all these contexts life world contexts.

When people are speaking as everyday people they use what we will call a "vernacular style" of language. People's vernaculars differ by dialect and sociocultural group. Further, we each have different versions of the vernacular—for example, less and more formal versions—that we use in different contexts.

In Section 3.2 you reflected on some data about a young woman talking to her boyfriend and to her parents. This woman, who I will call "Jane," was an upper middle-class, Anglo-American in her twenties. Jane was attending one of my courses on language and communication. The course was discussing the ways in which people varied how they spoke in different contexts to express different identities. Jane claimed that she herself did not do this. She said she was consistent from context to context in how she spoke and who she was. In fact, to do otherwise, she said, would be "hypocritical," a failure to "be oneself."

In order to support her claim that she did not switch her style of speaking in different contexts and for different conversational partners, Jane decided to record herself talking to her parents and to her boyfriend. In both cases, she decided to discuss a story the class had discussed earlier, so as to be sure that, in both contexts, she was talking about the same thing.

In the story, a character named Abigail wants to get across a river to see her true love, Gregory. A river boat captain (Roger) says he will take her only if she consents to sleep with him. In desperation to see Gregory, Abigail agrees to do so. But when she arrives and tells Gregory what she has done, he disowns her and sends her away. There is more to the story, but this is enough for our purposes here. Students in my class had been asked to rank order the characters in the story from the most offensive to the least.

In explaining to her parents why she thought Gregory was the worst (least moral) character in the story, the young woman said the following:

> Well, when I thought about it, I don't know, it seemed to me that Gregory should be the most offensive. He showed no understanding for Abigail, when she told him what she was forced to do. He was callous. He was hypocritical, in the sense that he professed to love her, then acted like that.

Earlier, in her discussion with her boyfriend, in an informal setting, she had also explained why she thought Gregory was the worst character. In this context she said:

> What an ass that guy was, you know, her boyfriend. I should hope, if I ever did that to see you, you would shoot the guy. He uses her and he says he loves her. Roger never lies, you know what I mean?

It was clear—clear even to Jane—that Jane had used two very different styles of language. The differences between these two styles are everywhere apparent in the two texts. To her parents, she carefully hedges her claims ("I don't know," "it seemed to me"); to her boyfriend, she makes her claims straight out. To her boyfriend, she uses terms like "ass" and "guy," while to her parents she uses more formal terms like "offensive," "understanding," "callous," "hypocritical" and "professed." She also uses more formal sentence structure to her parents ("it seemed to me that ...," "He showed no understanding for Abigail, when ...," "He was hypocritical in the sense that ...") than she does to her boyfriend (... "that guy, you know, her boyfriend," "Roger never lies, you know what I mean?").

Jane repeatedly addresses her boyfriend as "you," thereby noting his social involvement as a listener, but does not directly address her parents in this way. In talking to her boyfriend, she leaves several points to be inferred, points that she spells out more explicitly to her parents (e.g., her boyfriend must infer that Gregory is being accused of being a hypocrite from the information that though Roger is bad, at least he does not lie, which Gregory did in claiming to love Abigail).

All in all, Jane appears to use more "school-like" language to her parents. Her language to them requires less inferencing on their part and distances them as listeners from social and emotional involvement with what she is saying, while stressing, perhaps, their cognitive involvement and their judgment of her and her "intelligence." Her language to her boyfriend stresses, on the other hand, social and affective involvement, solidarity, and co-participation in meaning making.

This young woman is making visible and recognizable two different versions of *who* she is. She is enacting through talk two different identities. In one case she is "a dutiful, intelligent, and educated daughter having dinner with her proud parents" (who paid for her education) and in the other case she is "a girlfriend being intimate with her boyfriend." Of course, I should add, that while people like Jane may talk at dinner this way to their parents, not all people do. There are other identities one can take on for one's parents. And, indeed, Jane may very well speak differently to her parents in other contexts.

We will later call the different styles of language that Jane uses—and all such stylistic variation—different "social languages" (see Section 4.4). In her language to her boyfriend she uses an informal variety of her vernacular social language. In her language to her parents, she moves to a quite formal style of language that is "school-based." This style of language serves for many educated people as the most formal version of their vernacular, though we could also say that when people speak this way they are not really being everyday people, but "educated people." People who do not use this style of language, or at least not when engaged with family and friends, sometimes think that people who do use it in such contexts are "putting on airs." In any case, it is one place where the vernacular transitions into something on the border of being a "specialist" language (one associated with a good deal of education).

One way we enact an identity in language is to portray other people and their identities in certain ways that compare or contrast with the identity we want to take on or enact. In many cases a given identity cannot exist without other people taking up or being portrayed as having related identities. For example, the "Special Ed" teacher needs "Special Ed" ("SPED") students and talks about and acts in regard to students in such a way as to create and sustain this identity as well.

I have often heard teachers talk about "my low" and "my high" students. It is, of course, not clear that we really can rank students on one single scale as either high or low. Furthermore, there are those who argue that being "high" or "low" as a student is not something that resides in the student or the student's mental abilities, but in the contexts in which their schooling takes place and their relations to and within those contexts. On this view, a student could be "high" in one setting or set of relationships and "low" in another. Nonetheless, schools are often about ranking and sorting students and within this Discourse (see Section 4.8) the teacher takes on an identity as a sorter and the students take on—and sometimes are talked about by teachers in terms of—an identity as things to be sorted based on the basis of their fixed internal traits (e.g., being "smart" or "quick").

Jane above is not just enacting in language different identities for herself. She is also creating different identities for her boyfriend and her parents. She is "positioning" them in certain ways, that is, through her talk she is creating an identity "position" or "place" for them to take up and to talk within, for this time and place.

So we want to ask how people enact different identities, how they portray other people's identities, and how they position others to take up identities in response to them. Thus, we can state our next building tool, the Identity Building Tool:

Tool #16: The Identities Building Tool

For any communication, ask what socially recognizable identity or identities the speaker is trying to enact or to get others to recognize. Ask also how the speaker's language treats other people's identities, what sorts of identities the speaker recognizes for others in relationship to his or her own. Ask, too, how the speaker is positioning others, what identities the speaker is "inviting" them to take up.

Reading

Gumperz, J. J., Ed. (1982). *Language and social identity*. Cambridge University Press. [An important collection.]

Habermas, J. (1984). *Theory of communicative action*, Vol. 1, trans. by T. McCarthy. London: Heinemann. [Habermas uses the "life world" concept.]

3.9 Working with the Identities Building Tool

People use language to build different identities for themselves in different contexts. They also help build identities for other people that they "invite" them to take up. In turn, they often use the identities they are building for others to further the work they are doing building their own identity (in terms of comparison and/or contrast). Below I print two sets of data that will allow you to study both how a speaker constructs an identity for herself and uses identities she attributes to others to further the construction of her own identity.

Problem 24

The data below is from an interview with a White middle-school girl named Emily. Emily has fairly recently moved from a middle-class community to an upper-middle-class prestigious suburb. In the data below Emily is talking about her new best friend in the suburb, a White girl named Susie. Read and reflect on the data and then answer the questions below.

In the transcript, "/" makes a non-final intonation contour, "//" and "?" mark final contours. A comma represents a pause and "—" represents a place where the speaker breaks off and says something else.

1. Like, there's there was this girl / who was dressed / dressing really like like preppy //
2. And, and, she came up to me and I was talking with Susie //
3. And she's like, she's like, "Yeah" you know / "I really like the Grateful Dead //
4. I just got one of their albums and I like the song like KC Jones" //
5. Which is like, you know, the most popular song like in the world that the Dead ever wrote //
6. And um, she's like, "Yeah, they're really like cool and I wanna get their shirt and stuff"//
7. And so after she walked away / I was talking to Susie / And, and I was like / I was like, "Oh" //
8. And Susie's like "So what do you think about" like, "that girl, that she likes the Dead"?
9. I was like, "I think she's kind of a poser"//
10. And um, and Susie's like, "Well why do you say that? //
11. You know if she really likes the Dead what makes her a poser"?
12. So, I mean, it's like she has a point //
13. But she doesn't, like, even like—
14. And then I can't explain myself //
15. I'm just like, "Well, it's just how it is, you know," I mean //
16. And like, a lot of times she'll make comments that I take to be like, like, like, homophobic or something //
17. Like not really badly, like, she won't say that gay people are evil or something //
18. But you know, just like, sort of like innuendoes //
19. And um, I'll say like, "Oh Susie, you know, please don't say that / like, it bothers me" //
20. And, and she'll like, "Why? It's not bad / you know, like, I wasn't saying anything bad" //
    [short aside between Emily and interviewer, then Emily continues about Susie]
21. About people, like when I, when I was in Colorado / I came back and I was telling her about um, like, we went on a horse trip //
22. And we stayed with these like cowboys / and like, they were so cool //
23. They were like, right out of the movies //
24. And, right near us there was this shed / and there were like, where we were camping / which was 22 miles out of civilization t/ his little like run down like cabin shed thing //

25. And they told us all these ghost stories / about this guy who lived there / like Alfred Packer / who was a cannibal //
26. And so when I came back / I told Susie these stories //
27. And she's like, "Oh, they're just making that up to scare you //
28. They don't believe that and stuff / because, like, it's not true" //
29. And, you know, I said, "Maybe it's not true but they do believe it / because you know that's like, how they've been brought up //
30. And they like really are rednecks / and they like really say these things" //
31. And she's like, "No:o they aren't really like that / no, they're just saying that, they like—"
32. And I'm like, "Susie, you, you just don't understand that there are people like that"//
33. And so, I dunno //
34. She, she's, like doesn't understand some things //
35. But she, she's like really nice and really fun / and that's why we're friends //
36. So //

Questions:

1. What sort of identity is Emily building for herself? What sort of identity is she building for Susie? Go through the data and point to all the ways Emily is using language to build these identities. Tie all your observations to specific features of the language in the data.
2. What role does the identity Emily is building for Susie play in Emily's own identity building? That is, how does the identity that Emily attributes to Susie help build the identity she is attempting to construct for herself in this data?
3. In another part of the interview, Emily tells the interviewer that she considers the kids in her new town "sheltered" (by their parents) and not "worldly." She considers herself more "worldly" because in her old community she saw more diversity and was "less sheltered." How does the data above reflect these viewpoints Emily holds about her identity and that of the kids in her new town?
4. Do you see any tensions or contradictions in how Emily attempts to build her own identity both through talk about herself and through juxtaposing her identity to the one she attributes to Susie?

Problem 25

The data below is from an interview with a middle school Latina named Maria. Maria goes to school in a blue-collar industrial town that has lost a good deal of its industry and is in a poor economic condition. There are not a lot of jobs and those that still do exist often no longer carry good wages and medical benefits. Many of the parents in the town—(non-Hispanic), Black, or Hispanic—work more than one job to make ends meet and there is high unemployment. There are not a lot of wealthy people in the town. There are many working class and poor whites in the town and in the lower tracks at school, as well as Blacks and Hispanics. However, the small upper track in Maria's school is almost all white. At this point in the interview, Maria is talking about why there are so few professional Hispanics (e.g., doctors) compared to whites:

1. Because like white people get more education //
2. Like Hispanic people don't, don't / some of the Hispanic don't like go to college and stuff like that //
3. And, you know, just, the white people just like / they like to, they want a future //
4. You know they—
5. Some, some Hispanic and stuff they, they just—
6. I'm Hispanic but I'm saying—
7. Some um, they just like, like to hang around / they don't want to go to school / they don't you know //
8. So people don't, don't think like that //
9. They want to get an education / they want to have a good/ their life //
10. And they really don't care what people say / like if they make fun of em //
11. Like "gringos" and stuff like that //
12. They don't, they don't care / they just do their work and then, they see after / they're like, they're married /and they have their professions and stuff made, / then, let's see who's gonna like, be better //
13. Maybe the Hispanic boy that said that you gonna / that like you're a nerd or something //
14. Probably in the streets looking for sh, for money and stuff like that / sick / and you have a house / you have your profession / you got money //
15. So—

Questions:

1. What sort of identity is Maria building for herself, Hispanics, and whites?
2. Earlier in the interview Maria has said she thinks s are smarter than Hispanics. She goes on to say:

> They're just smart // ((slight laugh))
> I think they were born smart //
> There's something like, their moms or something they give em a little piece of smart or something // ((slight laugh))
> so they'll be smart //

How does what Maria says here fit with the way she treats identity in the data above?

3. What tensions or contradictions are present in the ways in which Maria is building identities for herself, Hispanics, and whites?

4. Maria talks little here directly about herself. How does this affect the identity or sense of self we as listeners attribute to her? What is the role of "I'm Hispanic but I'm saying—"?

5. The interviewer was a woman. Do you think this played a role in what Maria said? Why or why not?

6. Do you think the state of Maria's town plays a role in how she looks at identity here?

7. People often tend to blame social problems (like declining economic fortunes of a town in the global world) on other people and what they can see and not on larger global and institutional factors. How does this play a role in Maria's talk?

8. People get themes they use in building identities from somewhere. They usually don't just make them up on the spot. Where do you think Maria got some of her themes?

3.10 The Relationships Building Tool

We use language to build and sustain relationships of all different kinds. We use language to build relationships with other people and with groups and institutions. Clearly this building task is related to the Identities Building task, since the identity we construct for ourselves in any context is often defined, in part, by how we see and construe our relationships with other people, social groups, cultures, or institutions.

In turn, we relate to other people in terms of different identities we take them to have. I will talk and act towards someone differently if I see my relationship to them as one of being a professional colleague as against being a friend. I will even treat one and the same person differently when I relate to them as a professional colleague and when I relate to them as a friend.

Consider again the data we looked at in Section 3.8 when we were discussing the Identity Building Tool. There we looked at a young woman talking to her parents, in one case, and to her boyfriend, in the other case. I reprint the two communications below:

> To Parents:
> Well, when I thought about it, I don't know, it seemed to me that Gregory should be the most offensive. He showed no understanding for Abigail, when she told him what she was forced to do. He was callous. He was hypocritical, in the sense that he professed to love her, then acted like that.

> To Boyfriend:
> What an ass that guy was, you know, her boyfriend. I should hope, if I ever did that to see you, you would shoot the guy. He uses her and he says he loves her. Roger never lies, you know what I mean?

In Section 3.8 we said that this young woman is making visible and recognizable two different versions of *who* she is. She is enacting through talk two different identities. In one case she is "a dutiful, intelligent, and educated daughter having dinner with her proud parents" and in the other case she is "a girlfriend being intimate with her boyfriend." But, of course, these are two different sorts of relationships, as well. Jane is engaging in a relationship of solidarity and bonding with her boyfriend. She is engaging in a relationship of more formal deference and respect with her parents.

Identity and relationships go hand in hand. However, it is often useful to focus on them separately. Creating or taking on identity and creating and sustaining a relationship of a certain type are not the same, however closely related they are. Identities set up parameters for a relationship. As a professor (an identity) I can have different sorts of relationships with different sorts and types of students, though there are constraints I cannot breach without mitigating or destroying my identity as a professor. Furthermore, even though I am a professor I have had different sorts of relationships with the college and universities wherein I have been a professor.

Being a friend is a type of identity: it is a role to enact, a way of being a certain type of person. Nonetheless, I can form different sorts of relationships with different friends; for example, kidding and playful with one and more deferential and polite with another. Here, too, there are parameters beyond which I cannot go without mitigating or destroying my identity as a friend.

So, we always want to ask about both identity and relationships and how they interact. Thus, we can state another building tool:

> ## Tool #17: The Relationships Building Tool
>
> For any communication, ask how words and various grammatical devices are being used to build and sustain or change relationships of various sorts among the speaker, other people, social groups, cultures, and/or institutions.

Let's look at an example. In Section 3.2 we discussed a foreign doctoral student in graduate school in the United States who, after several years in the program, had lost her PhD advisor. She needed to get another one. She was talking to a professor who she wanted as an advisor, but who was reluctant to take her on as a student. She said: "It's your job to help me, I need to learn."

This student is construing the professor as being in what we might call a "helping profession": "It's your job to help me." We think of people in helping professions as obligated to help people who need help if their need falls into the domain of the professional's skills. Thus, we think that priests, doctors, nurses, and teachers are there to help people and are professionally and morally obligated to help people in need. Of course, not all people in these professions actually behave this way. There are doctors who will not treat people who cannot pay no matter how dire their need. But, at least, ideally we think of these professions as "helping professions."

By construing the faculty member as a member of a helping profession, the student is, of course, construing his relationship with the institution for which he works in a certain way. She is construing the university as the sort of institution that is there is to help people and pays its faculty to do so. That is why it is "his job." He is in a "helping profession," she believes.

By saying "I need help" the student is stating her need for help, a need that is supposed to necessitate that people in helping professions respond. She is construing her relationship to the faculty member as a needy person who will be helped by the professor in the way in which health professionals help sick people or elementary school teachers help children in need of extra aid.

When one construes the relationships between graduate student and professor in this way what is liable to happen if the professor says no? The student is liable to make herself yet more needy, to construe herself as worse off, so as to get the "helper" to help. This is what a sick patient might do if he or she did not get enough of a response or a quick enough response from a nurse. And this is, indeed, what the student did when the faculty member continued to resist her request to be her new advisor.

The faculty member did not view his relationship to his institution or to his students as one that was like a "helping profession." He saw himself as mentoring professionals who were already confident and skilled, much as a professional sports coach views his or her players. Thus, expressing need was not going to work. He expected an expression of confidence and skills, even if more skill building was still needed. Yet more neediness was going to work even worse.

This encounter did not work out well for the student (at least initially). Nonetheless, she can be seen as trying to get the faculty member to accept the sort of relationship she was seeking to build. This could have happened, of course. She might have gotten the faculty member to see his relationships with his institution and students in a new way. All building is a risk. It may not work. We can build buildings people refuse to live in.

At the same time this student could have tried to build relationships differently. She could have used language to seek a relationship with the faculty member that was, say, closer to the sort of relationship a coach has with a professional sports team than the one a caring nurse has with her patients. In this case, she would have had to have crafted herself as less needy and more confident, accomplished, and competent, inviting the professor to see the relationship as mutually beneficial.

3.11 Working with the Relationships Building Tool

Problem 26

Consider again the data below, which we also saw in Section 1.6. This is data from the history project we have discussed several times (e.g., see Section 1.4).

Here a teacher named Jane (a good friend of Karen's—who we saw in Section 1.4—Jane and Karen teach at the same school) is telling the historian Sara, and the representatives of the university research center helping with the project, about how the teachers are the ones who need to be contacted first if you want to involve the children in their classes in a project. It is not acceptable to go to an administrator first and not the teacher, as Sara has now twice done.

Jane is here talking in a context where Sara has written a grant proposal to continue the project in the next year and has, once again, gone to Mary Washington, an administrator, first and not the teachers. Joe is an administrator (and Su and Lucy are teachers at his school) who was also at the first meeting, the one from which the data from Karen in Section 1.4 above comes. Mary is, of course, Mary Washington, the same administrator who Sara called and who told Karen to call Sara:

> Well I think /
> one thing you need to recognize /
> about the STRUCTURE of the Middleview schools
> is that if Su, Lucy, Karen, and I /
> or any combination thereof /
> are involving our classrooms /
> we are the people who need to be asked /
> and to be plugged into it //
> Joe does /
> um as curriculum coordinator for Freeland Street /
> does not have the right to commit Su Wilson //
> Nor Linda Defoe //
> Nor does Mary /
> have the right to commit /
> or structure the grant for us //
> Uh it becomes a question /
> like Karen said /
> this isn't her priority area / [Because Karen teaches English, not History like Jane]
> that she wants to be in //
> If it is mine /
> or someone else /
> we are the direct people //
> In a sense we OWN the kids //
> If you want the children to be doing the work /
> You've got to get the classroom teacher /
> not the curriculum coordinator or [the next speaker interrupts Jane]

Questions:

1. Looking carefully at Jane's language, how is she building, constructing, or construing (however we want to put it) the sorts relationships she and teachers like her have to other sorts of people (e.g., children in her class

and school) and institutions? Point to specific things Jane says and the way she says them to answer this question.

2. What sort of relationship is Karen building to those present and listening to her through the way in which she is using language?

3. When Jane says "In a sense we OWN the kids," what do you think she means? Why does she use emphatic stress on "own"?

Problem 27

Below is a posting on a website made by a fifteen-year-old girl who writes stories ("fan fiction") using software that comes with the computer game *The Sims*. You will see this data again in Section 4.5 below. The girl's stories are made up of pictures (from the game) and words (each "slide" has an image and text beneath it). This girl writes novel-length stories of this sort, one of which is called Lincoln Heights ("LH"). She has a devoted following of fans that wait for each new chapter of the story to be posted. Below is a message she sent out to her fan base. Discuss how this girl (an author) is building her relationship with her fans (who are also teenage girls).

> *Sunday, 02 December 2007*
> *As u can see I gave my page a little makeover! I've had that oldd one for over a year! Needed a change! As 4 LH 1.3 I've got around thirty slides, working up to my usual 127! Patience is all it takes! I garentee it'll B out B4 Xmas though! ;)*
> *<3 A*
> [See the Sunday, 02 December 2007 entry from http://thesims2.ea.com/mysimpage/blog.php?user_id=2877919&date=all]

3.12 The Politics Building Tool

As I said in Section 3.3, I am going to use the term "politics" in this book in a special way. By "politics," I mean, not government and political parties, but any situation where the distribution of social goods is at stake. By "social goods" I mean anything a social group or society takes as a good worth having.

We use language to build and destroy social goods. There are lots of social goods in any society. Some are things that are viewed as social goods by nearly everyone in a society. Others are viewed as social goods only by some sub-group or sub-groups in the society. For example, in the United States, some people view being able to carry guns in public as a social good and others do not. When those who do not view carrying guns as a social good seek to deprive those who do of their guns, the gun carriers see themselves as having been deprived not just of guns but of a social good, one for which they are willing to fight. The gun opponents see the social good as a gun-free society.

Almost all humans view being treated with respect or deference as a social good. They also view being treated with solidarity by those they like as a social good. These can come into conflict. Being respectful and showing deference means being formal and creating a certain distance between people. If I expect solidarity from you and I get a respectful distance, I may be hurt. On the other hand, showing solidarity means being informal, friendly, and close. If I expect a respectful distance from you and I get solidarity, I may feel you are being too personal and assuming too much about our friendship.

All humans have what sociologists call "face needs." "Face" is the sense of worth or dignity each of us has and wants to be honored by others in society. Face is something that can be lost, maintained, or enhanced. We have such idioms as "losing face" and "saving face." There are two major types of "face needs" people have. Each person has what are called "negative face" needs. They want their privacy respected and they do not want others to impose on them. This is the face they turn away from others unless they choose to interact with them. But each person also has what are called "positive face" needs. They want to belong and to be involved and, thus, do not want people to leave them out. This is the face people turn toward others.

Different people, often based on cultural differences, but sometimes just as an individual matter, have a different balance between these two face needs. Some people prefer that others be very careful about imposing on them. They value negative face needs more than positive face needs. Other people prefer involvement and want people to err on the side of interacting and involving them in things. They value positive face needs more than negative face needs. Some cultures lean one way and other cultures the other way. All people have both needs, but they balance them differently and expect different things in different contexts.

Consider what can happen when two strangers are waiting at a bus stop. After a while some people feel it is rude not to talk to the other person. They favor involvement and think that ignoring the other person or being ignored by the other person is disrespectful. They expect positive face needs (needs for involvement) to operate in this situation. On the other hand, some people think that a stranger talking to them is being disrespectful of their right to be left alone and to determine how and when they get involved. They find a stranger talking to them an imposition. They expect negative face needs (needs for privacy) to operate in this situation.

Making a request of someone can be "face threatening," that is, seen as an imposition or a form of over-involvement. For example, in some circumstances if I say "Do you want to go to dinner," you might feel that the request has put you on the spot. It is hard to say "no" without harming my face need for involvement. You feel my question has imposed on you in a way that you don't like. So I have harmed your face need for privacy and not being imposed upon. At the same time, in some circumstances if I do not ask I will offend you because I have harmed your positive face needs by not including and involving you.

In a pluralistic society with many different types of people in it, it can be difficult for people to navigate face needs and not offend other people.

Sometimes we find we have been too personal and assumed a desire to be involved where there is none. Sometimes we find we have been too distant when there was a desire for more closeness and personal involvement.

Face needs are large and general categories of social goods. We can honor or dishonor these face needs in many different ways.

Another large and general category of social goods which can be given or withheld in many different ways are things like having ourselves, our behaviors, or our possessions treated as "normal," "appropriate," "correct," "natural," "worthy," or "good." Of course, standards for these can change in different contexts and across different social and cultural groups.

I once worked at a university where each year the school I was in had a conference where graduate students presented their work. The conference was organized by the graduate students themselves. When making the schedule one year, the organizers put together a session called "alternative research methods." One student whose paper was placed in this session was incensed. She felt insulted. She took the term "alternative" to mean she was not mainstream or "normal." She demanded an apology, as did others who supported her. On the other hand, some people would take the term "alternative research methods" to mean "better" or "newer" methods and be proud to be "special" and not classed with "mainstream" research in their area. Nonetheless, taking what people do or say, or what they are, as not normal, natural, acceptable, correct, good, or worthy when and where they view these things as social goods can be a source of major insult and conflict.

When we are using language, then, one thing we build is what counts for us as social goods. We also distribute these to or withhold them from others, as well as to the groups, cultures, and institutions to which people belong. And, finally, we build viewpoints about how we think social goods are or should be distributed in society or among social and cultural groups. This is, for me, how and where language is "political." I use the term "political" here because a great deal of the work of government, elections, and political parties at all levels is devoted to conflict and negotiation over social goods and how they should be distributed. So, too, are social interactions and conflicts throughout society.

So we can introduce another building tool:

Tool #18: The Politics Building Tool

For any communication, ask how words and grammatical devices are being used to build (construct, assume) what counts as a social good and to distribute this good to or withhold it from listeners or others. Ask, as well, how words and grammatical devices are being used to build a viewpoint on how social goods are or should be distributed in society.

Let's look at an example of the Politics Building Tool at work. Below I print data from an interview with a middle-school girl named Karin. Karin goes to a prestigious but public school in a very wealthy neighborhood in the United States. Students from her school go on to the country's best colleges. At this point in the interview Karin is being asked whether she believes that the quality of her school gives her advantages that kids at much poorer schools do not have.

> *Interviewer: ... just say that it's a really really poor neighborhood um or a ghetto school, and, um, do you feel like somebody who goes to school there would have a chance, um, to succeed or become what they want to become?*
> Not as good as they would in a good school system //
> It depends on—
> I know that they probably don't //
> If they don't have enough money /
> they might not have enough to put into the school system //
> and not, may not be able to pay the teachers and /
> um, the good supplies and the textbooks and everything //
> So maybe they wouldn't, they probably wouldn't have the same chance //
> But, I believe that every person has equal chances /
> um, to become what they want to be //

Karin is being asked an explicit question about social goods. Are children in poor schools denied social goods that they need for success in society? Karin first makes it clear that she thinks they are: "So maybe they wouldn't, they probably wouldn't have the same chance." She also makes clear that the social good they and their school lacks is money. Karin expresses a theory about good schools as a social good and poor schools as a lack of that social good: a lack of money leads to less good teachers and supplies and this can negatively affect the future chances of children who go to these schools.

At the end, however, Karin seems to contradict this view she has expressed. She says: "But, I believe that every person has equal chances / um, to become what they want to be." It is unclear how the children in the poor school "wouldn't have the same chance" and yet "every person has equal chances to become what they want to be." Karin, in the latter statement, is expressing a very different view of how social goods are distributed in society. Now, she construes the distribution as fair.

Notice, too, how Karin expresses her view that poor kids do not have equal chances in probabilistic terms: "I know that they probably don't" and "So maybe they wouldn't, they probably wouldn't have the same chance." Here we get "probably" and "maybe." On the other hand, she expresses her view about everyone having equal chances in much more certain terms: "I believe that every person has equal chances."

What is going on here? The viewpoint that every person has an equal chance to succeed if he or she tries hard enough is one of the most pervasive beliefs in American society. It is a common sense theory that many Americans hold about the distribution of social goods that heavily discounts the workings of poverty and discrimination (see Section 4.6 below on "social models" and "figured worlds"). Karin holds this view and expresses it clearly. At the same time, the interview has caused her to reflect a good deal on the advantages her school brings her and the disadvantages a much poorer school might bring others. Nonetheless, this reflection does not cause her to question her view about success and everyone having an equal shot at success in the United States.

We know from interviews with a number of young people at Karin's school that they were deeply concerned about being successful in society (which for them meant becoming professionals like their parents). They know that there is great competition for prestigious colleges and jobs. They also want badly to believe not only that they will be successful, but that they will have earned that success "fairly" through hard work and not just through the advantages of social class and wealth.

Thus, Karin wants to concede that poor kids are disadvantaged by poor schools, since she very much hopes her school and education will advantage her in the face of the stiff competition she will face to get into a good college and obtain a good job. At the same time, she wants also to believe that all people have fair chances, that hard work will bring her success, and that her success will have been "fairly" earned and stem from her worth and not her advantages. Indeed, to tell Karin that her success in school now and in the future is due not to her but to her circumstances would be to threaten her face needs for respect as a "worthy" and "good" human being.

It is common in communication for all of us that we seek to balance our conflicting desires, needs, and beliefs. Karin is not special or benighted in this respect at all. When we build with language we are often trying both to reflect reality as we see it and to see reality—and construe it—in ways that make us feel like humans worthy both of respect (for our achievements) and as involved with others (as one of them, not unfairly advantaged or set apart in any unfair way).

At the same time, Karin's interview shows that confronting people with "facts," even facts they concede, does not necessarily get them to change deeply seated theories about the world—and there are few theories as deep seated as our views about social goods and how they are and should be distributed. We will later discuss people's theories about the world and how these theories shape their language and actions when we introduce the terms "social models" and "figured worlds" for theories like Karin's model of success (i.e., the viewpoint that everyone has an equal chance in the United States if they work hard enough).

Reading

Brown, P. and Levinson, S. C. (1987). *Politeness: Some universals in language usage.* Cambridge: Cambridge University Press. [See the use of the concept of "face" in this book.]

Scollon, R. and Scollon, S. B. K. (1981). *Narrative, literacy, and face in interethnic communication.* New York: Ablex. [A wonderful and important book—often out of print, unfortunately, but a must read.]

3.13 Working with the Politics Building Tool

Problem 28

The data below is from an interview with a middle-school teacher. The teacher teaches in the town we discussed in Section 3.9 when we looked at Maria's data. As we said in Section 3.9, the town is a former blue-collar industrial town that has lost a good deal of its industry and is in a poor economic condition. There are not a lot of jobs and those that there are often no longer carry good wages and medical benefits. Many of the parents in the town—Asian, Black, or Hispanic—work more than one job to make ends meet and there is high unemployment.

The teacher has been asked about whether she ever discusses social issues with her students. A part of her response is printed below. In the transcript, "I" stands for "Interviewer." Words in brackets are guesses about what was said when it cannot be well heard on the tape. "[????]" means material is inaudible.

1. Uh so [what] you you need to do about job hunting /
2. You need to look the part // [I:mm hm]
3. You don't see anybody at any nice store dressed in jeans // [I: uh huh]
4. They're not gonna have a job if they do that // [I: uh huh]
5. And a lot of the kids question that //
6. uh I talk about housing /
7. We talk about the [????], we talk about a lot of the low income things //
8. I said "Hey wait a minute" /
9. I said, "Do you think the city's gonna take care of an area that you don't take care of yourself"? [I: uh huh]
10. I said, "How [many of] you [have] been up Saints Street"?
11. They raise their hands /
12. I say "How about Main Ave."?
13. That's where those gigantic houses are /
14. I said, "How many pieces of furniture are sitting in the front yard"? [I: mm hm]
15. "Well, none" //
16. I said "How much trash is lying around"?

17. "None" //
18. I said, "How many houses are spray painted"?
19. "How many of them have kicked in, you know have broken down cars in front of them"? [I: uh huh]
20. I said, "They take care of their area" /
21. I said, "I'm not saying you kids do this" /
22. I said, "Look at Great River Valley /
23. They burn the dumpsters //
24. That's your housing area" // [I: uh huh]
25. "Do you know how fast that can JUMP into someone's apartment or whatever else"?
26. I bring up the uh, they have in the paper /
27. Probably about two years ago /
28. The uh police were being sued—
29. Uh the fire department were being sued by a family that had a girl with asthma /
30. And the kids had lit the dumpster outside of their bedroom window /
31. And she had a severe asthma attack /
32. And the fire department would not come in /
33. So they couldn't get the police escort //
34. The fire department used to only go in with a police escort /
35. Because the people living there would throw bottles and cans at them // [I: uh huh]
36. And you know, again, the whole class would [???] //
37. I don't understand this //
38. Here is someone who's coming in here—
39. Maybe the police I could understand /
40. Because you feel like you're getting harassed by the police /
41. What has the fire department done to you /
42. That you're gonna throw bottles, rocks, cans at them? [I: uh huh]
43. And stop them from putting out a fire [I: uh huh] that could burn down your whole house? [I: uh huh]
44. Why do you burn the grass? [I: mm hm]
45. There's grass here that every single summer as soon as it turns green they burn /
46. And as soon as it grows back up they burn again //
47. Why do you do that?

Questions:

1. Go through this data line by line and discuss how this teacher is building or construing what count as social goods and how they are distributed.

2. Why are there broken down cars in front of the houses in some poor neighborhoods and not in richer ones? Where are the broken down cars in rich neighborhoods?

3. Some people would see what the teacher is talking about in terms of "social class." Socioeconomic classes in a society are inherently about social goods and their distribution. Does the teacher? How does the teacher construe social class?

4. The teacher at many points performs dialogue she has had in her classroom. This dialogue is, of course, being enacted here for the interviewer. However, she is depicting how she talks to her students. How does talking to the students in this way position them in terms of social goods and how they are distributed? Is the teacher "blaming the victim"?

5. In line 21 the teacher says: "I said, 'I'm not saying you kids do this'." What do you make of this? What is she saying about the children ("you kids")? What does this have to do with social goods?

6. At the end of the data above the teacher says:

Why do you burn the grass? [I: mm hm]
There's grass here that every single summer as soon as it turns green they burn /
And as soon as it grows back up they burn again //
Why do you do that?

Here "Why do you burn the grass?" seems to be a question that the teacher is pretending to put to the students. She then switches from "you" to "they" in "There's grass here that every single summer as it turns green they burn / And as soon as it grows back up they burn it again." She then switches back to "you" in "Why do you do that?." What do you think the teacher is trying to do here? Think about this question in relation to question 5 above. How is she positioning herself in relationship to the interviewer and to her students? How does she position the interviewer in relation to the students?

7. In line 35 the teacher says that "people" (not necessarily children) throw rocks at the firemen. Then she reverts to "you" and says things like "Maybe the police I could understand / Because you feel like you're getting harassed by the police / What has the fire department done to you? And stop them from putting out a fire [I: uh huh] that could burn down your whole house?." Who does "you" refer to in these sentences? Go through the whole data and discuss what "you" refers to in each case and how "you" is functioning in this communication as a whole (at time "you" may be ambiguous). What does this have to do with social goods?

3.14 The Connections Building Tool

Connections

Things in the world can be seen as connected and relevant to each other (or not) in a great many different ways. We use language to connect or disconnect things and to make things relevant to each other or not. If I say "The king and queen died," I treat the two deaths as simultaneous or, at least, as though the difference in timing did not matter. If I say "The king died and then the queen died," I imply the queen's death has something to do with the king's. If I say "The king died and then the queen died from grief" or "The queen died because the king died" I make the connection explicit.

Some things in the world are really connected, for example cigarette smoking really does cause cancer. However, we can still treat such connections in different ways in how we speak in different contexts. For example, consider the sentence below:

Lung cancer death rates are clearly associated with an increase in smoking.

Let's consider for a moment how this sentence uses wording and grammar to make connections. The phrase "are clearly associated with" does not say smoking causes lung cancer. It just says the two are correlated or associated in some way. The sentence also does not say who is getting lung cancer from smoking, whether it is just the smokers or non-smokers who inhale secondary smoke. It says nothing about the connections here. A version of this sentence like: "Lung cancer deaths of smokers and non-smokers (via second-hand smoke) are caused by increased smoking in a society" would make different and more direct connections.

Sometimes connections are not made explicit because the speaker assumes the listener will make them. The speaker leaves such connections to the Filling In Tool. At other times speakers want to manipulate more overtly how listeners think about particular connections and what connections they make in their minds, so they word what they have to say to accomplish these goals.

So we can state yet another of our building tools:

Tool #19: The Connections Building Tool

For any communication, ask how the words and grammar being used in the communication connect or disconnect things or ignore connections between things. Always ask, as well, how the words and grammar being used in a communication make things relevant or irrelevant to other things, or ignores their relevance to each other.

Let's look at one more example of how words and grammar are used to build connections and the Connections Building Tool in action. Consider the sentences below from a talk by the science fiction writer Philip K. Dick (Retrieved September 26 from http://deoxy.org/pkd_how2build.htm):

> The basic tool for the manipulation of reality is the manipulation of words. If you can control the meaning of words, you can control the people who must use the words.

This sentence first connects reality and words: words are tools for manipulating reality. But it isn't really words that manipulate reality, it is the manipulation of words and that is something speakers and writers do. The second sentence connects words and people: speakers or writers can control people through their control of the meanings of words. They do not control these people by controlling their non-verbal actions but by controlling what words they in turn use. Later in his talk Dick makes clear that the words people are manipulated to use (and he adds the images used in the media) affect reality by causing people to perceive reality in certain ways and to behave in certain ways.

By pairing "manipulation of reality" with "manipulation of words" in his first sentence and "control the meanings of words" and "control people" in his second sentence, Dick sets up an almost puppet like version of the connections between words and reality. The speaker or writer pulls (manipulates, controls) the strings and the puppet (people) say what he or she wants them to say. Speakers and writers who can manipulate words or control meaning (and Dick is a professional writer) put words into people's mouths and thereby control their perceptions and behavior and thus, too, reality.

Now presumably any and every speaker manipulates words and controls meanings whenever he or she speaks. That is what language is about after all. This common trait we all share cannot be what Dick is talking about or we would all be controlling reality and each other every time we speak and none of us would be more powerful than any others of us. Presumably he means to say that people who are good, adept, or skilled at manipulating words and controlling meanings are the powerful ones who control other people and reality. Dick's sentences are in that sense special pleading for the power of "professionals" of speaking (e.g., politicians) and writing (e.g., novelists) and image making (e.g., the media).

There is a paradox with the connections Dick has created. He sets up the following connections: Manipulate words (well) → control the meanings of words → control the words other people use → control their perceptions and behavior → control reality. But now that Dick has told us of this power of writers—and himself as a writer—why would we not think that anything he said or wrote was meant only to manipulate and control us? Would not he now have lost his power?

Dick, of course, wants us to trust him. His target is other manipulators:

> ...today we live in a society in which spurious realities are manufactured by the media, by governments, by big corporations, by religious groups, political groups—and the electronic hardware exists by which to deliver these pseudo-worlds right into the heads of the reader, the viewer, the listener.

But, then, the real question would become how do we know when we are being manipulated and when we are not? Is the (view of) reality Dick goes on to offer in his talk "spurious" or not? In the quote above Dick makes the connection between words (and images) and manipulation of people quite direct: "deliver these pseudo-worlds right into the heads of the reader, the viewer, the listener." The agency of the reader, the viewer, the listener is not mentioned; people's ability to think about, reflect on, and reject messages is not highlighted. Thus, agency is not rendered relevant to the way Dick sees words and images working in society.

At the same time, this view of manipulation leaves us as readers of Dick's talk to ask the following question: When and if we agree with his view of reality (which is a striking one), do we agree because we are being reflective agents or just because Dick has become a better wordsmith and manipulator than his enemies? How would we know? It is an interesting question whether the sorts of connections between words, reality, and people's perceptions and their behavior that Dick wants to make could have been made in a different way so as to have avoided this dilemma that Dick has created for himself.

Reading

Halliday, M. A. K. and Martin J. R. (1993). *Writing science: Literacy and discursive power*. Pittsburg, PA: University of Pittsburg Press [The sentence about lung cancer and smoking is from this book, p. 77.]

Grammar Interlude # 8: Cohesion

In Grammar Interlude #4 we talked about the way clauses can be integrated together into single sentences. But speakers and writers have to do more than connect clauses within sentences. They must also connect sentences across whole oral or written texts. The grammatical devices we use to create such connections are called *cohesive devices*. They signal to the listener or reader the connections among the sentences of a communication and are part of what makes a spoken or written communication sound like it "hangs together" (coheres).

There are six major types of cohesive devices. Examples of each of them (numbered in reference to the following discussion) are seen in the little discourse on the next page (note that the second sentence has been placed vertically):

The Federal Government expected Indian Nations to sign treaties.

<u>However, though</u>	=	6
<u>most of</u>	=	2
<u>them</u>	=	1
<u>had in fact</u>	=	6
<u>done so,</u>	=	3
<u>the</u>	=	2
<u>Seminoles</u>	=	5
<u>would not</u> .	=	4

Each of the numbered words or phrases is a cohesive device that signals to the hearer how the second sentence is linked (or how it coheres) with the preceding sentence. Below, I list the six major classes of cohesive devices and show how the member of that class represented in our example above functions. The numbers below correspond to those used in the example.

1. *Pronouns.* In the example, the pronoun "them" links back to the preceding sentence by picking up its reference from a phrase in that sentence ("Indian Nations").

2. *Determiners and Quantifiers.* The quantifier "most" links to the preceding sentence by indicating that we are now talking about a part ("most") of a whole that was talked about in the preceding sentence ("Indian Nations"). The determiner "the" in front of "Seminoles" links to the preceding sentence by indicating that the information it is attached to ("Seminoles") is information that is assumed to be predictable or known on the basis of the preceding sentence. In this case, it is predictable because the preceding sentence mentioned Indian Nations and Seminoles are an Indian Nation.

3. *Substitution.* The words "done so" are a dummy phrase that substitutes for (stands in for) "signed treaties" in the previous sentence. This allows us both not to repeat this information and to signal that the second sentence is linked to the preceding one.

4. *Ellipsis.* The blank after "would not" indicates a place where information has been left out (elided) because it is totally predictable based on the preceding sentence (the information is "sign a treaty"). Since we reconstruct the left out information by considering the preceding sentence this ellipsis is a linking device.

5. *Lexical cohesion.* The word "Seminoles" is lexically related to "Indian" since Seminoles are Indians. This links the two sentences together through the fact that they contain words that are semantically related. Lexical cohesion can involve exact repletion of words or repetition of words that are related to each other.

6. *Conjunctions, adjunctive adverbs, and other conjunction-like links.* The word "however" signals how the hearer is to relate the second sentence to the first. It signals that there is an adversative relation between the

two sentences. "In fact" also links the second sentence to the first, though in a way that is subtle enough and hard enough to describe that it is possible that only native speakers would get its placement just right in a variety of cases. Related to this category are "discourse particles," words like "so" and "well" that also help tie sentences together into meaningfully related chains of sentences that "sound" like they go together.

Let's consider a moment how cohesion works in the text below:

> Also secure, by 1689, was the principle of representative government, as tested against the two criteria for valid constitutions proposed in the previous chapter. As to the first criterion, there was a genuine balance of power in English society, expressing itself in the Whig and Tory parties. As narrowly confined to the privileged classes as these were, they nonetheless represented different factions and tendencies. Elections meant real choice among separate, contending parties and personalities.

The author devotes a great deal of the words and grammatical devices in this passage to cohesion. He uses the phrase "as to the first criterion" in his second sentence to tie back to the phrase "two criteria" in the first sentence. In the third sentence, he uses a pronoun inside a subordinate clause in its sentence ("as narrowly confined to the privileged classes as these were") and another pronoun in the main clause ("they") to tie back to "the Whig and Tory parties" in the preceding sentence. His final sentence about elections is not tied to the previous sentences in any explicit way (in fact, "elections" comes rather "out of the blue" here), for example, the author does not use any logical connectors like "and therefore."

The final sentence about elections is, however, tied to the previous sentences by lexical (word-level) relations. "Elections" is a word that is in the same semantic (meaning) family as the words in phrases like "different factions and tendencies," "the Whig and Tory parties," "balance of power," "constitutions," and "representative government" in the previous sentences (these are all words and phrases about governing and government). This connects "elections" back to these sentences. The author seems to suggest, by this tactic, that his claim about elections—i.e., that they constituted a "real choice"—follows rather straightforwardly from the very meaning of what he has previously said. He treats his claim about meaningful elections as needing no more explicit logical connection to what has come before than that. He treats it almost as a mere restatement of what he has already said, despite the fact that a critical reader might worry about how meaningful (and for whom) these elections among the "privileged classes" were.

Thus, we can state another grammatical tool:

> **Tool #20: The Cohesion Tool**
> For any communication, ask questions like: How does cohesion work in this text to connect pieces of information and in what ways? How does the text fail to connect other pieces of information? What is the speaker trying to communicate or achieve by using cohesive devices in the way he or she does?

Problem 29

Consider the utterance below. This is from a teacher in the history project we have discussed several times so far. She was supposed to bring maps to the meeting she is in so the people in the meeting could plan what neighborhoods children would study:

> I do have all the maps //
> Unfortunately, my source said that the city of Middleview no longer has any of the big ones //
> They're not being printed //
> I do have three or four //

Discuss how this speaker uses cohesion to tie her clauses and sentences together across her entire utterance. Check each word in each sentence (and what is left out—ellipsis) to see if it plays a role in tying sentences together.

Problem 30

The text below is from a young woman with schizophrenia who is telling a therapist a story about how much she loved horses as a kid and how she worked at a camp taking care of horses (so she is associated by the other girls at the camp with the horses):

1. That was at summer camp / Camp Quonset / a girl's camp I worked at //
2. And all the other girls my age / they were rich //
3. They were all going to camp there //
4. And they / uh most of them were sort of afraid of horses //
5. So I couldn't get to be very friendly with them / where they wanted to come around / and hang around with me or anything / because they were more or less afraid //

Counting each numbered line here as a sentence, discuss cohesion in this communication. What type of cohesion device is operating after the word "afraid" in (5)? There is a crucial ambiguity here. What is it? Why do you think it occurred? Has the speaker used this cohesive device to create this ambiguity as a form of communication?

Reading

Halliday, M. A. K. and Hasan, R. (1976). *Cohesion in English*. London: Longman [The example and discussion at the beginning of this section follows this classic source.]

Halliday, M. A. K. and Hasan, R. (1989). *Language, context, and text: Aspects of language as a social-semiotic perspective*. Oxford: Oxford University Press.

3.15 Working with the Connections Building Tool

In this section I will give you some data that you can use to work with the Connections Building Tool. When people speak and write they engage in several or all of the seven building tasks at once. So, too, we discourse analysts must often use several or all of the seven building tools at once. So here think, as you apply the Connections Building Tool, how all the other building tools you have seen so far would apply to the data below, as well. Remember that cohesion is only one way to signal connections. There are many others (though they do not fall into such a neat grammatical system as does cohesion). Pay attention to as many as you can.

Problem 31

Once again we will consider data below from the history project we have discussed in Section 1.6 and elsewhere in this book. The project involved an historian, an educational researcher, undergraduate students, and teachers working together. The historian (Sara) and the educational researcher (Ariel) had brought in two curriculum consultants to help them work with the teachers in building curriculum for the project. At a meeting where the teachers had objected to not having been consulted on a grant proposal that if successful would have involved children in their classrooms (see data in Section 3.11—where Jane was speaking), one of the two curriculum consultants tried to defend the project and the confusions that had been part of it. Part of her communication is printed below.

1. There's a there's a big complicated process /
2. Of working through the materials /
3. Figuring out how to teach it /
4. Which is called curriculum development //
5. And that's what we're involved in now /
6. And it's very murky /
7. And it's very complicated /
8. And we we don't know where we're going /

9. But that's an innate part of curriculum development /
10. Unfortunately /
11. Especially when you work with a group of people /
12. And you're not just doing it yourself //
13. Um so /
14. And that's where Sandy and I were hired /
15. As sort of the hired guns /
16. To come in and help facilitate it /
17. Because we know you don't have the time //
18. Um and and um Sara and Ariel /
19. Didn't don't have the experience /
20. Of working in the classroom /
21. And they teach in a different structure /
22. Which is very different //
23. And so /
24. So we're there as the helping hands to give you /
25. To to help you where you need /
26. And to act as sort of the interpreters /
27. And the shapers /
28. But in response to what is necessary //
29. I mean /
30. We're not coming in to do something that we want to do //
31. We're trying to facilitate what you want to do //

Questions:

1. What sorts of connections is this speaker (a curriculum consultant on the project) building? What sort of connection does she build between herself and the teachers? Between herself and the two academics (Sara and Ariel)? Between herself and curriculum development? Between teachers and curriculum development? Between the two academics and curriculum development?

2. Both Sara and Ariel are college professors and teach college students in classrooms, as the speaker concedes in line 12. So why does she say they don't have "the experience of working in the classroom" in lines 10 and 11? Why is the word "classroom" here used to mean only classrooms of teachers who do not teach at the college level, but not college professors? What does this tell you about the connections the speaker is building between teachers, professors, and classrooms? [Note how we often use "teacher" for non-college teachers and "professor" for people who teach in colleges and how "classroom teacher" seems never to mean a person teaching at the college level. Even when we say that someone teaches at a "teaching college" and not a research-based university, we still call him or her a professor and not a teacher.]

3. In lines 15 and 16 the speaker switches word choice from "give you" to "help you." Why? There is a certain tension here, what is it? Are there other indications of this tension in the data?
4. How does the Politics Building Tool apply to this data?

Problem 32

The data below is from a college professor being interviewed about her views on race in society. This professor works at a college in the town where the history project took place, but at a different college from Sara and Ariel.

Interviewer: . . . How, do you see racism happening, in society, let's put it that way.

1. Um, well, I could answer on, on a variety of different levels // [I: uh huh]
2. Um, at the most macro level /
3. Uum, I think that there's um, um /
4. I don't want to say this in a way that sounds like a conspiracy / [I: mm hm]
5. But I think um, that um, basically that the lives of people of color are are, are irrelevant to the society anymore // [I: mm hm]
6. Um, they're not needed for the economy because we have the third world to run away into for cheap labor // [I: uh huh]
7. Um, and I think that, that the leadership /
8. This country really doesn't care if they shoot each other off in in the ghettos / [I: uh huh]
9. Um, and, and so they let drugs into the ghettos /
10. And they, um, they, let people shoot themselves /
11. Shoot each other /
12. And they don't have, a police force that is really gonna, um, work /
13. And they cut the programs that might alleviate some of the problems //
14. And, um—
15. So I think there's /
16. That it's manifested at, at the most, structural level as, um, you know, a real hatred, of, of, of uh people of color //[I: uh huh]
17. And, and it's shown, in, the cutbacks and so forth //
18. And, um, I think that um, that, it's, it's reflected in, in the fact that, they're, they're viewed as, expendable / [I: mm hm]
19. By our leadership //
20. Um, and so I think, I see cutbacks in programs as just a, an example of, of a broader / [I: mm hm]
21. You know, sense, that, that, from the point of view of, of those in power /
22. People of color are expendable / [I: uh huh]
23. And, and irrelevant //

Questions:

1. How does this speaker build (see) the connections among "people of color," "society," the "third world," and "leadership" (of the country)?

2. In line 4 the speaker says "I don't want to say this in a way that sounds like a conspiracy." Why does she say this? Does she say it in a way that sounds like a conspiracy or not? How do connections work in so-called "conspiracy theories"?

3. This professor is being interviewed by the same interviewer who interviewed the teacher in Section 3.13 (Working with the Politics Building Tool). Go back and look at that data. Who gives the people they are talking about (in the case of the professor, "people of color," and in the case of the teacher, her working class students and the people who live where they do) more agency? How do the professor and the teacher see the world in terms of connections differently? Even though they live and work in the same town, the interviewer asked the professor how she thought about race in society and the teacher if she ever dealt with social issues like race and class in her classroom. Why this difference in questions? Does it surprise you? How does it help shape the sorts of answers the interviewees give and the connections they make?

3.16 The Sign Systems and Knowledge Building Tool

We use language to build up (or privilege) or denigrate various sign systems (communicational systems) and different ways of knowing the world. There are many different languages (e.g., Spanish, Russian, English). There are many different varieties of any one language (e.g., different dialects, as well language varieties like the language of lawyers, biologists, and hip-hop artists). There are communicative systems that are not language (e.g., equations, graphs, images) or at least not just language (e.g., hip hop, poetry, ads with pictures and words). These are all different sign systems.

All these different sign systems are important to the people who use them and at least partly define their identities in terms of them. People are often deeply connected to and committed to their dialect. Lawyers are committed to talking like lawyers. Hip hop fans are passionate about hip hop. There are even arguments over where and when Spanish should be spoken in the United States. Physicists believe the language of mathematics is superior to languages like English for explicit communication.

Furthermore, different sign systems represent different views of knowledge and belief, different ways of knowing the world. As we said, physicists believe the language of mathematics is superior to English for producing and communicating knowledge about the physical world. Poets believe poetry is a higher form of knowing and insight, as do, in another sense, people who use religious varieties of language. Speakers of Black Vernacular English believe there are some things that can be expressed or felt in that dialect better than they can in standard English. So, too, for Spanish–English bilinguals who favor one language or the other for different topics or emotions. Statisticians believe statistics is a deep way of understanding reality, while some qualitative researchers do not or, at least, believe the language of statistics has spread too far in our understanding of the social world.

We humans contest over the value of different languages and other sorts of sign systems. We contest, as well, over different ways of knowing the world. We can use language to make or construe certain sign systems and certain forms of knowledge and belief as better or worse than others, as relevant or privileged or not in a given context. We can build privilege or prestige for one sign system over others or for one way of claiming knowledge over other ways. For example, I can talk and act so as to make the knowledge and language of lawyers relevant (privileged) or not over "everyday language" or over "non-lawyerly academic language" in our committee discussion of facilitating the admission of more minority students.

So we can introduce the last of our seven building tools, the Sign Systems and Knowledge Building Tool:

Tool #21: Systems and Knowledge Building Tool

For any communication, ask how the words and grammar being used privilege or de-privilege specific sign systems (e.g., Spanish vs. English, technical language vs. everyday language, words vs. images, words vs. equations, etc.) or different ways of knowing and believing or claims to knowledge and belief?

The Sign Systems and Knowledge Building Tool is clearly closely related to the Politics Building Tool. This is so because the mastery, use, and maintenance of languages, dialects, sign systems, and ways of knowing the world are, for the people who "own" them, social goods. Thus, when we use language to build them up or tear them down, we are engaged in politics in the sense of building viewpoints on the distribution of social goods in society. But language, sign systems, and ways of knowing the world are so important to people and distinctive for human beings that we separate them out as particularly important social goods over which people negotiate and contest in the world.

Let's discuss an example of data where the Sign Systems and Knowledge Building Tool applies. Consider the two excerpts below written by the same biologist on the same topic. The first is for a scientific journal; the second is for a popular science magazine read by non-scientists (e.g., *National Geographic, Natural History*). These examples reflect two major styles within professional scientific writing, each of which uses distinct kinds of language and represents a distinctive way of knowing the world.

1.   Experiments show that *Heliconius* butterflies are less likely to oviposit on host plants that possess eggs or egg-like structures. These egg-mimics are an unambiguous example of a plant trait evolved in response to a host-restricted group of insect herbivores.
2.   *Heliconius* butterflies lay their eggs on *Passiflora* vines. In defense the vines seem to have evolved fake eggs that make it look to the butterflies as if eggs have already been laid on them.

Let's consider the differences between these two texts. The first excerpt, published in a professional scientific journal, is concerned with furthering conceptual understanding within a sub-discipline of biology. Its language is carefully developed to do this—to build evidence and marshal support for certain biological claims within particular parts of the biological community. The subject of its initial sentence is "experiments," a primary methodological tool in biology. The subject of the next sentence is "these egg mimics." Note here how parts of the plant ("these egg mimics") are named, not in terms of the plant itself, but in terms of the role they play in a particular theory of natural selection and evolution, namely, co-evolution of predator and prey (co-evolution means that two species interact with each other over a long period of time so as to mutually shape each other's evolution). Note, too, how they are framed as an "unambiguous example" of the relation in question, a linguistic turn that underscores the importance of the experiments being reported.

Looking further into this text, the butterflies are referred to as "a host-restricted group of insect herbivores," which points simultaneously to an aspect of scientific methodology (as "experiments" did) and to the logic of a theory (as "egg mimics" did). Scientists arguing for the theory of co-evolution face the difficulty of demonstrating a causal connection between a particular plant characteristic and a particular predator when most plants have many different animals attacking them. To overcome this problem, they use a strategic methodological technique: they study plant groups that are preyed on by only one or a few predators (i.e., "host-restricted"). "Host-restricted group of insect herbivores," then, refers both to the relationship between plant and insect that is at the heart of the theory of co-evolution and to the methodological technique of focusing research on plants and insects that are restricted to each other. This first excerpt, then, is concerned with addressing a particular problem and advancing knowledge within biology; the language of the text has been carefully shaped to communicate these concerns.

The second excerpt, published in a popular science magazine, is about animals in nature, not methodology and theory or claims and arguments. Scientists write for popular magazines to inform the public and to build public support for their work and the field at large. Here, too, they shape their language to meet these purposes. The language in the second example focuses on nature itself as the subject, rather than the activity of science as in the first text. In the second text, the subject of the first sentence is "butterflies" and the subject of the second is "the vine." In contrast with the first text, the butterflies and vine are both labeled as such, rather than being described in terms of their role in a particular theory. This second text is a story about the struggles of insects and plants that are transparently open to the trained gaze of the scientist (as opposed to inferences derived from clever experimental manipulation, as suggested in the first text). The plant and insect are dramatically represented as intentional actors: The plants act in their own "defense" and things "look" a certain way to the insects, who are deceived by appearances as humans sometimes are.

Interestingly, these two excerpts reflect a historical shift in the relationship between the scientist and nature. In the history of biology, the biologist's relationship with nature has gradually changed from telling stories about direct observations of nature (as in the excerpt from the popular science magazine) to carrying out complex experiments to test complex theories (as reflected in the excerpt from the professional journal). These two texts also reflect a shift in curricular focus from early elementary science, where direct observation is usually stressed, to upper level science education, where experiment grows in importance. A shift in the academic nature of the language used in the science classroom, from conversational, story-like styles to more academic styles, likewise accompanies the transition from elementary to high school.

Thus, these two texts, though written by the same person and about "the same thing" (in one sense), are not the same. Each uses a distinctive style of language—and each style is used in a different communication system (i.e., professional science, popular science)—and each represents and privileges, as well, a different but distinctive way to know the world and make claims about it. It is interesting that the way of knowing the world and the style of language in the more popular text, the one for wider consumption, represents a way of knowing and a style of language that the author and his discipline would "dismiss" as "wrong" (perhaps, "misleading") or "immature" in their more professional disciplinary identities. The two texts are built to privilege two different ways of knowing (theoretically-driven experimentation versus observation in the world) and two different styles of language (specialist scientific language versus popular science language).

Reading

Myers, G. (1990). *Writing Biology: Texts in the social construction of scientific knowledge.* Madison: University of Wisconsin Press [This book is the source of the passages from professional science and popular science, see p. 150.]

3.17 Working with the Sign Systems and Knowledge Building Tool

Problem 33

The data below is once again from the history project. The group has had a
long and contentious meeting. This is the same meeting from which the data
in Sections 3.11 and 3.15 were taken. The meeting is now over and only Karen
and Jane (two teachers), Joe (an administrator from a school involved in the
project, though not Karen and Jane's school), and Sara (the university
historian) are still present. They are engaging in "small talk"—no longer
talking about the project—before themselves leaving.

Karen, Jane, and Joe were all born in Middleview. So were their parents. Sara
was born and educated elsewhere, worked at Woodson University in Middleview
at the time of this project, and is now at another university in another state.

Read and reflect on the data below. Then answer the questions following
the data.

KAREN:
1.   My mother used to talk about in the 40s /
2.   You'd hang around at Union Station /
3.   And anybody would just pick you up /
4.   Because everybody was going down to dance at Bright City /
5.   Whether you knew them or not //

JOE:
6.   Lakeside Ballroom //

JANE:
7.   Yeah definitely //

JOE:
8.   My father used to work there //

JANE:
9.   And also, once you finally get into the war situation /
10.   Because you have Fort Derby /
11.   Everybody would get a ride in to come to Bright City /
12.   To the amusement park //
13.   So it was this influx of two, three cars worth of guys /
14.   That were now available to meet the girls that suddenly were there //

SARA:
15.   Well actually street, street cars had just come in in this /
16.   And as I recall um from a student who wrote a paper on this /
17.   Bright City and Park was built by the street car company /
18.   In order to have it a sort of target destination for people to go to /
19.   And to symbiotically make money off of this //

JANE:
20. Because once you got there /
21. You could take a boat ride /
22. And go up and down a lake /
23. And there were lots of other ways to get the money from people //

Questions:

1. How does the way in which Sara builds and privileges knowledge of the world differ from how Karen, Jane, and Joe do? How does their ways of using language build and privilege their different ways of claiming knowledge about the world here?
2. What do Karen, Jane, and Joe base their claims on? What does Sara base her claims on?
3. Is what Sara says potentially disruptive or rude in this context? Why is or isn't it?
4. What do you think of Jane's remarks after Sara has spoken? Are they responsive to Sara? How does what Jane says here connected to what Sara said? To what Karen and Joe has said before?
5. In what ways is Sara at a disadvantage in this discussion?
6. Can you see any differences in the styles of language (the "social languages") Sara uses and the longtime Middleview residents use in this episode of "small talk"?

Problem 34

In several states in the United States, bilingual education has become controversial. Some people argue that immigrant children should be allowed to learn school content (such as science and math) in their native language while they are also learning English. Others argue that immigrant children should learn English immediately and quickly and then be exposed to school content only in English.

The point of the data and questions below is to study how viewpoints on language and languages are expressed (including your own). The point is not to convince you here of one viewpoint on bilingual education or "English-only" as policy. If you are doing this exercise collaboratively, pay attention to how you express your viewpoints and respect other people's viewpoints (while insisting, of course, that everyone offer fair arguments for those viewpoints).

In the state of Arizona, immigrant students are grouped in classrooms based on English language proficiency determined by a test (the Arizona English Language Learner Assessment—AZELLA). In these classrooms, the children receive four hours of mandated skill-based English language instruction each day. Teaching and learning does not include the content areas, such as science or social studies. Students are segregated from native English speaking students in these four-hour blocks. No bilingual education is allowed.

A proposition passed by voters (Proposition 203) led to the implementation of this system. Here is part of what the proposition said:

> The English language is the national public language of the United States of America and the state of Arizona …. Immigrant parents are eager to have their children acquire a good knowledge of English, thereby allowing them to fully participate in the American Dream of economic and social advancement…. Therefore it is resolved that: all children in Arizona public schools shall be taught English as rapidly and effectively as possible. (Retrieved September 24, 2009 from www.azsos.gov/election/2000/Info/pubpamphlet/english/prop203.htm)
> Here is how the Arizona Department of Education frames the four-hour block policy:
> The year of intensive instruction is designed to advance a student to English language proficiency, thereby moving the student into the mainstream classroom where they [sic] will have access to the curriculum allowing for academic success. The language skills are pre-requisite skills to academic content. (Retrieved September 24, 2009 from www.ade.state.az.us/oelas/sei/SEIModelsFAQs.doc)

Finally, printed below is one teacher's view of the policy from an interview:

> It's racism. Blatant racism. There's no other way to describe it. It's against the 14th amendment [of the U.S. Constitution]. It's made specifically to isolate children who are immigrants to this country. And that's what it is, because if you're an immigrant, you're coming in this class. And to say that there's no time to teach them science and social studies is against the 14th amendment of the Constitution. It is segregation at its finest, because you are not providing the same educational opportunities for the kids in that class that you are providing to native English speakers. (Data from: Heineke, A. J. (2009). *Teacher's discourse on English language learners: Cultural models of language and learning.* Unpublished doctoral dissertation. Mary Lou Fulton College of Education, Tempe, Arizona, p. 162)

Questions:

1. How does the language in the first two excerpts build a view of English in relation to immigrant children and their families? What is that view?

2. Not saying something—staying silent about it—can be a way of privileging what you do say, since you leave unsaid information that might make the listener or reader think differently about your viewpoint. The third excerpt from the teacher brings up things that are unsaid in the two earlier excerpts. What are these? How do they change (if they do) how a reader might respond to the two earlier excerpts if that reader kept this unsaid information in mind?

3. Many people argue that in a global world, all children should know at least two languages, both orally and for writing and reading. Skill with language learning is seen as an important twenty-first century skill in a global world. This is not said in any of the excerpts above. One could imagine it as a state policy. If one accepts this claim about the importance

of being bilingual and bi-literate in a global world, how might this change the way in which one responds to the excerpts above?

4. The second excerpt above says "The language skills are pre-requisite skills to academic content." This clearly means in context "English language skills." Why doesn't it say so? If language skills are a pre-requisite to [learning] academic content, then why would that not be an argument to start teaching content in Spanish, for example, for Spanish speaking children, while they are also learning English? Wouldn't this also mean these children would acquire literacy in Spanish and thus end up bilingual and bi-literate in two languages (a seemingly good thing in a global world)? Is this a contradiction in the text? Why or why not?

5. It is clear that being silent about certain things—children being segregated away from peers who are native speakers of English and thus models for learning English; children not receiving school content instruction to keep up with other students in a school; children not gaining literacy in their native language or learning more than one language—is one device to enhance building the importance of an English only policy in the two earlier policy excerpts. If readers do not think of what is unsaid, the two excerpts sound more convincing and "natural" than they otherwise would. The issue here is not what viewpoint you should have on bilingual education or English only. The issue is how you can defend your views in fair and convincing ways. Write a short policy statement about language learning policy or goals for immigrant children that is not silent on the issues we have just mentioned. How has your text used language to build a viewpoint on languages and aspects of language (e.g., literacy) in the world as social goods?

Grammar Interlude #9: Topic Flow or Topic Chaining

Earlier, we discussed subjects, topics, and themes, as well as cohesion. Now we take up topic-comment structure and topic chaining. People do not just introduce a topic in a single sentence and then drop it. They usually continue to talk about the same topic for a while. Further, when they switch topics they must signal this in some way.

When one speaker speaks after another, the second speaker usually has to either continue talking about the same topic as the first speaker or at least tie or relate to that topic in some way before introducing a new topic. When one speaker or a second speaker continues to talk about the same topic, we will say that they are speaking "on topic." When they switch topics but try in some fashion to relate the new topic to the old, we will say they are speaking "topically."

English clauses and sentences usually have a topic-comment structure. The subject is normally in first position which makes it both topic and theme (if something is in front of the subject, then that is the theme and the subject is just the topic). What follows the subject is the comment, what is being said about it. Normally the subject/topic is old information, that is, information that has already been talked about or is assumed by the speaker to be known already to the listener. Normally the comment is, or at least contains, new information, information that moves the communication along and that is not already known or assumed to be known by the listener. As we pointed out in Grammar Interlude #3 on intonation, where in a clause the major pitch change (which demarcates the focus of the clause) is placed determines what constitutes the new information and this is usually some place in the comment.

Of course, some subject/topics are new information when we start a new topic. If we continue talking about it, it is thereafter old information. So I could say "A unicorn is in the garden. It is really beautiful." Here "a unicorn" is a new topic and new information (in fact, everything in the sentence is new information), and "it" continues talking about it and is old and assumed information.

A structure like "There is a unicorn in the garden" has a "dummy subject" (a meaningless subject) and shifts the old subject ("a unicorn") towards the back of the sentence. This is a way of introducing and emphasizing topics that are new information. Structures like "It is clear that John lied" do a similar thing. This could be said as "That John lied is clear," but here the subject/topic ("that John lied") is heavy and a lot of new information for subject position. So English can move it towards the back of the sentence where new information more normally occurs. We can call these structures ("There is a unicorn in the garden," "It is clear that John lied") topic shifted structures, since the normal subject/topic is not in first position but shifted towards the back of the sentence.

Consider the written passage below. This is from a paper written by a Mexican-American academic about a controversy that arose in a court of law as to whether a burrito was a sandwich or not (Richard Ruiz, "The ontological status of burritos," 2008, unpublished paper, University of Arizona, Tuscan, Arizona). I have numbered each sentence and placed material on different lines to make the data easier to read. I have capitalized and underlined the subject/topics of main clauses. These are the most prominent topics in a communication. I have bolded the subject/topics of embedded and subordinate clauses. These are less prominent topics, sort of sub-topics. There are three cases (in 2, 5, and 6) where heavy subject/topics with lots of new information have been shifted.

First Paragraph:

1. A few months ago, <u>A JUDGE IN MASSACHUSETTS</u> declared that a **burrito** was not a sandwich.
2. It is not clear WHAT **HIS CREDENTIALS** WERE TO MAKE THIS DECISION.
3. <u>HIS NAME</u> does not lead me to conclude that **he** had the kind of intimate personal experience with Mexican food that **I and many others like me** have had, although **I** fully acknowledge that **names** are not **a good way** to determine national origin

4. (I went to school with a **Mexican-American** named Plunkett and I work with a **Puerto Rican** who counts Schwartzkopf as one of his family names.)

5. THE JUDGE'S DECISION was explicitly legal, but IT still brings **us** to question **what social and cultural considerations** might have gone into this determination.

Paragraph 2:

6. It is not new THAT **JUDGES AND COURTS** DECIDE QUESTIONS FOR WHICH **THEIR BACKGROUND** MAY BE DEEMED INADEQUATE.

7. SOME OF THESE DECISIONS are much more important than resolving the ontological status of burritos.

8. In 1896, A COURT decided that **a law** requiring **Black and White people** to use separate public facilities was constitutional.

9. THE PLAINTIFF was Homer Plessy, **a man** who was one-eighth Black.

The first paragraph starts with the topic "a judge in Massachusetts." The indefinite article "a" tells us this topic is new information and not already assumed known (if it were already assumed known, the author would have said "The judge in Massachusetts). The second sentence has a dummy subject, the word "it" and shifts the subject "what his credentials were to make this decision" towards the back of the sentence. "His credentials" is the subject/topic of this embedded clause (the clause is itself a shifted subject). In "his credentials," "his" refers back to "a judge in Massachusetts." Sentence (3) has the topic "his name," with "his" once again linking back to the judge. So we get the chain: "a judge in Massachusetts" ↔ "his credentials" ↔ "his name," all of which are about the judge. This chain of topics all referring to the judge creates a coherent sense that the paragraph so far is about one thing.

The shifted subject structure in (2) is a way to introduce "what his credentials were to make this decision" as both a topic and important new information. In fact, it is the central idea around which the whole paragraph turns. The paragraph is about the judge's lack of cultural credentials and the fact that the author does have such credentials.

Then we get an aside, placed in parentheses in sentence (4). Here we have a two conjoined clauses (both main clauses, then), both of which have the topic "I." These two "I" topics follow a number of mentions of the author himself in the preceding sentence. In fact, we get a run of "I" subjects in subordinated or embedded clauses preceding the conjoined clauses in (4), which constitutes "I" as a sort of sub-topic in this paragraph. And, indeed, the author is trying to try a comparison and contrast between the judge and himself:

> ... that **I and many others like me** have had
> although **I** fully acknowledge
> that **names** are not
> **a good way** to determine national origin
> (**I** went to school with a **Mexican-American** named Plunkett
> and **I** work with a **Puerto Rican** who counts Schwartzkopf as one of his family names).

(5) is another sentence made up of two conjoined clauses. The topic of the first conjoined clause is "the judge's decision" and the topic of the second is the pronoun "it" referring to the judge's decision. So, after the aside we return to the judge as the overall topic of the paragraph. The embedded topic "social and cultural considerations" in (5), which is new information, introduces in a subordinated way a topic that will become prominent later in the essay.

In this first paragraph the author is saying things about the judge that question his credentials, especially his cultural credentials. A sub-theme in the paragraph is about the author himself ("I"). About himself, the author says things that make clear his own cultural credentials as a Mexican-American, but one with sophistication about culture in a cosmopolitan country like the United States. He thus, juxtaposes his cultural competence against his suspicion of the judge's lack of such competence.

In the second paragraph the author wants to change topics away from the judge to a list of court decisions. He does this by using a shifted subject structure: "It is not new THAT **JUDGES AND COURTS** DECIDE QUESTIONS FOR WHICH **THEIR BACKGROUND** MAY BE DEEMED INADEQUATE." This allows him to introduce the embedded clause "that judges and courts decide questions for which their background may be deemed inadequate" as an important topic and new information. In fact, it is the topic of the next paragraph as a whole. The subject/topic of this embedded clause ("judges and courts") links back to the topic of the first paragraph (the judge) and, thus, speaks topically.

In sentence (7) the subject/topic is "some of these decisions," which links back to "that judges and courts decide questions for which their background may be deemed inadequate" via the "decide"/"decisions" relationship. The author then lists several decisions (I quote only one) where courts made culturally insensitive decisions of much greater consequence than the decision about burritos. The topics of sentence (8)—"court"—and (9)—"plaintiff"— are terms that link back to "some of these decisions," since legal decisions involve courts and plaintiffs. So, again, we get a chain of topics that give coherence and unity to the paragraph.

The author both controls topic flow—or chains topics—and introduces topics that are new information in lucid ways that help focus and guide the attention of his reader. It should be clear, too, that topic chaining or topic flow is a form of creating cohesion and, in turn, uses several of the cohesive devices we discussed in Grammar Interlude #8. Topic chaining ties sentences together across an oral or written text and helps listeners organize information in their minds.

In doing a discourse analysis it is always a good idea to map topics as I have done, since topic flow or topic chaining is one key way speakers and writers create a perspective and seek to control their listeners and readers attention.

This allows us to introduce another grammatical tool:

> ### Tool #22: The Topic Flow or Topic Chaining Tool
>
> For any communication, ask what the topics are of all main clauses and how these topics are linked to each other to create (or not) a chain that creates an overall topic or coherent sense of being about something for a stretch of speech or writing. Topics in subordinated and embedded clauses represent less prominent topics that are subordinated to the main chain of topics in main clauses, but it is useful to ask how they relate to the main chain of topics. Ask, as well, how people have signaled that they are switching topics and whether they have "spoken topically" by linking back to the old topic in some first. Look, as well, for topic shifted structures and how they are being used.

Problem 35

Below is data from the history project we have discussed several times before. You saw this data before in Section 3.17. Karen, Jane (teachers), and Joe (an administrator) work in the Middleview schools. They were born in Middleview and they intend to stay there and want their children to stay there. Sara is a university professor not born in Middleview (or the state it is in) and not intending to stay there (and she eventually moved to another university to advance her career).

How are topics and topic chaining working in this conversation? How do topics and topic chaining work here to communicate a sense of identity? How are topic shifted structures being used? Does Sara speak topically (i.e., tie back to the topic being talked before or while introducing a new topic)? Does Jane in her last contribution speak topically by linking back to Sara's topic? How so?

I have capitalized and underlined the subject/topics of each idea unit (tone unit). I have not here considered the topics of subordinate and embedded structures that are not tone units by themselves, nor made a distinction between tone units that are main clauses and ones that are not. (13) and (14) make up a complex shifted subject structure ("it was …" is a colloquial version of "there was …"). (23) is another shifted subject structure. In two cases, I have placed information in brackets that was not said but which is understood:

KAREN:
1. MY MOTHER used to talk about in the 40s /
2. YOU'd hang around at Union Station/
3. And ANYBODY would just pick you up /
4. Because EVERYBODY was going down to dance at Bright City /
5. Whether YOU knew them or not //

JOE:
6. LAKESIDE BALLROOM //

JANE:
7.   Yeah definitely //

JOE:
8.   <u>MY FATHER</u> used to work there //

JANE:
9.   And also, once <u>YOU</u> finally get into the war situation /
10. Because <u>YOU</u> have Fort Derby /
11. <u>EVERYBODY</u> would get a ride in to come to Bright City /
12. To the amusement park //
13. So it was this <u>INFLUX OF TWO, THREE CARS WORTH OF GUYS</u> /
14. [GUYS] That were now available to meet the girls that suddenly were there //

SARA:
15. Well actually street, <u>STREET CARS</u> had just come in in this /
16. And as I recall um from a student who wrote a paper on this /
17. <u>BRIGHT CITY AND PARK</u> was built by the street car company /
18. In order to have <u>IT</u> [as] a sort of target destination for people to go to /
19. And [for the <u>STREET CAR COMPANY</u>] to symbiotically make money off of this //

JANE:
20. Because once <u>YOU</u> got there /
21. <u>YOU</u> could take a boat ride /
22. And (<u>YOU</u> could) go up and down a lake /
23. And there were <u>LOTS OF OTHER WAYS TO GET THE MONEY FROM PEOPLE</u> //

Reading

Erteschik-Shir, N. (2007). *Information structure: The syntax-discourse interface*. Oxford: Oxford University Press.

Smith, C. S. (2003). *Modes of discourse: The local structure of texts*. Cambridge: Cambridge University Press.

Van Dijk, T. A. (1980). *Macrostructures: An interdisciplinary study of global structures in discourse, interaction, and cognition*. Hillsdale, N. J.: Erlbaum.

UNIT 4

Theoretical Tools

4.1 Six Theoretical Tools

We turn now to six tools that are centered in different theories (core ideas) about how language ties to the world and to culture. First, we will draw on a theory from cognitive psychology about how meaning works. We will introduce the notion of "situated meanings" and argue that we humans actively build meanings "live on line" when we use language in specific contexts.

Second, we will draw on a theory from sociolinguistics about how different styles or varieties of using language work to allow humans to carry out different types of social work and enact different socially significant, socially-situated identities. We will introduce the notion of "social languages" and argue that any language (like English or Russian) is composed of a great many different social languages. Each of these is connected to meanings and activities associated with particular social and cultural groups.

Third we will draw on theories from literary criticism to introduce the notion of "intertextuality." When anyone speaks or writes they often make reference to what other people or various texts (like the Bible) or media (like movies) have said or meant. They may quote or just allude to what others have said. This means that one "text" (where the word here means any stretch of spoken or written language) refers to or points to another "text" (words from what others have said or written). Thus, if I say "Even though life is sweet sorrow, I prefer it to the alternative," I am alluding to (for those in the know) Shakespeare's quote that "love is such sweet sorrow" and mixing these words from Shakespeare into my "text." Plagiarism is, of course, an extreme and "stealth" version of such "intertextual" references (that is, references, quotations, or allusions in one text to another text).

Fourth, we will draw on a theory from psychological anthropology about how humans form and use theories to give language meaning and understand each other and the world. Here we will introduce the notion of "figured worlds." Figured worlds are narratives and images different social and cultural groups of people use to make sense of the world. They function as simplified models of how things work when they are "normal" and "natural" from the perspective of a particular social and cultural group. They are meant to help people get on with the business of living and communicating without having to explicitly reflect in everything before acting.

Fifth, we will draw on theories from a variety of areas (cultural anthropology, cultural psychology, sociolinguistics, and philosophy) about how meaning goes well beyond human minds and language to involve objects, tools, technologies, and networks of people collaborating with each other. Here we will introduce the notion of "Discourses" with a capital "D" (so-called "big 'D' Discourses"). Discourses are ways of enacting and recognizing different sorts of socially situated and significant identities through the use of language integrated with characteristic ways of acting, interacting, believing, valuing, and using various sorts of objects (including our bodies), tools, and technologies in concert with other people.

Finally, we will draw on history and the nature of public debates and social change. Here we will introduce the notion of "Conversations" with a capital "C" (so-called "big 'C' Conversations"). It is not just people that have conversations with each other. Discourses—historically different kinds of people enacting and recognizing different socially significant identities—use people, texts, and media to carry on historically significant Conversations (debates) among different themselves. Often when I talk as a professor, a (video) gamer, an environmentalist (a "green"), or as a Baby Boomer what I say relates to, assumes, and contributes to relatively widely known and recognized historically evolving topics, issues, debates, controversies, and different sides in debates.

4.2 The Situated Meaning Tool

Meaning is a very complicated concept. One important distinction we can make is between the general meaning a word or utterance has (sometimes called "utterance type meaning") and the specific meaning a word or utterance takes on in a specific context of use (sometimes called "utterance token meaning").

When we interpret any piece of language we have *general expectations* about how our language is normally used. Another way to put this is to say that any word or structure in language has a certain "meaning potential," that is, a range of possible meanings that the word or structure can take on in different contexts of use. Thus, for example, the word "cat" has to do, broadly, with the felines; the (syntactic) structure "subject of a sentence" has to do, broadly, with naming a "topic" in the sense of "what is being talked about." This is general meaning (utterance-type meaning.) Such meanings are connected to the prototypical situations in which a word or structure is usually used.

Such general meanings are what word definitions in dictionaries try to capture. For example, a definition of "cat" might be something like:

> 1 a : a carnivorous mammal (*Felis catus*) long domesticated as a pet and for catching rats and mice b : any of a family (Felidae) of carnivorous usually solitary and nocturnal mammals (as the domestic cat, lion, tiger, leopard, jaguar, cougar, wildcat, lynx, and cheetah) [Retrieved September 24, 2009 from www.merriam-webster.com/dictionary/cat]

No one knows exactly how definitions work in our heads, though psychologists and linguists have long studied the matter. Definitions like the one above are certainly not typical of what is in heads. Few people know cats are classified as "Felis catus" and not everyone knows cats are carnivorous (or what "carnivorous" really means, i.e., that cats cannot survive with meat, not just that they happen to eat or like meat). What is in our heads is probably a combination of the following things: images or prototypes of what is typical of the things the word refers to; information and facts we know (but which not all of us share exactly); and typical uses of the word and the typical range of contexts in which the word is normally used.

In any case, we will just talk about "general meanings," meaning by this the range of typical meanings a word (or structure) has. This is the "meaning potential" of the word or the "meaning resources" it represents. Such meaning potential or meaning resources can, of course, change as we hear the word used in more contexts or as people change how they use the word.

In actual situations of use, words and structures take on much more specific meanings within the range of (or, at least, related to the range of) their meaning potentials. This is what I will call "situated meaning." Thus, in a situation where we are discussing species of animals and say something like "The world's big cats are all endangered," "cat" means things like lions and tigers; in a situation where we are discussing mythology and say something like "The cat was a sacred symbol to the ancient Egyptians," "cat" means real and pictured cats as symbols; and in a situation where we are discussing breakable decorative objects on our mantel and say something like "The cat broke," "cat" means a statue of cat.

Turning to structures, rather than words: while the subjects of sentences are always "topic-like" (this is their general meaning), in different situations of use, subjects take on a range of more specific meanings. In a debate, if I say, "The constitution only protects the rich," the subject of the sentence ("the constitution") is an entity about which a claim is being made; if a friend of yours has just arrived and I usher her in saying "Mary's here," the subject of the sentence ("Mary") is a center of interest or attention; and in a situation where I am commiserating with a friend and say something like "You really got cheated by that guy," the subject of the sentence ("you") is a center of empathy (signaled also by the fact that the normal subject of the active version of the sentence—"That guy really cheated you"—has been "demoted" from subject position through use of the "get-passive").

So words do not have just general meanings. They have different and specific meanings in different contexts in which they are used and in different specialist domains that recruit them. This is true of the most mundane cases. For instance, notice the change in meaning in the word "coffee" in the following utterances which refer to different situations: "The coffee spilled, go get the mop" (coffee as liquid), "The coffee spilled, go get a broom" (coffee as grains), "The coffee spilled, stack it again" (coffee in cans). Or notice the quite different meanings of the word "work" in everyday life and in physics (e.g., I can say, in everyday life, that I worked hard to push the car, but if my efforts didn't move the car, I did no "work" in the physics sense of the word).

In actual contexts, people do not just look up the meanings of words in their heads, like a dictionary. They know the possible range of the meanings of a word, but they also know this can change with new uses. People must in context actively "make up" (guess) the meanings of the words and phrases they hear. Often this is fairly routine, since they have heard meanings like this before. But sometimes they must do more work and actively seek to ask what people must mean here and now if they have said what they said in the context in which they have said it.

For example, if someone says "The cat is floating away," in some contexts they may be referring to a "cat-shaped cloud." The phrase "things you would save first from your house in a fire" will mean different specific things to different people in different contexts (e.g., would you take your cat or your expensive painting?). To know what it means to you, you have to think about what meaning you would give it in the context of a fire and your own life. What does someone mean in the context of current political debates in the United States by the word "democracy" if they say: "The United States will not really be a democracy until we have real campaign finance reform."

So we can introduce the first of our four theoretical tools, the Situated Meaning Tool:

Tool #23: The Situated Meaning Tool

For any communication, ask of words and phrases what situated meanings they have. That is, what specific meanings do listeners have to attribute to these words and phrases given the context and how the context is construed?

The Situated Meaning Tool is obviously closely related to the Filling In Tool. It is part of what we fill in from context. But it is a particularly crucial part of the filling in process. Words and phrases in actual contexts of use do not always have clear dictionary like meanings. Listeners have to figure out— guess—what they mean based on what else has been said and other aspects of the context. So do we discourse analysts. Meaning making is not a "look up" process. It is an active process.

There is one important aspect of situated meaning to keep in mind. One way we as listeners situate the meanings of words and phrases is to use our previous experience of—and knowledge of—what is being talked about. Speakers have to make assumptions about what sorts of experience and knowledge are shared or shared enough with others to communicate. If you have never heard about campaign finance reform and know nothing about U.S. politics, then you cannot situate a meaning for "democracy" in an utterance like "The United States will not really be a democracy until we have real campaign finance reform."

All utterances make assumptions about people's previous experiences and knowledge. They assume certain experiences and knowledge in order to be understood. In that sense, any utterance, in terms of how it is formulated, makes assumptions about the "kind of person" who is an "appropriate" or "acceptable" listener (and maybe even person). We will see this aspect of language more when we discuss figured worlds and Discourses below.

4.3 Working with the Situated Meaning Tool

The Situated Meaning Tool tells us to ask what words and phrases mean in specific contexts. In many cases, the meanings of words and phrases in context are clear and well within the normal and routine range of meanings these words and phrases typically have. But this is not always the case and we want to be on the watch for cases where words and phrases are being given situated meanings that are nuanced and quite specific to the speaker's worldview or values or to the special qualities of the context the speaker is assuming and helping to construe or create (remember the reflexive property of context).

In this section we will look at cases where the Situated Meaning Tool applies in important ways.

Problem 36

A typical dictionary definition of "democracy" is "government by the people; a form of government in which the supreme power is vested in the people and exercised directly by them or by their elected agents under a free electoral system" (http://dictionary.reference.com/browse/democracy). This definition captures pretty well what we have called the general meaning of the word "democracy." However, a word like "democracy" is what we might call a "contested word." People argue a good bit about what political systems "really" deserve to be called a "democracy." People use the word with specific nuances of meaning that reflect their viewpoints and values.

Consider the quotes below. Each uses the word "democracy." First, ask yourself how the definition of democracy, its general meaning, does or does not fit with the way the word is being used in the quote. Then specify what situated meaning the word has in each quote (what additional meanings, connotations, and nuances the word is being given). What does each author mean in specific terms by the word? Finally, what does the way the author has used the word "democracy" tell you about his or her value system and political viewpoint? The quote in (4) is from a ruling of the Israeli Supreme Court. In (3) you want to analyze what Penalosa has to say about "democracy."

1. … yet I believe [Milton] Friedman is right that thoroughgoing restrictions on economic freedom would turn out to be inconsistent with **democracy** (Retrieved Sept. 24, 2009 from www.becker-posner-blog.com/archives/2006/11/on_milton_fried.html).

2. If **democracy** is about creating processes that allow people to empower themselves, then pirates [people running illegal pirate radio channels] are clearly the perfect catalyst for such processes (Mason, M., 2008, *The pirate's dilemma: How youth culture is reinventing capitalism*. New York: Free Press, p. 47).

3. Penalosa [Mayor of Bogota, Columbia] observes that "high quality public pedestrian space in general and parks in particular are evidence of true **democracy** at work" (Brown, L. R., 2008, *Plan B 3.0: Mobilizing to save civilization*. Revised and Expanded Edition. Washington, DC: Earth Policy Institute, p. 193).

4. That is the fate of **democracy**, in whose eyes not all means are permitted, and to whom not all the methods used by her enemies are open (*The Public Committee Against Torture in Israel v The State of Israel*, cited in Weisberg, J., 2008, *The Bush tragedy*. New York: Random House. pp. 181–82).

Problem 37

In the state of Arizona in the United States, immigrant children take a test of their English proficiency. Based on their scores they are put into classes that meet four hours every day where they are taught English language skills only in English. The teacher below teaches children classified as "4" by the test. If a child does better than 4 they are consider proficient in English and do not need to take the four-hour English language classes. Read the teacher's quote and say what you think her situated meaning for "gifted" is. Why is the teacher using hedges like "pretty" in "pretty advanced," "pretty gifted," "pretty high" and "per se" in "don't have gifted kids per se"? This teacher can be seen as creating a situated meaning for "fours." What is it? Can one tell whether a child is "gifted" or not by how well they speak a language they don't yet fully know? Do all "gifted" people learn second languages quickly? How are the situated meanings this teacher is creating for "gifted," "pretty gifted," "pretty high," and "fours" related to an implicit contrast she is drawing to kids who scored lower on the test (and, thus, aren't in her classroom)?

> They're fours. So they're pretty advanced actually. They're pretty gifted, not gifted. I don't have any gifted kids per se, but I think they're pretty high. Like just when we were sorting out the whole second grade, they're pretty high. They have a lot of their basic phonics and they've been reading their books pretty well in the second grade text. [Data from: Heineke, A. J. (2009). *Teacher's discourse on English language learners: Cultural models of language and learning*. Unpublished doctoral dissertation. Mary Lou Fulton College of Education, Tempe, Arizona, p. 119.]

4.4 The Social Languages Tool

People do not speak any language "in general." They always speak a specific variety of a language (which might actually mix together more than one language, e.g., English and Spanish) and they use different varieties in different contexts. There are social and regional varieties of language that are called "dialects" (see Section 1.1), such as African-American Vernacular English, Appalachian Vernacular English, or different working class varieties of English in different parts of the United States. However, we are going to concentrate here on what I will call "social languages" (many linguists use the term "register" in a somewhat similar way).

To understand what a speaker says, a listener needs to know who is speaking. But it is not enough to know, for example, that Mary Smith is the speaker. I need to know what identity Mary is speaking out of. Is she speaking to me as a teacher, a feminist, a friend, a colleague, an avid bird watcher, a political liberal, or a great many other possible identities or roles?

Listeners need to know who speakers are. Is my doctor saying I look "stressed" just as a friend or is he speaking as a doctor? When the policeman says "I think you should move your car" is she speaking as a policeman and ordering me to move the car or speaking as a helpful fellow citizen giving me advice?

I will define social languages as styles or varieties of a language (or a mixture of languages) that enact and are associated with a particular social identity. All languages, like English or French, are composed of many (a great many) different social languages. Social languages are what we learn and what we speak. Here are some examples of social languages: the language of medicine, literature, street gangs, sociology, law, rap, or informal dinner-time talk among friends.

Even within these large categories there are sub-varieties. Not all types of gangs or sociologists speak the same when they are speaking as gang members or sociologists. To know any specific social language is to know how its characteristic lexical and grammatical resources are combined to enact specific socially-situated identities (that is, being, at a given time and place, a lawyer, a gang member, a politician, a literary humanist, a bench chemist, a radical feminist, an everyday person, or whatever). To know a particular social language is either to be able to "do" a particular identity or to be able to recognize such an identity, when we do not want to or cannot actively participate.

Dialects can be seen as social languages as well. Southern English is a way to mark oneself as a southerner. African-American Vernacular English is a way to mark oneself as an African-American of a certain sort (at a certain time and place).

Let me give two examples, both of which we have seen earlier. First, a young woman, telling the same story to her parents and to her boyfriend, says to her parents at dinner: "Well, when I thought about it, I don't know, it seemed to me that Gregory should be considered the most offensive character," but later to her boyfriend she says: "What an ass that guy was, you know, her boyfriend." In the first case, she uses distinctive lexical and grammatical resources to enact "a dutiful and intelligent daughter having dinner with her proud parents" and in the other case to enact "a girlfriend being intimate with her boyfriend."

Note, by the way, that the particular labels I use here are not important. Many social languages have no names and names need not be used by people overtly. People who use a given social language may differ on what they call it. The point just is that people must have some, however tentative, unspoken, and sometimes problematic, idea of who is speaking in the sense of what social identity is at play.

Second, to take an example from Myers 1990 book *Writing Biology: Texts in the social construction of scientific knowledge*, an example which we saw in Sections 3.16 and 3.17, a biologist writing in a professional science journal writes: "Experiments show that Heliconius butterflies are less likely to oviposit on host plants that possess eggs or egg-like structures"; writing about the same thing in a popular science magazine, the same biologist writes: "Heliconius butterflies lay their eggs on Passiflora vines." The first passage uses distinctive lexical and grammatical resources to enact "a professional adaptationist biologist of a certain type engaged in managing uncertainty through the manipulation of theory and experiment"; the second passage uses distinctive lexical and grammatical resources to enact "a highly trained observer looking at animals and plants in nature."

Within any social language, as the speaker acts out a particular type of *who*—a particular socially-situated identity—the speaker must also make clear what he or she is doing, what action or activity, appropriate to that identity, he or she is carrying out. Listeners need to know not only who is talking but *what* they are seeking to accomplish. So speakers always use social languages to enact specific actions or activities as well.

For example, a listener needs to know if a doctor who says "Have you been stressed lately" is asking a diagnostic question as a doctor or showing concern (or even just making "small talk") as a friend. If a policeman says "I think you should move your car" I need to know if she is giving me a polite but official order or just offering helpful advice as a fellow but well informed citizen. If a professor asks a student "What does 'democracy' mean?," the student needs to know if this is "test" (and the answer has to be the one the professor thinks is correct) or a request for an considered opinion that might further class discussion. We need to know both who is speaking and what they are doing.

Each social language has its own distinctive grammar. However, two different sorts of grammars are important to social languages, only one of which we ever think to study formally in school. One grammar is the traditional set of units like nouns, verbs, inflections, phrases and clauses. These are real enough, though quite inadequately described in traditional school grammars. Let's call this "grammar 1."

The other—less studied, but more important—grammar is the "rules" by which grammatical units like nouns and verbs, phrases and clauses, are used to create *patterns* which signal or "index" characteristic social identities and social activities. That is, we speakers and writers design our oral or written utterances to have patterns in them in virtue of which interpreters can attribute situated identities and specific activities to us and our utterances. We will call this "grammar 2."

These patterns are called "collocational patterns." This means that various sorts of grammatical devices "co-locate" with each other. The patterns I am trying to name here are "co-relations" (correlations) among many grammatical devices, from different "levels" of grammar 1. For example, in Jane's utterance to her boyfriend, "What an ass that guy was, you know, her boyfriend," note how informal terms like "ass" and "guy," the vague reference "that guy," the informal parenthetical device "you know," and the informal syntactic device of "right dislocation" (i.e., letting the phrase "her boyfriend" hang out at the end of the sentence) all pattern together to signal that this utterance is in an informal social language used to achieve solidarity.

The situation here is much like choosing clothes that go together in such a way that they communicate that we are engaged in a certain activity or are taking up a certain style connected to such activities. For example, consider how flip-flops, bathing suit, tank top, shades, and sun hat "co-locate" together to "signal" to us things like outdoor and water activities and the situated identities we take up in such situations.

To see another example of how different word choices and grammatical structures pattern together to signal a given social language, consider the two sentences below:

1. Hornworms sure vary a lot in how well they grow.
2. Hornworm growth displays a significant amount of variation.

The first sentence is a vernacular style of language, a vernacular social language. Everyone who is a native speaker of English, regardless of their dialect, can utter some equally good variant of this sort of sentence (if they know what hornworms are—green caterpillar-like creatures with yellow horns).

The second sentence is in an academic social language. While every native speaker's grammar contains all the grammatical structures that this sentence contains (e.g., nominalizations), not every speaker knows that *combining them in just this way* is called for by certain social practices of certain academic (and school-based) domains (what we will later call "Discourses"). This has to be learned and this knowledge is not acquired on the basis of any biological capacity for language, as is our knowledge of the vernacular. It is manifestly the case that many children in school struggle to acquire forms of language like that in sentence 2, though none (if they are native speakers) struggle with the forms of language like that in sentence 1.

Again, every native speaker of English has a grammar that contains all of the sorts of grammatical structures that are used in sentence 2. All of them are used at times in vernacular forms of language. However, to produce a sentence like 2 you must know more than this. You must know that, in this style of language, verbs naming dynamic processes (e.g., "grow" and "vary") are often turned into nouns naming abstract things (e.g., "growth" and "variation"). You have to know that in this form of language emotive markers like "sure" are not used. You have to know that in this form of language a vague phrase like "a lot" must be replaced by a more explicit one like "significant variation" (where "significant" has a fairly precise definition in areas like biology). You have to know that subjects of sentences in this form of language will very often not be simple nouns (like "hornworms"), but nominalizations (like "hornworm growth") expressing a whole clause worth of information (i.e., hornworms grow) as an abstract concept. *And most importantly you have to know all these things together and that these linguistic features, in fact, tend to go together—to pattern together—in this form of language.*

The term "social language" applies to specific varieties of language used to enact specific identities and carry out specific sorts of practices or activities. A single written or oral text can be in one social language or it can switch between two or more or even mix them up pretty thoroughly.

For example, consider the warning on an aspirin bottle that you saw in Section 3.7:

> Warnings: *Children and teenagers should not use this medication for chicken pox or flu symptoms before a doctor is consulted about Reye Syndrome, a rare but serious illness reported to be associated with aspirin.* Keep this and all drugs out of the reach of children. In case of accidental overdose, seek professional assistance or contact a poison control center immediately. As with any drug, if you are pregnant or nursing a baby, seek the advice of a health professional before using this product. IT IS ESPECIALLY IMPORTANT NOT TO USE ASPIRIN DURING THE LAST 3 MONTHS OF PREGNANCY UNLESS SPECIFICALLY DIRECTED TO DO SO BY A DOCTOR BECAUSE IT MAY CAUSE PROBLEMS IN THE UNBORN CHILD OR COMPLICATIONS DURING DELIVERY. See carton for arthritis use+ and Important Notice.

There are two different social languages or varieties of language in this warning. The first is made up of the following sentences:

> *Children and teenagers should not use this medication for chicken pox or flu symptoms before a doctor is consulted about Reye Syndrome, a rare but serious illness reported to be associated with aspirin.* IT IS ESPECIALLY IMPORTANT NOT TO USE ASPIRIN DURING THE LAST 3 MONTHS OF PREGNANCY UNLESS SPECIFICALLY

DIRECTED TO DO SO BY A DOCTOR BECAUSE IT MAY CAUSE PROBLEMS IN
THE UNBORN CHILD OR COMPLICATIONS DURING DELIVERY.

Here things are referred to quite specifically ("children or teenagers," "this
medication," "chicken pox," "flu," "Reye Syndrome," "aspirin," "last 3
months," "unborn child," "delivery"), doctors are called "doctor," and matters
are treated emphatically (italics, capitals, "should not," "rare but serious,"
"especially important," "specifically directed").

The second social language is made up of the following sentences, placed in
the middle of the other two:

> Keep this and all drugs out of the reach of children. In case of accidental overdose,
> seek professional assistance or contact a poison control center immediately. As
> with any drug, if you are pregnant or nursing a baby, seek the advice of a health
> professional before using this product.

Here things are referred to more generally and generically ("this and all
drugs," "any drug," and "this product," rather than "this medication" and
"aspirin"; "children" rather than "children and teenagers," "pregnant" rather
than "last 3 months of pregnancy"), doctors are not mentioned, rather the
health profession is referred to more generally ("professional assistance,"
"poison control center," "health professional"), and matters are treated less
stridently with the exception of the word "immediately" (here we get small
print and the less strident phrases "keep out of reach," "accidental overdose,"
"seek ... assistance," "seek advice," rather than the more direct "should not"
and "important not to use" of the other part of the warning).

These two social language "feel" different. They are authorized and issued
by different "voices" to different purposes and effects. The first speaks with a
lawyerly voice responding to specific potential legal problems and court cases;
the second speaks with the official voice of a caring, but authoritatively
knowledgeable company trying to protect and advise people, especially
women and children, while still stressing that aspirin is not particularly special
or dangerous compared to drugs in general.

Of course, this second social language sits in some tension with the first. By
the way, the second social language on the aspirin bottle used to be the only
warning on the bottle (with the order of the sentences a bit different). And,
indeed, the warning has changed yet again on newer bottles.

This warning, like all utterances, reflects the company it has kept, or, to put
the matter another way, it reflects a history that has given rise to it. In this
case, presumably, the new sterner, more direct social language was added to
the more general and avuncular one because the company got sued over things
like Reye's syndrome.

The warning on the aspirin bottle is heteroglossic. That is, it is "double-
voiced," since it interleaves two different social languages together. Of course,

in different cases, this sort of interleaving could be much more intricate, with the two (or more) social languages more fully integrated, and harder to tease apart.

We can now state the second of our theoretical tools, The Social Languages Tool:

Tool #24: Social Languages Tool:

For any communication, ask how it uses words and grammatical structures (types of phrases, clauses, and sentences) to signal and enact a given social language. The communication may mix two or more social languages or switch between two or more. In turn, a social language may be composed of words or phrases from more than one language (e.g., it may mix English and Spanish).

Reading

Biber, D. and Conrad, S. (2009). *Register, genre, and style*. Cambridge: Cambridge University Press. [Biber has pioneered work on corpus linguistics, style, and registers.]

Gee, J. P. (2011). *Social linguistics and literacies: Ideology in Discourses*. Fourth Edition. London: Falmer.

Halliday, M. A. K. and Hasan, R. (1989). *Language, context, and text: Aspects of language as a social-semiotic perspective*. Oxford: Oxford University Press.

Hoey, M. (2005). *Lexical priming: A new theory of words and language*. New York: Routledge. [See this source for the notion of collocation.]

Joos, M. (1961). *The five clocks*, New York: Harcourt, Brace and World.

Wardhaugh, R. (1986). *Introduction to sociolinguistics*. Second Edition. Cambridge: Blackwell.

4.5 Working with the Social Languages Tool

Problem 38

The text below is from a published article in a journal on child development. Read it and think about how what sort of social language and identity this text represents.

The present study sought to clarify and extend previous work suggesting that physically abused children develop perceptual sensitivity to anger. First, we sought to further examine the ways in which physically abused children can regulate attentional processes when confronted with anger or threat. Second, because prior research suggested that physically abused children would be especially sensitive to anger, the anger-related stimuli presented to the children occurred in the background and were irrelevant to the child's purported task and not personally meaningful. This created a relatively conservative test of children's attentional regulation. The present data suggest that once anger was introduced, abused children maintained a state of anticipatory monitoring of the environment. In contrast, non-abused children were initially more aroused by the introduction of anger, but showed better recovery to baseline states once anger was resolved. (Pollak, S. D., Vardi, S., Putzer Bechner, A. M., and Curtin, J. J. (2005). Physically abused children's regulation of attention in response to hostility." *Child Development* 76.5: 968–77—see p. 974)

Questions:

1. List some of the features in terms of word choice, grammatical structures, and patterns of grammatical structures that make this a distinctive social language.
2. This type of language is often referred to as "academic language." However, there are many different varieties of academic language (e.g., physics, sociology, linguistics, etc.). How would you characterize the academic area this social language is connected to?
3. What is the situated meaning of the phrase "not purposefully meaningful" in the text? Are their senses (situated meanings) of "personally meaningful" in which anger, even if not expressed directly at them, could be "personally meaningful" to a child who has been physically abused by angry parents (as were these children)?
4. How would you characterize the identity that the authors of this text are enacting or expressing through this social language?

Problem 39

In Section 3.13 we looked at data from an interview with a middle-school teacher. As we said earlier, this teaches lives in a town that is a former blue-collar industrial town that has lost a good deal of its industry and is in a poor economic condition. There are not a lot of jobs and those that still do exist often no longer carry good wages and medical benefits. Many of the parents in the town—Black or Hispanic—work more than one job to make ends meet and there is high unemployment.

The teacher was asked about whether she ever discussed social issues with her students. A part of her response is reprinted below. In the transcript, "I" stands for "Interviewer." Words in brackets are guesses about what she said when it cannot be well heard on the tape. "[????]" means material is inaudible.

1. Uh so [what] you you need to do about job hunting /
2. You need to look the part // [I:mm hm]
3. You don't see anybody at any nice store dressed in jeans // [I: uh huh]
4. They're not gonna have a job if they do that // [I: uh huh]
5. And a lot of the kids question that //
6. uh I talk about housing /
7. We talk about the [????], we talk about a lot of the low income things //
8. I said "Hey wait a minute" /

9. I said, "Do you think the city's gonna take care of an area that you don't take care of yourself"? [I: uh huh]

10. I said, "How [many of] you [have] been up Saints Street"?

11. They raise their hands /

12. I say "How about Main Ave."?

13. That's where those gigantic houses are /

14. I said, "How many pieces of furniture are sitting in the front yard"? [I: mm hm]

15. "Well, none" //

16. I said "How much trash is lying around"?

17. "None" //

18. I said, "How many houses are spray painted"?

19. "How many of them have kicked in, you know have broken down cars in front of them"? [I: uh huh]

20. I said, "They take care of their area" /

21. I said, "I'm not saying you kids do this" /

22. I said, "Look at Great River Valley /

23. They burn the dumpsters //

24. That's your housing area" // [I: uh huh]

25. "Do you know how fast that can JUMP into someone's apartment or whatever else"?

26. I bring up the uh, they have in the paper /

27. Probably about two years ago /

28. the uh police were being sued—

29. uh the fire department were being sued by a family that had a girl with asthma /

30. And the kids had lit the dumpster outside of their bedroom window /

31. And she had a severe asthma attack /

32. And the fire department would not come in /

33. So they couldn't get the police escort //

34. The fire department used to only go in with a police escort /

35. Because the people living there would throw bottles and cans at them // [I: uh huh]

36. And you know, again, the whole class would [???] //

37. I don't understand this //

38. Here is someone who's coming in here—

39. Maybe the police I could understand /

40. Because you feel like you're getting harassed by the police /

41. What has the fire department done to you /

42. That you're gonna throw bottles, rocks, cans at them? [I: uh huh]

43. And stop them from putting out a fire [I: uh huh] that could burn down your whole house? [I: uh huh]

44. Why do you burn the grass? [I: mm hm]

45. There's grass here that every single summer as soon as it turns green they burn /
46. And as soon as it grows back up they burn again //
47. Why do you do that?

Questions:

1. Much of the language of this data, at least in terms of word choice, is in the teacher's vernacular English. While some university academics who had been interviewed in the same study often answered the questions in academic forms of language or mixtures of academic language and the vernacular, this teacher stays pretty close to the vernacular. Yet she uses a certain style of speaking—uses patterns of words and grammar—that are pretty distinctive. Her style is a form of "teacher talk" in this town. She and other teachers in this town often used this style. So this is really not just her vernacular. How would you characterize this social language—point to specific stylistic features the teacher uses. What do you think the function of this style of language is? What is the teacher trying to say and do by speaking this way?
2. The university academics we interviewed often based what they said on the authority of their disciplines, which is why they often used academic language in the interviews when they were asked social and political questions. What is the source of the teacher's authority for the things she says in the communication above?
3. What is the situated meaning of "the low income things" in the communication above?
4. How would you characterize the identity this teacher is enacting or expressing through this social language?

Problem 40

Below is a posting on a website made by a fifteen-year-old girl who writes stories using software that comes with the computer game *The Sims*. The stories are made up of pictures (from the game) and words (each "slide" has an image and text beneath it). This girl writes novel-length stories of this sort, one of which is called Lincoln Heights ("LH"). She has a devoted following of fans that wait for each new chapter of the story to be posted:

> *Sunday, 02 December 2007*
> *As u can see I gave my page a little makeover! I've had that oldd one for over a year! Needed a change! As 4 LH 1.3 I've got around thirty slides, working up to my usual 127! Patience is all it takes! I garentee it'll B out B4 Xmas though! ;)*
> <3 A
> [See the Sunday, 02 December 2007 entry from http://thesims2.ea.com/ mysimpage/blog.php?user_id=2877919&date=all]

Questions:

1. How would you characterize this social language? Point to specific lexical and grammatical features? What is its function or functions?
2. How would you characterize the identity that this girl is enacting or expressing through this social language?

4.6 The Intertextuality Tool

When we speak or write, we often quote or allude to what others have said. Here I will use the word "text" in a special way to mean what someone has said or written, a stretch of speech or writing. When one text (in this sense) quotes, refers to, or alludes to another text (that is, what someone else has said or written), we will call this "intertextuality." We can expand this to cover references or allusions to media (television, film, video games, etc.), treating these as "texts" too.

There are obviously lots of ways one text can quote, refer to, or allude to another one. One way is direct quotation as in "It's funny that Bob said 'I'll never give up' and then gave up." Another way is indirect quotation as in "It's funny that Bob said he would never give up and then gave up." Yet another way is just to allude what hearers or readers in the know will realize are words taken from some other source as in "Even if life is sweet sorrow, I prefer it to the alternative," where "sweet sorrow" echoes a quote from Shakespeare: "love is such sweet sorrow." If I say that "When John fought with the boss, it was David against Goliath," the mere mention of David and Goliath is enough (again, for people who know the reference) to make reference to the Biblical story where the young David defeats the giant Goliath with his sling shot. Here my speech (my "text") has alluded to (made an intertextual reference to) a Biblical text.

Another type of intertextuality occurs when a text written in one style (in one social language associated with one identity) incorporates a style of language (a social language) associated with a different identity. For example, *Wired* magazine once printed a story with this title: "The New Face of the Silicon Age: Tech jobs are fleeing to India faster than ever. You got a problem with that?" (February 2004). The sentence "You got a problem with that?" reminds us of "tough guy" talk we have heard in many movies or read in books. It intrigues us that such talk occurs in a magazine devoted to technology and otherwise written in popular culture high-tech magazine style.

Finally, one text can refer or allude to another text or style of language (social language) by using or mimicking the grammar or phrasing, but not necessarily the words, of another text or style of language. For example, I could write a letter in Biblical sorts of prose or in iambic pentameter verse thereby making reference to the Bible or traditional English poetry, but with very different content.

Thus, we can state another tool for discourse analysis:

Tool #25: The Intertextuality Tool:

For any communication, ask how words and grammatical structures (e.g., direct or indirect quotation) are used to quote, refer to, or allude to other "texts" (that is, what others have said or written) or other styles of language (social languages).

Reading

Allen, G. (2000). *Intertextuality*. London: Taylor & Francis.

Bakhtin, M. M. (1986). *Speech genres and other late essays*. Austin: University of Texas Press. [A much discussed and highly influential book.]

Bauman, R. (1998). *A world of others' words: Cross-cultural perspectives*. Malden, MA: Blackwell.

Fairclough, N. (1992). *Discourse and social change*. Cambridge: Polity Press.

Fairclough, N. (2003). *Analyzing discourse: Textual analysis for social research*. London: Routledge.

Kristeva, J. (1980). *Desire in language: A semiotic approach to literature and art*. New York: Columbia University Press.

4.7 Working with the Intertextuality Tool

In this section you will work with the intertextuality tool. Here you will be looking for any "echoes" of any sort in one text to another, whether these be as direct as quotation or as indirect as allusion. You also want to ask how intertextuality is used to engage in our various building tasks.

Problem 41

Consider the data below from an article about sports (the World Series in baseball) on the internet (the author is talking about the New York Yankees beating the Philadelphia Phillies in the 2009 World Series):

> Sometimes Goliath wins, or, if you prefer the most appropriate analogy after World Series Game 6, Godzilla kicks butt.

> After years of seeing upstarts, hot teams and cursebreakers win the World Series and playoff baseball reduced to "a crapshoot," we got an old fashioned, the-best-team-won World Series.
>
> (From: http://sportsillustrated.cnn.com/2009/writers/tom_verducci/
> 11/05/five.cuts/index.html?eref=sihp)

Questions:

1. Find and discuss all the intertextual references here. What is being referred to? What function or role does each such reference play in the data? [By the way "crapshoot" is in "scare quotes." If you do not know what scare quotes are, look it up. Why is "crapshoot" in scare quotes? Some editors do not approve of scare quotes. Why do you think that is?]
2. Why does it seems sports reporting in newspapers and in other popular media (e.g., television) is so prone to the sorts of intertextual references in the data below?
3. If you do not follow baseball, sports, or U.S. sports, pair up with someone who does and ask whether an "insider" gets more in terms of intertextual references or what they mean or are doing in this data than does someone who is an "outsider."
4. Find other examples of intertextuality in sports writing or reporting. It would be interesting to compare writing about different sports or about sports in different countries in this regard.

Problem 42

You saw the data below in Section 1.4 and 1.6 where you were given some context for the data. A teacher (Karen) is telling a story of how the curriculum coordinator in her school told her to call an historian at a local university. Consulting the context you have been given in Section 1.4 and 1.6, discuss how direct quotation works here as a form of intertextual reference. Why didn't the speaker use indirect quotation (e.g., Mary said that Sara is interested in …" or "Mary said a person from Woodson who is interested in …")? What differences would direct or indirect quotation make here?

> LAST YEAR /
>   Mary Washington /
> who is our curriculum coordinator here /
> had a call from Sara //
> at Woodson //
>   And called me /
> and said (pause) /
> "We have a person from Woodson /
> Who's in the History Department /
> She's interested in doing some RESEARCH /
> into BLACK history //
> And she would like to get involved with the school /
> And here's her number /
> Give her a call" //

Problem 43

The text below is from George Saunders' book *The Braindead Megaphone: Essays* (New York: Riverhead Books, p. 251). Discuss all the intertextual references in this text. They require that you have kept up with the news over the last decade. This is taken from a literary essay. What is the author trying to accomplish? How does he use intertextuality to accomplish his literary and political goals?

> Now it can be told.
>
> Last Thursday, my organization, People Reluctant To Kill For An Abstraction (PRKA), orchestrated an overwhelming show of force around the globe.
>
> At precisely nine in the morning, working with focus and stealth, our entire membership succeeded in simultaneously beheading no one. At nine-thirty, we embarked on Phase II, during which our entire membership simultaneously did not force a single man to simulate sex with another man. At ten, Phase III began, during which not a single one of us blew himself/herself up in a crowded public place. ... In addition, at eleven, in Phase IV, zero (0) planes were flown into buildings.

4.8 The Figured Worlds Tool

Is the Pope a bachelor? Though the Pope is an unmarried man—and "bachelor" as a word is defined as "an unmarried man"—we are reluctant to call the Pope a bachelor. Why? The reason is that we do not use words just based on their definitions or what we called earlier (see Section 4.2) their "general meanings." We use words based, as well, on stories, theories, or models in our minds about what is "normal" or "typical."

It is typical in our world that men marry women. A man who is somewhat past the typical age when people marry we call a "bachelor," assuming he is open to marriage but has either chosen to wait or has not found the "right" person. The Pope is both well past the normal age for marriage and has vowed never to marry. He just does not fit the typical story in our heads.

We use words based on such typical stories unless something in the context makes us think the situation is not typical. If the issue of gay marriage or the chauvinism of calling men "bachelors" and women "spinsters" comes up, then we have to think more overtly about matters and abandon, if only for the time, our typical picture. Indeed, things can change in society enough that what counts as a typical story changes or becomes contested. People may even stop using words like "bachelor" based on the typical story and form a new typical story—and, thus, start calling marriage-eligible women "bachelors" as well.

We use such typical pictures so that we can go on about the business of communicating, acting, and living without having to consciously think about everything—all the possible details and exceptions—all the time. This is good for getting things done, but sometimes bad in the ways in which such typical stories can marginalize people and things that are not taken as "normal" or "typical" in the story.

What counts as a typical story for people differs by their social and culture groups. For example, some parents confronted by a demanding two-year-old who angrily refuses to go to bed take the child's behavior as sign of growth towards autonomy because they accept a typical story like this: Children are born dependent on their parents and then grow towards individual autonomy or independence. On their way to autonomy, they act out, demanding independence, when they may not yet be ready for it, but this is still a sign of development and growth. Other parents confronted by the same behavior take the behavior as a sign of the child's willfulness because they accept a typical story like this: Children are born selfish and need to be taught to think of others and collaborate with the family rather than demand their own way.

It is, perhaps, not surprising that this latter typical story is more common among working class families where mutual support among family and friends is important. The former story is more common among middle and upper-middle-class families with many more financial resources where people are expected to grow into adults who have the resources to go it more on their own.

Such typical stories are not "right" or "wrong." For example, children are, of course, born dependent on their parents. But are children primarily inherently selfish and in need of being taught how to cooperate with others or are they inherently reliant on caregivers and in need of learning to be independent? The different stories we discussed are probably both true in some sense, but one or the other can be stressed and help form the main parenting style in the home. They are simplified theories of the world that are meant to help people go on about the business of life when one is not allowed the time to think through and research everything before acting. Even theories in science are simplified views of the world meant to help scientists cope, without having to deal with the full complexity of the world all at once.

These typical stories have been given many different names. They have been called "folk theories," "frames," "scenarios," "scripts," "mental models," "cultural models," "social models," "discourse models," and "figured worlds" (and each of these terms has its own nuances). Such typical stories are stored in our heads (but we will see in a moment that they are not always only in our heads) in the form of images, metaphors, and narratives.

We will use the term "figured world" here for these typical stories. The term "figured world" has been defined in Dorothy Holland's influential 1998 book, written with several colleagues, *Identity and agency in cultural worlds*, as follows:

> A socially and culturally constructed realm of interpretation in which particular characters and actors are recognized, significance is assigned to certain acts, and particular outcomes are valued over others. Each is a simplified world populated

by a set of agents who engage in a limited range of meaningful acts or changes of state as moved by a specific set of forces. (p. 52)

A figured world is a picture of a simplified world that captures what is taken to be typical or normal. What is taken to be typical or normal, as we have said, varies by context and by people's social and cultural group (as we saw in the example of acting out two-year-olds above). For example, if I ask you to imagine a suburban bedroom you will populate the room with people and things in a quite different way than if I ask you to imagine a bedroom in a college dorm. You base what you take to be typical on your experiences and since people's experiences vary in terms of their social and cultural groups, people vary in what they take to be typical. And, again, as society changes what people take as typical can and does change. Figured worlds are not static.

To give another example, consider the figured world (or typical story) that might arise in someone's mind if they think about an elementary school classroom: Typical participants include one teacher (a female) and a group of kids of roughly the same age and some support staff including teachers who help kids with special problems (e.g., learning disabilities, reading problems, or who are learning English as a second language), sometimes by pulling them out of the classroom. The kids are sitting in desks in rows facing the teacher, who is doing most of the talking and sometimes asks the kids questions to which she knows the answers. There are activities like filling our sheets of paper with math problems on them. There are regular tests, some of them state standardized tests. There is an institution surrounding the teacher that includes a principal and other teachers as well as curriculum directors and mandates from officials. Parents are quasi "outsiders" to this institution. There are labels for individual kids, labels such as "SPED" (special education), "LD" (learning disabled), and "ESL" (English as a Second Language).

This figured world—with its typical participants, activities, forms of language, and object and environments—is, of course, realized in many actual classrooms. However there are many exceptions, as well, but they do not normally come to mind when we think and talk about schools. In fact, every aspect of this figured world is heavily contested in one or more current school reform efforts (e.g. age grading, lots of testing, skill sheets, too much teacher talk, children in rows, etc.). The taken-for-granted nature of the figured world, however, often stands in the way of change. Reforms just do not seem "normal" or "right" or "the ways things should be." For example, today it is not uncommon that young children can teach adults things about digital technology, but the child teaching and the teacher learning violates our typical story. It also violates the values and structures of authority this typical story incorporates.

I have said that these typical stories—what we are calling figured worlds— are in our heads. But that is not strictly true. Often they are partly in our heads and partly out in the world in books and other media and in other people's heads, people we can talk to. The figured world in which children are born dependent and development is progress towards individual autonomy and independence as eventual adults who can manage their own lives based on their own resources is a model that is found in lots of child-raising self-help books and in the talk and actions of many parents who are professionals (e.g., doctors, lawyers, professors, executives, and so forth) with whom we can interact if we live in the right neighborhood.

Thus, we can state out third theoretical tool, the Figured World Tool. It is clear that this tool is related to the Filling In Tool, since assumptions about shared figured worlds is a part of context and what speakers assume listeners will be able to fill in:

Tool #26: Figured World Tool

For any communication, ask what typical stories or figured worlds the words and phrases of the communication are assuming and inviting listeners to assume. What participants, activities, ways of interacting, forms of language, people, objects, environments, and institutions, as well as values, are in these figured worlds?

In Section 3.10 we discussed a foreign doctoral student in graduate school in the United States who has, after several years in the program, lost her PhD advisor. She needed to get another one. She was talking to a professor who she wanted as an advisor, but who was reluctant to take her on as a student. She said: "It's your job to help me, I need to learn." While we talked about this utterance in terms of the Relationships Building Tool, we can also see a conflict of figured worlds here.

The student was using a figured world of the relationship between professors and students in which professors were in a helping profession and the students were the ones they helped. In this figured world there are helpers who have the skill to help and who are obligated to help if someone needs their help. The more in need of help the person is, the more the helper is morally and professionally obligated to help. This figured world fits some professions (e.g., doctors, nurses, teachers) better than it does others (e.g., professional sports, accountants, bookies). And since all figured worlds are oversimplified, it does not always actually fit well the professions for which it is a best fit (e.g., doctors and hospitals who will not treat poor people who are sick).

The professor's figured world of the relationship between professors and students was different, perhaps based on his own graduate education and his years in the profession. He saw the professor as training students who are already well on their way to being professionals and who, if they succeeded as researchers themselves, would be his legacy. The relationship was mutually beneficial. This is not an uncommon model for professors in disciplines like physics, say, though professors in education (and in ESL) sometimes do adopt the helping profession model.

The conflict in the student and professor's figured worlds could best have been resolved if it had risen to consciousness and been overtly discussed. Then the student could have had the opportunity to rephrase her request or the professor could have rethought the role of helping in his profession. But figured worlds (typical stories of how things typically are in the world) are usually unconscious and taken-for-granted. It can be an important strategy for people to seek to understand them better and bring them to overt attention when there are conflicts in communication.

Reading

Fillmore, C. (1975). An alternative to checklist theories of meaning. In C. Cogen, H. Thompson, G. Thurgood, K. Whistler, and J. Wright, Eds., *Proceedings of the First Annual Meeting of the Berkeley Linguistics Society*. Berkeley, Calif.: University of California at Berkeley, pp. 123–31. [The example of the Pope is from this source.]

Harkness, S., Super, C., and Keefer, C. H. (1992). *Learning to be an American parent: how cultural models gain directive force*. In R. D'Andrade and C. Strauss, Eds., *Human motives and cultural models*. Cambridge: Cambridge University Press, pp. 163–78. [The example of the two year old is from this source.]

Holland, D. and Quinn, N, Eds. (1987). *Cultural models in language and thought*. Cambridge: Cambridge University Press.

Holland, D., Skinner, D., Lachicotte, W., and Cain C. (1998). *Identity and agency in cultural worlds*. Cambridge, MA: Harvard University Press.

Strauss, C. and Quinn, N. (1997). *A cognitive theory of cultural meaning*. Cambridge: Cambridge University Press.

4.9 Working with the Figured Worlds Tool

Figured worlds are "theories" or models or pictures that people hold about how things work in the world when they are "typical" or "normal." We all hold a myriad of such figured worlds. We all use them so that we do not have to consciously think about everything before we talk and act. The best way to get at what figured worlds a speaker is assuming in a given context is to ask the following question: What must this speaker assume about the world—take to be typical or normal—in order to have spoken this way, to have said these things in the way they were said? Often interviewing people is a good way to uncover figured worlds (e.g., people's assumptions about what typical schools and schooling look like).

Because figured worlds deal in what is taken as typical or normal, they can sometimes become means to judge and discriminate against people who are taken as untypical or not normal. Often the sense of typical or normal that is captured in a figured world lapses over into a notion of what is "appropriate" or "good."

Problem 44

Below are two excerpts from interviews or working men in Rhode Island from Claudia Strauss's important 1992 paper "What makes Tony run?" (see Reading at end of this Section for citation). Reflect on the data and answer the questions below.

> I believe if you put an effort into anything, you can get ahead. ... If I want to succeed, I'll succeed. It has to be, come from within here. Nobody else is going to make you succeed but yourself... And, if anybody disagrees with that, there's something wrong with them. (p. 202)

> [The worker is discussing the workers' fight against the company's proposal mandating Sunday work] But when that changed and it was negotiated through a contract that you would work, so you had to change or keep losing that eight hours pay. With three children, I couldn't afford it. So I had to go with the flow and work the Sundays. (p. 207)

Questions:

1. State the figured world (the picture of the world or a story about the world each speaker takes for granted as expressing what is "typical" or "normal"; how the speaker assumes "things work" in the world) expressed in each excerpt. How do they differ?
2. The figured world or cultural model expressed in the first excerpt has been called "the success model" and is held by a great many people in the United States. The figured world or cultural model expressed in the second excerpt has been called "the good provider model." Strauss found that the working class men she interviewed held both models, though they were often in conflict in their lives. When their lives did not lead to success (often because they had chosen to support their families over their own interests as individuals) in larger societal terms (e.g., having to do with things like income) who do you think they blamed?
3. Strauss found that upper-middle-class men often sacrificed the needs of their families when they moved in order to take better jobs in order to achieve success. Why do you think they did this? She found that the working class men she interviewed did not do this and sometimes gave up promotions and new job opportunities rather than harm their families other interests. Why do you think they did this?

Problem 45

In Section 3.15 you worked with some data from a college professor being interviewed about her views on race in society. This data is reprinted below. Though this speaker is using academic language, there are, of course, still figured worlds at play in her talk. Indeed, these figured worlds are influenced by her academic discipline, but also carry over into her views of the world around her in her own town.

When academic disciplines develop theories of the world, especially in the social sciences, they are like figured worlds, but usually more explicit and we hope more open to evidence and falsification. We call them "theories" (but, remember, theories are themselves simplified views of the world used to help us understand the world better by leaving aside some of its complexity).

It is, of course, possible that an academic discipline claims that something is a theory that really just replicates the figured worlds of some group of people in society. This most certainly happened in psychology when psychologists in the first half of the twentieth century claimed, often in textbooks, that African-Americans were inferior to Whites and women inferior to men in many respects.

The speaker's reference to different levels of reality is a core theme of much work in the social sciences. The distinction between the "macro" level (the level of institutions and large social trends) and the "micro" level (the level of human social interactions) has been deeply important to the social sciences. At the same time it is a major problem in the social sciences as to how to understand the relationship between the macro level and the micro level. Do larger institutional and social forces cause individuals' social actions and interactions or are larger institutional and social forces simply made up of these social actions and interactions? There are important questions here. We are concerned in analyzing the data below in the uses the speaker makes of "levels."

Reflect on the data and then answer the questions below.

> Interviewer: . . . How, do you see racism happening, in society, let's put it that way.
> 1. Um, well, I could answer on, on a variety of different levels // [I: uh huh]
> 2. Um, at the most macro level /
> 3. Uum, I think that there's um, um /
> 4. I don't want to say this in a way that sounds like a conspiracy / [I: mm hm]
> 5. But I think um, that um, basically that the lives of people of color are are, are irrelevant to the society anymore // [I: mm hm]
> 6. Um, they're not needed for the economy because we have the third world to run away into for cheap labor // [I: uh huh]
> 7. Um, and I think that, that the leadership /
> 8. This country really doesn't care if they shoot each other off in in the ghettos / [I: uh huh]
> 9. Um, and, and so they let drugs into the ghettos /
> 10. And they, um, they, let people shoot themselves /
> 11. Shoot each other /
> 12. And they don't have, a police force that is really gonna, um, work /
> 13. And they cut the programs that might alleviate some of the problems //
> 14. And, um—

15. So I think there's /
16. That it's manifested at, at the most, structural level as, um, you know, a real hatred, of, of, of uh people of color //[I: uh huh]
17. And, and it's shown, in, the cutbacks and so forth //
18. And, um, I think that um, that, it's, it's reflected in, in the fact that, they're, they're viewed as, expendable / [I: mm hm]
19. By our leadership //
20. Um, and so I think, I see cutbacks in programs as just a, an example of, of a broader/ [I: mm hm]
21. You know, sense, that, that, from the point of view of, of those in power /
22. People of color are expendable / [I: uh huh]
23. And, and irrelevant //

Questions:

1. State the basic figured world this speaker is using in terms of how people, activities, institutions, and environments function in this picture of the world (e.g., Who or what are the actors and what do they do?).
2. Would you call the picture of the world behind this speaker's communication here a "theory" or a "figured world" (which are theories or pictures of the world that are more tacit, taken-for-granted and often more simplified than academic theories) or some of both?
3. What is the situated meaning of the phrase "people of color" here (e.g., consider the use of the word "ghetto"). Who are being taken as typical "people of color"? Why?
4. Can you think of figured worlds (picture of the world) that some people might hold that would be quite different than the one expressed by the speaker above? Who might these people be and why would they hold a different model?
5. What would social activism look like if one accepts the figured world expressed by this speaker? What are some different figured worlds an activist for causes concerned with poverty and equity in society might assume as a starting point?

Reading

Strauss, C. (1992). What makes Tony run? Schemas as motives reconsidered. In R. D'Andrade and C. Strauss, Eds., *Human motives and cultural models*. Cambridge: Cambridge University Press, pp. 197–224.

4.10 The Big D Discourse Tool

People talk and act not just as individuals, but as members of various sorts of social and cultural groups. We do not invent our language, we inherit it from others. We understand each other because we share conventions about how to use and interpret language. We can most certainly innovate within these conventions—create new words, give new situated meanings to words, find new ways of saying things—but these innovations must be shared with others in order to be understood and to survive. Furthermore, our innovations are carried out against the background of shared conventions about how to use and interpret language.

The social groups with which we share conventions about how to use and interpret language are many and varied. These groups include cultures; ethnic groups; professions like doctors, lawyers, teachers, and carpenters; academic disciplines; interest-driven groups like bird watchers and video gamers; and organizations like street gangs, the military, and sports teams. There are yet many other sorts of social groups. Each of them has distinctive ways with words associated with distinctive identities and activities.

There is no one word for all these sorts of groups within which we humans act out distinctive identities and activities. People have tried various names for them: "cultures" (broadening the term), "communities of practice," "speech communities," "discourse communities," "activity systems," "actor-actant networks," and others. Each label is meant to capture just some such groups or just some aspects of such groups.

I will use the term "Discourse" with a capital "D" (so-called "big D Discourses"). I use this term because such groups continue through time—for the most part, they were here before we arrived on earth and will be here after we leave—and we can see them as communicating (discoursing) with each other through time and history, using us as their temporary mouthpieces.

We introduced the term "social language" earlier for distinctive styles or varieties of language with which people enact specific socially recognizable identities and actions or activities. Social languages allow people to speak as certain types of African-Americans, Anglo-Americans, doctors, soldiers, gamers, mathematicians, gang members, bird watchers, politicians, or any of a great many other things. However, when we enact an identity in the world, we do not just use language all by itself to do this. We use language, but we also use distinctive ways of acting, interacting with others, believing, valuing, dressing, and using various sorts of objects and tools in various sorts of distinctive environments.

If you want to show me you are a basketball player you cannot just talk the talk, you have to walk the walk and do that with a basketball on a basketball court in front of other people. If you want to get recognized as a devout Catholic, you cannot just talk the "right" way about the "right" things, you also have to engage in certain actions (like going to Mass) with the "right" people (e.g., priests) in the "right" places (e.g., church) and you have to display the "right" sorts of beliefs (e.g., about the virgin birth of Christ from his mother Mary) and values (e.g., deference to the Pope). The same is true of trying to get recognized as a "Native American," a "good student," a "tough policeman," or a "competent doctor." You need to talk the talk and walk the walk.

A Discourse with a capital "D" (I will use "discourse" with a little "d" just to mean "language in use" or stretches of oral or written language) is composed of distinctive ways of speaking/listening and often, too, distinctive ways writing/reading. These distinctive ways of speaking/listening and/or reading/ writing are *coupled* with distinctive ways of acting, interacting, valuing, feeling, dressing, thinking, and believing. In turn, all of these are coupled with ways of coordinating oneself with (getting in synch with) other people and with various objects, tools, and technologies. All this is in the service of enacting specific socially recognizable identities. These identities might be things like being–doing a Los Angeles Latino street-gang member, a Los Angeles policeman, a field biologist, a first-grade student in a specific classroom and school, a "SPED" student, a certain type of doctor, lawyer, teacher, African-American, Mexican-American, worker in a "quality control" workplace, man, woman, boyfriend, girlfriend, or regular at the local bar, etc., through a nearly endless list.

Discourses are about being "kinds of people." There are different ways to be an African-American, Latino, or Anglo. Thus, there are different kinds of African-Americans or different kinds for any other social or cultural group. Being a policeman is to act out a kind of person. So is being a "tough cop," which is to talk and act as sub-kind of person within the kind of being a policeman. Being a SPED student ("Special Ed") is one way to be a kind of student, it is one kind of student. There are kinds within kinds.

Kinds of people appear in history and some disappear. At one time in history, in England and the United States, you could be recognized as a witch, if you talked the talked and walked the walk (and you might in some cases do so unintentionally). Now it is much harder to get recognized as a witch in many of the places where it was once much easier, though there are still places in the world where you can get recognized as a witch. That "kind of person" has pretty much disappeared in England and the United States.

The whole point of taking about Discourses is to focus on the fact that when people mean things to each other, there is always more than language at stake. To mean anything to someone else (or even to myself) I have to communicate *who* I am (in the sense of what socially-situated identity am I taking on here and now). I also have to communicate *what* I am doing in terms of what socially-situated activity I am seeking to carry out, since Discourses (being and doing kinds of people) exist in part to allow people to carry out certain distinctive activities (e.g., arresting people for a policeman, taking communion for a Catholic, getting an "A" for a good student).

Language is not enough for this. We have to get our minds and deeds "right," as well. We also have to get ourselves appropriately in synch with various objects, tools, places, technologies, and other people. Being in a Discourse is being able to engage in a particular sort of "dance" with words, deeds, values, feelings, other people, objects, tools, technologies, places and times so as to get recognized as a distinctive sort of *who* doing a distinctive sort of *what*. Being able to understand a Discourse is being able to recognize such "dances."

Discourses are not units or tight boxes with neat boundaries. Rather they are *ways of recognizing and getting recognized* as certain sorts of *whos* doing certain sorts of *whats*. One and the same "dance" can get recognized in multiple ways, in partial ways, in contradictory ways, in disputed ways, in negotiable ways, and so on and so forth through all the multiplicities and problematics that work on postmodernism has made so popular. Discourses are matters of enactment and recognition, then.

All recognition processes involve satisfying a variety of constraints in probabilistic and sometimes partial ways. For example, something recognized as a "weapon" (e.g., a baseball bat or a fireplace poker) may share some features with prototypical weapons (like a gun, sword, or club) and not share other features. And there may be debate about the matter. Furthermore, the very same thing might be recognized as a weapon in one context and not in another. So, too, with being in and out of Discourses, e.g., enacting and recognizing being–doing a certain type of street gang member, Special Ed student, or particle physicist.

While there is an endless array of Discourses in the world, nearly all human beings, except under extraordinary conditions, acquire an initial Discourse within whatever constitutes their primary socializing unit early in life. Early in life, we all learn a culturally distinctive way of being an "everyday person" as a member of our family and community. We can call this our "primary Discourse." Our primary Discourse gives us our initial and often enduring sense of self and sets the foundations of our culturally specific vernacular language (our "everyday language"), the language in which we speak and act as "everyday" (non-specialized) people.

As a person grows up, lots of interesting things can happen to his or her primary Discourse. Primary Discourses can change, hybridize with other Discourses, and they can even die. In any case, for the vast majority of us, our primary Discourse, through all its transformations, serves us throughout life as what I will call our "life world Discourse." Our life world Discourse is the way that we use language, feel and think, act and interact, and so forth, in order to be an "everyday" (non-specialized) person. In our pluralistic world there is much adjustment and negotiation as people seek to meet in the terrain of the life world, given that life worlds are culturally distinctive (that is, different groups of people have different ways of being–doing "everyday people").

All the Discourses we acquire later in life, beyond our primary Discourse, we acquire within a more "public sphere" than our initial socializing group. We can call these "secondary Discourses." They are acquired within institutions that are part and parcel of wider communities, whether these be religious groups, community organizations, schools, businesses, or governments.

As we are being socialized early in life, secondary Discourses very often play an interesting role. Primary Discourses work out, over time, alignments and allegiances with and against other Discourses, alignments and allegiances that shape them as they, in turn, shape these other Discourses.

One way that many social groups achieve an alignment with secondary Discourses they value is by incorporating certain aspects of the practices of these secondary Discourses into the early (primary Discourse) socialization of their children. For example, some African-American families incorporate aspects of practices and values that are part of African-American churches into their primary Discourse, as my family incorporated aspects of practices and values of a very traditional Catholicism into our primary Discourse. This is an extremely important mechanism in terms of which bits and pieces of a valued "community" or "public" identity (to be more fully practiced later in the child's life) is incorporated as part and parcel of the child's "private," "home-based," life world identity.

Social groups that are deeply affiliated with formal schooling often incorporate into the socialization of their children practices that resonate with later school-based secondary Discourses. For example, their children from an early age are encouraged (and coached) at dinner time to tell stories in quite expository ways that are rather like little essays, or parents interact with their children over books in ways that encourage a great deal of labeling and the answering of a variety of different types of questions, as well as the forming of intertextual relationships between books and between books and the world.

There are, of course, complex relationships between people's primary Discourses and the secondary ones they are acquiring, as well as among their academic, institutional, and community-based secondary Discourses. For example, children acquire a secondary Discourse when they go to school, a Discourse that involves the identity of being a student of a certain kind and using certain kinds of "school language" (this Discourse can change across grades and levels of schooling). This identity and these forms of language can, at points, conflict with the identities, values, and ways with words some children have learned at home as part of their primary Discourse. For other children there is a much better fit or match.

Here is one example of such a conflict. In some Native American groups, people in a subordinate status stay quiet in the presence of elders or people of higher status who speak and display their knowledge. School often requires children to talk and display their knowledge to the teacher so she can assess it. But the teacher is higher status, the authority figure, and the child's home-based Discourse dictates listening and not speaking and displaying in this sort of context.

We can now introduce our last theoretical tool, the Big "D" Discourse Tool. Keep in mind that Discourses can mix or be ambiguous. For example, an African-American running for office might, in giving a talk in a church, be speaking and acting from a mixture of a church Discourse—seeking to get recognized as a Christian of a certain sort—and a political Discourse—seeking to get recognized as a politician of a certain sort. Or there may be ambiguity about which Discourse is in play at which time. When people speak and act they are "bidding" to get recognized as a certain kind of person and the "bid" may not always be successful (and may be successful in some contexts and not in others) or the person may get recognized in different ways than he or she intended.

Tool #27: The Big D Discourse Tool

For any communication, ask how the person is using language, as well as ways of acting, interacting, believing, valuing, dressing, and using various objects, tools, and technologies in certain sorts of environments to enact a specific socially recognizable identity and engage in one or more socially recognizable activities. Even if all you have for data is language, ask what Discourse is this language part of, that is, what kind of person (what identity) is this speaker or writer seeking to enact or get recognized. What sorts of actions, interactions, values, beliefs, and objects, tools, technologies, and environments are associated with this sort of language within a particular Discourse?

Reading

Bourdieu, P. (1990b). *In other words: Essays towards a reflexive sociology*. Stanford: Stanford University Press.

Fairclough, N. (1992). *Discourse and social change*. Cambridge: Polity Press.

Fleck, L. (1979, org. 1935). *The genesis and development of a scientific fact*. Chicago: University of Chicago Press. [A classic, as modern today as when it was written.]

Foucault, M. (1969). *The archeology of knowledge*. New York: Random House.

Gee, J. P. (2011). *Social linguistics and literacies: Ideology in Discourses*. Fourth Edition. London: Taylor and Francis.

Hacking, I. (1986). Making up people, in T. C. Heller, M. Sosna, and D. E. Wellbery, with A. I. Davidson, A. Swidler, and I. Watt Eds. *Reconstructing individualism: Autonomy, individuality, and the self in Western thought*. Stanford, Calif.: Stanford University Press, pp. 222–36. [Hacking's work on identity as a whole—he has several fascinating books—is worth reading, but start here.]

Latour, B. (2005). *Reassembling the social: An introduction to actor-network-theory*. Oxford: Oxford University Press.

Scollon, R. and Scollon, S. W. (1981). *Narrative, literacy, and face in interethnic communication*. Norwood, N.J.: Ablex.

4.11 Working with the Big D Discourse Tool

Discourses take us beyond language. In order to study them we have to research both language and people's actions, interactions, values, beliefs, and uses of objects, tools, and environments within social or institutional settings. This, though, is part of a job we have seen we already have as discourse analysts, namely to study the context in which a spoken or written communication occurs.

We can analyze communications in terms of the Discourses they express (what identity the speaker is trying to get recognized) or in terms of how they talk about and imply things about Discourses and how Discourses inter-relate in the world. Often when we speak we not only speak out of a given Discourse (e.g., biology) but also say or imply things about other, sometimes competing, Discourses (e.g., creationism).

Problem 46

In Section 3.17 we discussed the state of Arizona's policy on teaching immigrant children. Immigrant students are grouped in classrooms based on English language proficiency determined by a test (the Arizona English Language Learner Assessment—AZELLA). In these classrooms, the children receive four hours of mandated skill-based English language instruction each day. Teaching and learning does not include the content areas, such as science or social studies. Students are segregated from native English speaking students in these four-hour blocks. No other language than English and no bilingual education are allowed in these classrooms. On the basis of the AZELLA test children are given a score between 1 and 4 and placed with students with the same number. If the children do not make fairly rapid progress to learning English and move on to regular mainstream classrooms the teachers and their schools can be sanctioned in various ways.

Below several teachers are talking to researcher (Amy) about these classrooms in which they teach. Read and reflect on the data and then answer the questions following [Data from: Heineke, A. J. (2009). *Teacher's discourse on English language learners: Cultural models of language and learning.* Unpublished doctoral dissertation. Mary Lou Fulton College of Education, Tempe, Arizona, p. 63.]

Erica: But I think that I've probably seen this difference [linguistic] because I [my classroom] am the mix, I have threes and fours, so I can see like those [students] who – and I have some threes that I swear could be fours, I don't think they're three.

Amy: What do you see as the distinction between [a three and four]?

Erica: Like they learn, well, I won't say they learn things faster, but they do seem to pick up a little faster, and then their output [spoken English] is so different.

Joni: Between a four and a three? Yeah.

Erica: Oh, yes. Like the output is different. Like they're the kind of kids that will take the language objectives and remember to use it, they are the ones that are a little bit more self-initiated. They will try to read, if you say point to the words and follow me, they will, these are seen as differences between a three and a four.

Joni: My home base is fours, and I mean, they rock, most of my kids rock.

Questions:

1. The Arizona policy is only a few years old. However it is creating a new Discourse. Students and teachers must find ways to be the "kinds of students" and "the kinds of teachers" that this policy and its implementation has required. To be these kinds, the students and teachers must talk, act, interact, value, think, and relate to various objects and environments in certain ways. From what I have told you about the policy and from the language above what are some of the ways of talking, acting, interacting, thinking and valuing that this Discourse does or probably will involve? What sorts of objects and environments play roles in this Discourse and what sort of roles do they play?
2. How is this emerging Discourse changing language, giving rise to what might be aspects of a new social language?
3. How does the concept of figured worlds relate to this data? Discourses recruit favored figured worlds (that is models or pictures of what is typical in the world). What figured worlds are expressed or assumed by the way these teachers are communicating?
4. Erica seems to equate a child's level of English, intelligence, and willingness to follow instructions. Why does she do this? Are the three really things that go together?

Problem 47

The text below is from a paper written by Richard Ruiz called "The Ontological Status of Burritos" (see Grammar Interlude #9). In the paper, he says that in his Mexican family they called anything rolled in a tortilla a "taco." They did not use the word "burrito." He goes on to say:

> In fact, many Mexicans in my circle would say that "taco" is metaphorical (actually metonymic—the Mexicans I know tend to be precise in their use of classical root-words), an icon that stands for much more than a piece of food. *Vamos a echarnos un taco*, literally "let's go throw a taco on ourselves," means something like "let's do lunch" or, more liturgically, "let us break bread together." Here, no one is really talking about bread. It is a way of indicating an interest in establishing or reinforcing a friendship beyond whatever formal roles the participants may be playing. In this, "taco" may be sociolinguistically unique; you don't hear people inviting someone to throw an enchilada or tamale (sic) on each other, thankfully. (If they did, I imagine it would be taken as an invitation to some sort of kinky Mexican duel—but that would be different.)

Questions:

1. How does the concept of Discourse we have developed apply to this text? What aspects of a certain type of "being a Mexican" Discourse is Ruiz pointing to?

2. What objects, ways of acting, interacting, valuing, objects, and environments play a role in this Discourse and what role do they play?

Problem 48

Pick a Discourse of which you are a member and detail some of the ways of talking, acting, interacting, believing, valuing, and using objects, tools, and environments that help people in this Discourse recognize others as in it or bidding to be in it. For example, if you were Native American or an avid gamer how do you get recognized as a Native American or gamer and how do you recognize others as Native Americans or gamers? Feel free to write a piece along the lines of Ruiz's text above where he uses some telling details to spell out a little piece of a Discourse (in Ruiz's case, of what it means to be a Mexican of a certain sort, namely the sort he and others in his "circle" are).

4.12 The Big C Conversation Tool

Big D Discourses—socially recognizable ways of being different kinds of people—often existed before we were born and will go on existing long after we die. Discourses are partly defined in terms of their relationships of allegiance and opposition to each other. It is as if they use us humans (for our time on earth) to talk to, with, and against each other. Historically, Jews, Muslims, Catholics, and Protestants; capitalists, socialists, Marxists, and anarchists; different races, ethnic groups, nations, and cultures, and even the fans of competing sports teams, television shows, or video games have defined themselves in relations to each other.

When we humans talk about the public debates that swirl around us in the media, in our reading, and in our interactions with other people, we are talking and taking part in debates among the Discourses that make up society. On certain large issues (e.g., abortion, smoking, gambling, feminism, affirmative action, etc.) nearly everyone in the society know what the "sides" are, how these sides are talked about and argued for, and what sort of people tend to be on specific sides. Some such issues are known by nearly everyone in a society, but others are known only by specifically defined groups (e.g., the ongoing big controversies in a given academic field, controversies which can be debated over a great many years). This knowledge about public issues and their sides is an ever present background people bring to their interpretations of what they hear and read or in terms of which you can formulate their own talk and writing.

I will call such public debates, arguments, motifs, issues, or themes "Conversations" with a capital "C," speaking metaphorically as if the various sides in debates around issues like abortion or smoking were engaged in one grand conversation (or debate or argument, whatever we want to call it). Of course, this big Conversation is composed of myriad of interactional events taking place among specific people at specific times and places and within specific institutions.

Let me give you an example of what I am trying to get at here. It has for some time now been fashionable for businesses to announce (in "mission statements") their "core values" in an attempt to create a particular company "culture" (see Collins and Porras 1994; examples below are from pp. 68–69). For instance, at one time, the announced core values of Johnson & Johnson, a large pharmaceutical company, included "The company exists to alleviate pain and disease" and "Individual opportunity and reward based on merit," as well as several others.

One might wonder, then, what the core values of a cigarette company might be. Given the Conversations that most of us are familiar with—about the U.S. and its history, as well as about smoking—we can almost predict what they will be. For example, the espoused core values of Philip Morris, a large company which sells cigarettes among a great many other products, once included "The right to personal freedom of choice (to smoke, to buy whatever one wants) is worth defending," "Winning—being the best and beating others," and "Encouraging individual initiative," as well as (in a statement similar to one of Johnson & Johnson's statements) "Opportunity to achieve based on merit, not gender, race, or class."

We all readily connect Philip Morris's core value statements to themes of American individualism and freedom. We can interpret these statements in light of what we know about various Conversations that have gone on historically in the United States not just over smoking itself, but also over freedom, individuality, government, and other topics. Conversations interact and affect each other. Note how the values of "individual initiative" and "reward for merit," which are part of the core values of both Johnson and Johnson and Philip Morris, take on a different coloring in the two cases. In the first case, they take on a humanistic coloring and in the other the coloring of "every man for himself." This coloring is the effect of our knowledge of the two sides to the "smoking Conversation" in which, we all know, individual freedom is pitted against social responsibility. This debate has gone on now for decades and is, perhaps, near its end in places like the United States where social responsibility, coupled with heath issues and health care costs are close to winning out and closing the historical debate over smoking.

Note here, then, how values, beliefs, and objects play a role in the sorts of Conversations I am talking about. We know that in this Conversation some people will hold values and beliefs consistent with expressions about individualism, freedom, the "American way," and so forth, while others will express values and beliefs consistent with the rights of others, social responsibility, and protecting people from harm, even harm caused by their own desires. In turn, these two value and belief orientations can be historically tied to much wider dichotomies centering around beliefs about the responsibilities and the role of governments.

Furthermore, within this Conversation, an object like a cigarette or an institution like a tobacco company, or an act like the act of smoking itself, take on meanings—symbolic values—within the Conversation, but dichotomous meanings. Smoking can be seen as an addiction, an expression of freedom, or a lack of caring about others. The point is that those familiar with the Smoking Conversation and the other Conversations it engages with, know the possible meanings of cigarettes, tobacco companies, and smoking.

The themes and values that enter into Conversations circulate in a multitude of texts and media. They are the products of historical disputes between and among different Discourses. Think, for example, of the historic debate between the Discourse of evolutionary biologists and the Discourse of fundamentalist creationists. This debate, over time, has constituted a Conversation that many people in society know something about. For that reason it is hard for a newspaper to discuss evolution in any terms without triggering people to think about this debate and to try to interpret what the newspaper is saying in terms of it.

People are often unaware of specific historical clashes among Discourses (e.g., the Reformation, the history of creationism, the changing nature of feminist Discourses). Often they are only aware of the residue of issue, debates, claims, and clashes that make up Big C Conversations. Historical interactions of Discourses leads to certain debates ("Conversations"), (for example, debates over smoking, race, evolution, global warming, and "nature" of men and women, males, females, and gays) being known widely by people in a society or social group, even by people who are not themselves members of those Discourses or even aware of their histories.

Big C Conversations—the topics, issues, sides, and debates that have become widely known in society at large or among large groups of people as they have enacted their Discourses (multiple identities) through history in talk, texts, and media—gives us our last tool:

Tool #28: The Big C Conversation Tool

For any communication, ask what issues, sides, debates, and claims the communication assumes hearers or readers know or what issues, sides, debates, and claims they need to know to understand the communication in terms of wider historical and social issues and debates. Can the communication be seen as carrying out a historical or widely known debate or discussion between or among Discourses? Which Discourses?

Reading

Bakhtin, M. M. (1986). *Speech genres and other late essays*. Austin: University of Texas Press.

Billig, M. (1987). *Arguing and thinking: A rhetorical approach to social psychology*. Cambridge: Cambridge University Press.

Collins, J. C. and Porras, J. I. (1994). *Built to last: Successful habits of visionary companies*. New York: Harper Business.

4.13 Working with the Big C Conversation Tool

I am using the term ("Big C") "Conversation" here because I want to stress that sometimes as members of a wider society and other times as members of social or cultural groups we realize or can come to realize that our everyday conversations and what we hear and react to in books and/on media constitutes Conversations among Discourse in history and not just talk and texts in the here and now. Often we understand issues in society in terms of at least partial understandings of how different kinds of people have talked, acted, and argued in history.

Problem 49

Discuss how the election of Barack Obama and the controversies it caused can be understood in terms of different kinds of peoples'—different Discourses'—interactions now and in history. What different historical kinds of people or Discourses are involved? What are the issues and the "sides" in the debate?

Problem 50

Discuss the issue of how global warming caused by human activities can be understood in terms of different kinds of peoples'—different Discourses'—interactions now and in history. What different historical kinds of people or Discourses are involved? What are the issues and the sides in the debate? Can you name any actual people alive today who are strongly associated with particular Discourses with a stake in the issue of global warming?

Problem 51

Below is a quote from an interview I once gave about using video games for learning and education:

> All technologies can be good or bad depending on how they are used. Textbooks are pervasive in schools but one of the worst learning technologies ever invented, because they try to do everything with one tool, standardized for everyone, with no care about context and individual differences in learning. We need to be

careful not to see technology as the main focus, but rather to see the main focus as creating good interactive learning systems in and out of classrooms, learning systems that stress participation, deep understanding, problem solving, and innovation.

People from different backgrounds will read this passage in relation to different controversies over education, technology, learning, and schools. What are some of the issues and sides in debates among Discourses that this passage might be seen as relevant to and in part contributing to? What are the larger Conversations it engages?

Conclusion

The "tools" approach in this book is meant to stress that speakers and writers are active designers and builders. They are making things, acting on others and on the world, and simultaneously reproducing social order, institutions, and cultures. They are making history as they enact and recognize—and thereby keep alive—a great variety of different Discourses, different ways of being in the world, different ways of being certain kinds of people.

All of our tools are basically about "recipient design," that is, designing for who we take our listeners or readers to be or who we want them be as we interact with them. All our tools are also basically about the related notion of "response design," that is, designing not just for who we take our listeners and readers to be or who we want them to be, but designing for what we want them to do in the world in response to what we have said or written. Here "who" means "socially recognizable and socially significant types of people," identities that in interaction make the social world and make history.

This book is meant to be a beginning to discourse analysis for its readers. Now that beginning is nearly at an end. The best way for readers to end this book would be to choose a topic of their own, collect their own data, and engage in their own discourse analysis. Readers can use each of the 28 tools we have introduced. This will lead them to ask 28 questions. As I said in the Introduction, there is no necessary order to the tools. Indeed, it is often useful to go through them backwards from 28 to 1, or to choose an order that works for the data and the researcher.

What makes a discourse analysis valid? I take validity to be something that different analyses can have more or less of, i.e., some analyses are more or less valid than others. Furthermore, validity is never "once and for all." All analyses are open to further discussion and dispute, and their status can go up or down with time as work goes on in the field. Validity for discourse analysis is based on the following four elements:

1. *Convergence*: A discourse analysis is more, rather than less valid (i.e., "trustworthy"), the more the answers to the 28 questions *converge* in the way they support the analysis or, put the matter the other way round, the more the analysis offers *compatible* and *convincing* answers to many or all of them.
2. *Agreement*: Answers to the 28 questions above are more convincing the more "native speakers" of the social languages in the data and "members"

of the Discourses implicated in the data agree that the analysis reflects how such social languages actually can function in such settings. The native speakers do not need to know why or how their social languages so function, just that they can. Answers to the 28 questions are more convincing the more other discourse analysts (who accept our basic theoretical assumptions and tools), or other sorts of researchers (e.g., ethnographic researchers), tend to support our conclusions.

3. *Coverage*: The analysis is more valid the more it can be applied to related sorts of data. This includes being able to make sense of what has come before and after the situation being analyzed and being able to predict the sorts of things that might happen in related sorts of situations.

4. *Linguistic Details*: The analysis is more valid the more it is tightly tied to details of linguistic structure. All human languages have evolved, biologically and culturally, to serve an array of different communicative functions. For this reason, the grammar of any social language is composed of specific forms that are "designed" to carry out specific functions, though any form can usually carry out more than one function. Part of what makes a discourse analysis valid, then, is that the analyst is able to argue that the communicative functions being uncovered in the analysis are linked to grammatical devices that manifestly can and do serve these functions, according to the judgments of "native speakers" of the social languages involved and the analyses of linguists.

Why does this constitute validity? Because it is *highly improbable* that a good many answers to 28 different questions, the perspectives of different "inside" and "outside" observers, additional data sets, and the judgments of "native speakers" and/or linguists *will* converge unless there is good reason to trust the analysis. This, of course, does not mean the analysis is true or correct in every respect. Empirical science is social and accumulative in that investigators build on each other's work in ways that, in the long run, we hope, improves it. It does mean, however, that a "valid" analysis explains things that any future investigation of the same data, or related data, will have to take seriously into account.

Well that is the end of this book. This book is about "preparation for future learning." I have given you one theory of discourse analysis to use for practice and for getting a bit familiar with the area. The purpose has not been to get you to stop here and believe me. It is to prepare you to read further, confront other perspectives, and reflect on your own views. The book itself, in this sense, is meant to be a tool to get some initial work done, initial work that will lead you to yet other tools and other work.

For those who will not themselves be discourse analysts, the goal is to deepen your view of language in use and to push you to go on to read and think more about language. For those who will do discourse analysis professionally, the goal is to show you the territory with the hope that you come to make your maps and find your way—and eventually make better and more novel contributions than this book. For all readers, I hope that I have added to—and not detracted from—the wonder that is language in human hands and minds.

What response have I designed my text to get from you? I have wanted readers to see that language is a force for action, for good or bad, that they are or can be active designers and makers, and that through language and understanding Discourses they can change the world for the better. The world badly needs it. And it is to this identity—as a powerful maker in your own right, bearing powerful tools—that I hope I have summoned you.

APPENDIX
List of Tools

Tool #1: The Diexis Tool

For any communication, ask how deictics are being used to tie what is said to context and to make assumptions about what listeners already know or can figure out. Consider uses of the definite article in the same way. Also ask what deictic like properties any regular words are taking on in context, that is, what aspects of their specific meanings need to be filled in from context (we will see this latter task again later in the Situated Meaning Tool in Section 4.2).

Tool #2: The Fill In Tool

For any communication, ask: Based on what was said and the context in which it was said, what needs to be filled in here to achieve clarity? What is not being said overtly, but is still assumed to be known or inferable? What knowledge, assumptions, and inferences do listeners have to bring to bear in order for this communication to be clear and understandable and received in the way the speaker intended?

Tool #3: The Making Strange Tool

For any communication, try to act as if you are an "outsider." Ask yourself: What would someone (perhaps, even a Martian) find strange here (unclear, confusing, worth questioning) if that person did not share the knowledge and assumptions and make the inferences that render the communication so natural and taken-for-granted by insiders?

Tool #4: The Subject Tool

For any communication, ask why speakers have chosen the subject/topics they have and what they are saying about the subject. Ask if and how they could have made another choice of subject and why they did not. Why are they organizing information the way they are in terms of subjects and predicates?

Tool #5: The Intonation Tool

For any communication, ask how a speaker's intonation contour contributes to the meaning of an utterance. What idea units did the speaker use? What information did the speaker make salient (in terms of where the intonational focus is placed)? What information did the speaker background as given or old by making it less salient? In dealing with written texts, always read them out loud and ask what sort of intonation contour readers must add to the sentences to make them make full sense.

Tool #6: The Frame Tool

After you have completed your discourse analysis—after you have taken into consideration all the aspects of the context that you see as relevant to the meaning of the data—see if you can find out anything additional about the context in which the data occurred and see if this changes your analysis. If it doesn't, your analysis is safe for now. If it does, you have more work to do. Always push your knowledge of the context as far as you can just to see if aspects of the context are relevant that you might at first have not thought were relevant or if you can discover entirely new aspects of the context.

Tool #7: The Doing and Not Just Saying Tool

For any communication, ask not just what the speaker is saying, but what he or she is trying to do, keeping in mind that he or she may be trying to do more than one thing.

Tool #8: The Vocabulary Tool

For any English communication, ask what sorts of words are being used in terms of whether the communication uses a preponderance of Germanic words or of Latinate words. How is this distribution of word types functioning to mark this communication in terms of style (register, social language)? How does it contribute to the purposes for communicating?

Tool #9: The Why This Way and Not That Way Tool

For any communication, ask why the speaker built and designed with grammar in the way in which he or she did and not in some other way. Always ask how else this could have been said and what the speaker was trying to mean and do by saying it the way in which he or she did and not in other ways.

Tool #10: The Integration Tool

For any communication, ask how clauses were integrated or packaged into utterances or sentences. What was left out and what was included in terms of optional arguments? What was left out and what was included when clauses were turned into phrases? What perspectives are being communicated by the way in which information is packaged into main, subordinate, and embedded clauses, as well as into phrases that encapsulate a clause's worth of information?

Tool #11: The Topic and Theme Tool

For any communication, ask what the topic and theme is for each clause and what the theme is of a set of clauses in a sentence with more than one clause. Why were these choices made? When the theme is not the subject/topic, and, thus, has deviated from the usual (unmarked) choice, what is it and why was it chosen?

Tool #12: The Stanza Tool

In any communication (that is long enough), look for stanzas and how stanzas cluster into larger blocks of information. You will not always find them clearly and easily, but when you do, they are an important aid to organizing your interpretation of data and of how you can display that interpretation.

Tool #13: The Context is Reflexive Tool

When you use the Fill in Tool, the Doing and Not Just Saying Tool, the Frame Problem Tool, and the Why This Way and Not That Way Tool, and all other tools that require that you think about context (and not just what was said), always ask yourself the following questions:

1. How is what the speaker is saying and how he or she is saying it helping to create or shape (possibly even manipulate) what listeners will take as the relevant context?
2. How is what the speaker is saying and how he or she is saying it helping to reproduce contexts like this one (e.g., class sessions in a university), that is, helping them to continue to exist through time and space?
3. Is the speaker reproducing contexts like this one unaware of aspects of the context that if he or she thought about the matter consciously, he or she would not want to reproduce?
4. Is what the speaker is saying and how he or she is saying it just, more or less, replicating (repeating) contexts like this one or, in any respect, transforming or changing them?

Tool #14: The Significance Building Tool

For any communication, ask how words and grammatical devices are being used to build up or lessen significance (importance, relevance) for certain things and not others.

Tool #15: The Activities Building Tool

For any communication, ask what activity (practice) or activities (practices) this communication is building or enacting. What activity or activities is this communication seeking to get others to recognize as being accomplished? Ask also what social groups, institutions, or cultures support and norm (set norms for) whatever activities are being built or enacted. (The Doing and Not Saying Tool in Section in Section 2.1 deals with actions; this tool deals with activities/practices.)

Tool #16: The Identities Building Tool

For any communication, ask what socially recognizable identity or identities the speaker is trying to enact or to get others to recognize. Ask also how the speaker's language treats other people's identities, what sorts of identities the speaker recognizes for others in relationship to his or her own. Ask, too, how the speaker is positioning others, what identities the speaker is "inviting" them to take up.

Tool #17: The Relationships Building Tool

For any communication, ask how words and various grammatical devices are being used to build and sustain or change relationships of various sorts among the speaker, other people, social groups, cultures, and/or institutions.

Tool #18: The Politics Building Tool

For any communication, ask how words and grammatical devices are being used to build (construct, assume) what count as a social good and to distribute this good to or withhold it from listeners or others. Ask, as well, how words and grammatical devices are being used to build a viewpoint on how social goods are or should be distributed in society.

Tool #19: The Connections Building Tool

For any communication, ask how the words and grammar being used in the communication connect or disconnect things or ignore connections between things. Always ask, as well, how the words and grammar being used in a communication make things relevant or irrelevant to other things, or ignores their relevance to each other.

Tool #20: The Cohesion Tool

For any communication, ask questions like: How does cohesion work in this text to connect pieces of information and in what ways? How does the text fail to connect other pieces of information? What is the speaker trying to communicate or achieve by using cohesive devices in the way he or she does?

Tool #21: Systems and Knowledge Building Tool

For any communication, ask how the words and grammar being used privilege or de-privilege specific sign systems (e.g., Spanish vs. English, technical language vs. everyday language, words vs. images, words vs. equations, etc.) or different ways of knowing and believing or claims to knowledge and belief?

Tool #22: The Topic Flow or Topic Chaining Tool

For any communication, ask what the topics are of all main clauses and how these topics are linked to each other to create (or not) a chain that creates an overall topic or coherent sense of being about something for a stretch of speech or writing. Topics in subordinated and embedded clauses represent less prominent topics that are subordinated to the main chain of topics in main clauses, but it is useful to ask how they relate to the main chain of topics. Ask, as well, how people have signaled that they are switching topics and whether they have "spoken topically" by linking back to the old topic in some first. Look, as well, for topic shifted structures and how they are being used.

Tool #23: The Situated Meaning Tool

For any communication, ask of words and phrases what situated meanings they have. That is, what specific meanings do listeners have to attribute to these words and phrases given the context and how the context is construed?

Tool #24: Social Languages Tool

For any communication, ask how it uses words and grammatical structures (types of phrases, clauses, and sentences) to signal and enact a given social language. The communication may mix two or more social languages or switch between two or more. In turn, a social language may be composed of words or phrases from more than one language (e.g., it may mix English and Spanish).

Tool #25: The Intertextuality Tool

For any communication, ask how words and grammatical structures (e.g., direct or indirect quotation) are used to quote, refer to, or allude to other "texts" (that is, what others have said or written) or other styles of language (social languages).

Tool #26: Figured World Tool

For any communication, ask what typical stories or figured worlds the words and phrases of the communication are assuming and inviting listeners to assume. What participants, activities, ways of interacting, forms of language, people, objects, environments, and institutions, as well as values, are in these figured worlds?

Tool #27: The Big "D" Discourse Tool

For any communication, ask how the person is using language, as well as ways of acting, interacting, believing, valuing, dressing, and using various objects, tools, and technologies in certain sorts of environments to enact a specific socially recognizable identity and engage in one or more socially recognizable activities. Even if all you have for data is language, ask what Discourse is this language part of, that is, what kind of person (what identity) is this speaker or writer seeking to enact or get recognized. What sorts of actions, interactions, values, beliefs, and objects, tools, technologies, and environments are associated with this sort of language within a particular Discourse?

Tool #28: The Big C Conversation Tool

For any communication, ask what issues, sides, debates, and claims the communication assumes hearers or readers know or what issues, sides, debates, and claims they need to know to understand the communication in terms of wider historical and social issues and debates. Can the communication be seen as carrying out a historical or widely known debate or discussion between or among Discourses? Which Discourses?

Index

Page numbers in **bold** show information contained in a text box.